CAMBRIDGE ASIA SERIES – 1
Series Editor: R.C. Jamieson
University of Cambridge

Pseudo Sahib

Major Sydney Bolt, Bombay, April 1946

Pseudo Sahib

Sydney Bolt

Hardinge Simpole

Hardinge Simpole Ltd,
Aylesbeare Common Business Park,
Exmouth Road,
Aylesbeare,
Devon,
EX5 2DG,
England

http://www.hardingesimpole.co.uk
admin@hardingesimpole.co.uk

First published 2007

ISBN-10   1 84382 183 4 Paperback
ISBN-13   978 1 84382 183 0 Paperback

Contents

List of Photographs

Acknowledgements

My sincere thanks are due to Caroline Stone, Kevin Greenbank and Rachel Rowe, without whose constant help these memoirs would not have been published.

The original manuscript of *Pseudo Sahib* is held in the Library and Archive at the Centre of South Asian Studies, University of Cambridge, where it may be consulted by prior appointment. Please address enquiries to the

Library,
Centre of South Asian Studies,
Laundress Lane,
Cambridge,
CB2 1SD,

tel: + 44 (0) 1223 338094,
fax: +44 (0)1223 767094,

website:http://www.s-asian.cam.ac.uk,
where contact details are available
for individual members of staff.

Preface

As a young man Sydney Bolt witnessed some of the most remarkable events in recent world history. He reached India at a time when the Japanese armed forces were powering through Southeast Asia and dealing a humiliating blow to European colonial empires from which they would never recover. His memoir covers the period of the rise of nationalist revolt in India and the climax of Gandhi's civil disobedience movement. He was on the Burma front as British and Indian armies began finally to push the Japanese back in some of the bloodiest fighting of the Second World War.

He remained in South Asia after Partition and Independence in 1947 watching the stumbling steps of India and Pakistan as they experimented with freedom but also came to blows over Kashmir. Sixty years ago, these events seemed dramatic enough: the end of Britain's long tenure of an Indian Empire. But today they seem even more epochal: some of the first small beginnings of the transformation that will make Asia the dominant continent of the twenty-first century.

What makes Mr Bolt's memoir so significant is the perspective from which he viewed these events. Most memoirs of this period were written by soldiers, administrators and journalists, who accepted or at least acquiesced in the existence of the British Empire. Mr Bolt did not. He was a communist who had struck up friendships with Indian communists while he was at Cambridge University. Despatched to the East by the authorities, his aim was to 'bore into the British Empire from within.'

During the Second World War, the Indian Communist Party reluctantly suspended its war against 'imperialism' to conduct one against an even more dangerous enemy, 'fascism.' Mr Bolt therefore worked within the British civil and military apparatus, but at every point he tried to plan and argue for the day when the left's war against empire would resume. Many British servicemen held left-wing views at this time and it was they, of course, who voted in the Labour government of 1945.

Few played such an active role in underground wartime politics in India as Mr Bolt. Herein lies the fascination of this important memoir.

C.A. Bayly,
Centre of South Asian Studies,
University of Cambridge,
September 2006.

Map of Assam, showing places mentioned in the text.

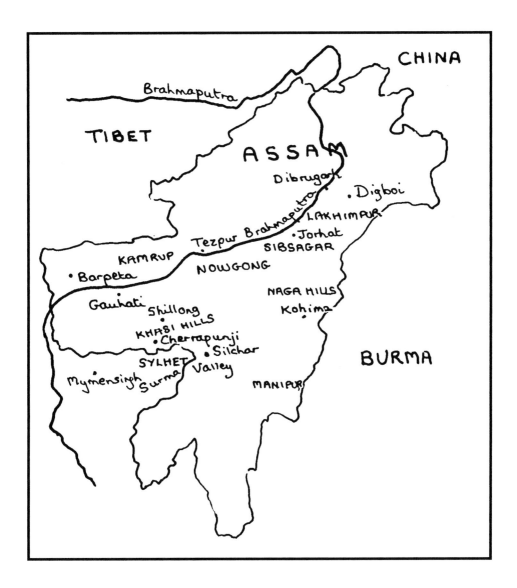

Map of Pre-Independence India, showing places mentioned in the text.

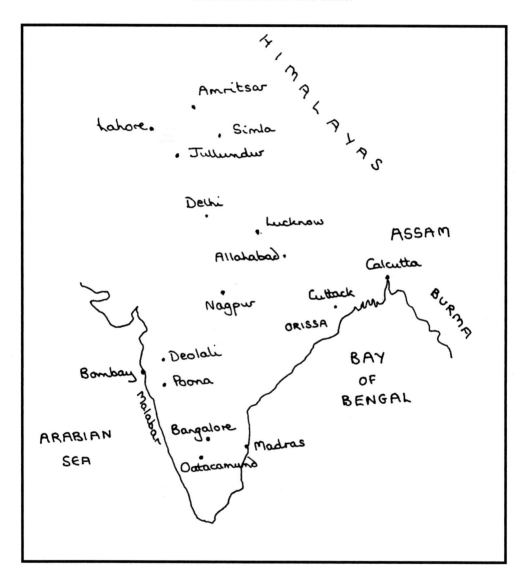

1: Initiation

It was not only to Indians that the British in India felt superior in the days of the Raj. They also felt superior to most of their compatriots. They were what was known as 'the Right Type'. In other words they had either attended what were known as 'the right schools' or wished they had. When war broke out in 1939, however, the Indian Army began recruiting Indians in such large numbers that there were not enough of the Right Type available to command them. Nevertheless, in 1940 an attempt was made to find them. The War Office invited public school leavers in Britain to volunteer for direct commissions in the Indian Army instead of joining the ranks at home, and the response was so encouraging that in January 1941 the Commandant of the Officers Training School in Bangalore assured the British staff sergeants, who were going to train them, that nine hundred cadets already on their way there were 'the cream of British youth'. And so most of them were.

'What kind of an officer do you think you're going to be, if you can't obey an order?' I heard an officer ask one of them, on the troopship that was taking them to India. (He had just caught him sleeping under a lifeboat, in defiance of a standing order.) 'Oh, I'll be alright' came the reassurance. 'I was at Marlborough.'

But I had been at a grammar school. The War Office had extended their offer to university students regardless of their schooling. My family background, too, was undesirable. During the Boer War my grandfather had stood up for the enemy and suffered accordingly and although he had volunteered in 1914 my father had refused the offer of a commission and was in the Etaples mutiny[1]. As for me, when war was declared in 1939 I had volunteered for the Royal Artillery and joined the Officers Training Corps, only because I was a card-carrying communist, and saw the war as the long delayed showdown with Fascism.

A few weeks later there occurred what Marxist dialecticians then called a 'qualitative' change – and perhaps still do. A war could not be an anti-fascist struggle unless an enemy of fascism was engaged in it and the only enemy of fascism – to wit the Soviet Union – was not involved in this one, thanks to a sudden non-aggression pact with Germany. This war was therefore no better than its 1914 predecessor.

We might never have worked this out for ourselves, but the Party leadership did it for us. Even so, I doubt whether many of us would have about-turned if we had still been on vacation at the time of this revelation. By then, however, we were back in Cambridge where we engaged in what were known as 'full and frank discussions' which meant listening closely to each other in case anyone sang out of tune. Primed to make any sacrifice for the revolution, most of us sacrificed our common sense, unhappy only to find ourselves ranked with pacifists. Pacifists had fixed principles. We believed in a fluid process of self-contradiction, called History.

Before the summer term had ended, however, as news of German victories poured in, some of us began to hope that once again the situation might 'change into its opposite' so that the war could be 'progressive' again. Comrades versed in Marxist theory spoke of 'revolutionary defenceism'. When I repeated this phrase to an erudite Indian Marxist student, called Arun Bose, however, he told me – sympathetically but firmly – that there was no hope that way. Revolutionary defenceism did indeed involve supporting the losing side in an imperialist war, but only when its proletariat had seized power.

Back in Manchester, while invasion loomed, perplexed I waited for my call-up, without reporting to the local Communist Party branch, as I had done on previous vacations. The excuse I made to myself for this dereliction was that my field of revolutionary activity was not the street now but the army, but what revolutionary activity in the army might involve was something I had no conception of. At Cambridge, although we had known that we would soon be in uniform, we had never discussed what we would do in it.

Presumably the answer was – to use the jargon – 'boreing from within', or in plain English, spreading disaffection. This would not be difficult, if a lecture on morale delivered by a regular artillery officer to the Cambridge O.T.C. was anything to go by. 'Before you take a bath when you come in from riding, you make sure your horse is taken care of. It's the same thing with your men. . . . . And you mustn't forget psychology. Suppose you send a chap to a forward observation post, and he gets shot, and you send another chap to the same F.O.P., and the same thing happens again, you wouldn't send a third chap there. That's psychology.'

But when a gleeful comrade told me that the morale of London was cracking in the blitz his glee repelled me and I refused to believe him. When he praised the German Radio's attacks on social inequality in Britain, I had no wish to emulate Lord Haw-Haw. But what was I to do? Leaving the Party would mean deserting people I admired when the going got rough.

The War Office solved my dilemma for me by notifying me that I would have to wait a year to join the artillery, but would be taken immediately if I applied for an emergency commission in the Indian Army. I had no qualms about boreing the Indian Army from within. I saw it as an occupation force, fighting peasant guerrillas in the mountains and slaughtering demonstrators in the streets, so I volunteered immediately. Simultaneously I reported this to the Party, and eventually received in return – by hand – the names and addresses of three contacts in India, to be memorised and destroyed, together with a copy of Palme Dutt's *India Today* to smuggle in with me.

This last item turned my trip into a mission. Palme Dutt's pronouncements were venerated by the Party faithful at the time. I believed that I was going to arrive in India bearing the sacred Truth. I wonder whether his book was even banned. Censorship in India was spasmodic. To protect cinema audiences from the sight of a black challenger flooring a white champion, importation of the Jack Johnson fight had been prohibited since 1909, but they watched black Joe Louis flooring white challengers throughout the war. Communists, however, mistakenly supposed that imperialists were as systematic as they themselves were.

I read Dutt's book dutifully, believing it would tell me all I needed to know about India. Nevertheless I also read Hindu legends and W.B. Yeats's version of the principal Upanishads. The prospect of visiting India had re-awakened an earlier fascination. When I was a six-year-old male chauvinist, the only feminine presence I welcomed in a story was that of an Indian princess, who was abandoned in the jungle where she was protected by a tiger. Later, hearing my father speak longingly of *nirvana* when harassed, I had equated it with the pleasant stupor I used to escape into, staring out of the school window. Exotic experiences awaited me!

When I reported for duty in Aldershot, just before Christmas, I found that I was not the only party member who had volunteered for India. Morris Jones, an L.S.E. communist student whom I had met in Cambridge when London University was evacuated there, was even in the same platoon.

We confronted our first *sahib* together on the voyage. In addition to nine hundred cadets, our troopship was carrying a contingent of retired Indian Army officers back to India. For weeks we saw nothing of them. They had been installed, along with our own officers, in the passenger accommodation, on the upper decks. We were stowed in the cargo space and allowed only on the well deck, where there was just room for us all to stand every morning to be inspected. Our voyage to India took us round Africa, however, and as we approached the Equator the Medical Officer decided that we needed air, so we were admitted to the lower promenade deck. Most officers reacted to this invasion by abandoning the lower promenade deck in favour of higher ones which were still barred to us, but on the evening of our first day up there, undeterred by a bugle sounding in the background, Morris and I were chatting by the rail, when I noticed that an Indian Army dug-out colonel, who had been strolling past, had halted and come to attention right next to us. For a moment he just stood there, but when we continued with our conversation he murmured, 'That's the Retreat.'

Those melancholy notes must have sounded in the first-class accommodation every evening since we weighed anchor, but this was the first time we had heard them and they meant nothing to either of us. Nevertheless I detected reproof in our informant's tone, so as he was standing to attention I followed suit. Morris on the other hand, took the words as a friendly offer of information, and feigned interest. 'Is it really? Thanks for telling us!'

The ageing colonel blinked and then walked off without another word, no doubt with renewed fears for the future of the land he still called 'home'. His real home was where he found himself at that moment – at sea between two worlds. Later in India I met a dug-out colonel who had realised this. Instead of settling in Britain, when he retired from service in India three years before the war, he had spent his time sailing to and fro between them. This arrangement, as he explained it, had three things to be said for it – exemption from income tax in both countries, a supply of reliable bridge-partners and duty-free drinks. Most important of all, however, it guaranteed him the company of fellow *sahibs*.

Before a British subject had ever set foot in India, *sahib* was a title bestowed by Indians on Indians, and it still is. It acknowledges a claim to deference. Some Indians like Tippu Sahib, the eighteenth century Sultan of Mysore, claimed the title by right of birth, but it can also be earned as a token of public respect. My friend Mian Iftikar-ud-din, an influential figure in the Punjab, was generally referred to as 'Mian Sahib'. Other applications were less specific. It could be used as a respectful form of address, as the English word 'sir' can be applied to the undubbed. Local communities might honour local notables with the title as a matter of course. An argumentative speaker might even apply it for the nonce to his listener to indicate that he thinks none the less of him although he disagrees with him – rather as the protestation 'with respect' is used in English. In brief, addressing a man as '*sahib*' is an acknowledgement of one of various different claims to respect, ranging from the institutional to the personal. It is not a recognition of his race.

Nevertheless, the British in India attempted to monopolise it – presumably in the belief that the respect its use implied was something no Indian was entitled to while every Briton was. A hundred odd years ago, *Hobson-Johnson*[2] – 'a glossary of colloquial Anglo-Indian words and phrases' – accordingly defined it as : 'a title by which, all over India, European gentlemen, and it may be said Europeans generally, are addressed, and spoken of, when no disrespect is intended, by natives'. (The word 'European' here means 'white'. It was Indians, not Americans and Australians, who were barred from membership of 'European' clubs.) It will be noted that *Hobson-Jobson* implies that a European was a *sahib* even when he was not a gentleman, and that to fail to address him as such was disrespectful – if you were an Indian.

Whatever might have been the case in the days of Hobson-Jobson, by the time I went to India, the only Indians who addressed Europeans as *sahib* were menials or *sepoys*. Nevertheless – just as an echo of a nobler, older sense still clings occasionally to the title 'gentleman'– expectations of lordliness did hang about some applications of *sahib* to Europeans, especially in the Indian Army where *sepoys* sometimes really did regard an officer as a sort of lord and themselves as his vassals. If he was ready to use his influence on their behalf – and even bend the rules a little – they might even rate him as a *pukka* (i.e. ripe or full-blown) *sahib*.

Some Indian Army officers did deserve this title. Some had even been born in India to fathers who had served in the same regiment, and therefore were truly native Indians. If they were unquestioningly loyal to the King-Emperor, so too were the ethnic Indians under their command, and they also resembled other Indians in being members of an exclusive group, with specific obligations and taboos. What was peculiar to them was the practice of retiring to die in a distant land, to which they also sent their children to be trained and educated. The cardinal virtue of *pukka sahibs* was personal loyalty to those for whom they were immediately responsible. That is why they were more plentiful in the Indian Army. It is easy to be loyal to a small group. A district magistrate might be responsible for a million or more people. In the Indian Civil Service, therefore, personal loyalty had to be replaced by devotion to duty, and often was.

As for the third group of Europeans – '*box-wallahs*' as business-men were called in the Army – few could conceive of ties to Indian subordinates beyond the terms of their employment, witness the reaction of a Calcutta *box-wallah* and his wife when an Indian Army widow told them what had happened to a *pukka sahib* she knew. When he was a subaltern he sometimes came home from the mess to his quarters drunk, and his bearer, an elderly Moslem, would then give him a sermon on the evils of drink as he put him to bed, until on one such evening he kicked the old man half-way through his homily and called him a pig. The old man went straight to the bathroom, ran a cold bath and, returning to the slumped *sahib* who was expecting to be put to bed now, dragged him to the bath and plunged him into it. 'Do you realise what you've done?' he asked.

'I do,' the suddenly sober young man admitted, 'and I ask you to forgive me.'

'What use is that?', his bearer answered. 'When it is told in the bazaar that you have kicked me and called me a pig, my name will be as dirt – unless I kill you – and I'm a Pathan, so I am going to kill you.'

The young man admitted that he could understand that.

'On the other hand,' the bearer continued, 'if the *sahibs* in the mess hear about what I just did to you, your name will be as dirt too, won't it?'

The young man agreed again.

'Then if you don't tell anyone,' the bearer offered, 'neither will I.'

'Of course, he sacked the fellow', was the *box-wallah*'s comment when the widow finished her story. She was stupefied.

For the remainder of the voyage the retired Indian Army colonels introduced us to their culture when we spent an hour each day in small groups, sitting on the deck at their feet, while they taught us Urdu from deck-chairs. The linguistic results were marginal, except in the case of one cadet, who had spent his early childhood in India, in the company of Indian servants. One morning he awoke to find that he spoke Urdu fluently. The moral result, however, was considerable.

Colonel Kelly, our own tutor, was the authentic voice of the Raj. His glosses on vocabulary usually took the form of reminiscences. Many of these were of wild life, especially bird life, although his very best story was about a cobra[3], but what most interested us was the human scene of which he gave us glimpses. He had commanded Punjabi Musalmans. They were quite like us, he assured us, and in some ways better. The Punjabi peasant had a sense of decency which Europeans would do well to imitate. Even in the Punjab, however, the same could not be claimed for city-dwellers. In the mouth of Colonel Kelly the word *shahr* ('city'), as distinguished from *chhaoni* (cantonment) had the same ring that *casbah* has in a tale of the French Foreign Legion. The garrison towns in which we would be stationed were divided into two parts, each with its own railway station. One where the general population lived – was the teeming city, only to be visited when it was unavoidable. Europeans lived with the necessary attendants in the military cantonment – in tidy bungalows if they were officers and in barracks if they were B.O.R.s (British Other Ranks).

According to Colonel Kelly, an Indian city was a powder keg. Even in the Punjab its inhabitants were prone to riot and it was infested with Congress Party politicians – lawyers for the most part. The Congress Party was a pack of self-important *babus* who wanted to step into our shoes, and no trick was too low for them to stoop to. Once a pious old Moslem villager he was chatting with had demanded to know why the government had put 'a good Moslem like Gandhi' into jail. Gandhi was in fact a fervent Hindu, but this simple old man had been tricked into believing that he was a Moslem, just to make him anti-British. Incidentally, not only was Gandhi a Hindu, but he was a *banya* by caste, and had therefore inherited the cunning of a money-lender.

When Colonel Kelly described cities as explosive, however, he was thinking less of anti-British political activity than of communal riots between Hindus and Moslems – a subject which Morris and I were sure that we knew more about than he did. Nevertheless, when he informed us that it was only the British presence that prevented Hindu-Moslem tension from erupting into massacre, we held our peace. This view had been imposed on him, we told ourselves. It did not occur to us that our own view of Hindu-Moslem relations might have been imposed on us. We understood the 'logic of history' – the Marxist equivalent of the will of God – and the logic of history united Hindus and Moslems in opposition to British exploitation, under the banner of the Indian National Congress. Little did we know that before the war was over the Indian Communist Party would endorse the opposite view of Mohammed Ali Jinnah, that Indian Moslems were a distinct nation.

Colonel Kelly commended anything Indian that was not an innovation, and anathematized anything Indian that was – especially the growth of a westernised middle class. In his view, western education destroyed Indians' traditional good qualities. The way to treat Indians was to leave them to do things as they always had done, apart from one or two practices which had already been prohibited. Hindus could not be allowed to go on immolating widows on their husbands' funeral pyres, for instance. Other customs, however, were not as bad as they might sound, so on the whole it was best to leave Indians to pursue their own time-honoured ways except for their habit of chewing *pan*. Something really must be done about that. We would find the pavements, passages and walls of Indian cities stained with splashes of what looked like blood, but was spittle, reddened as a result of chewing a preparation composed of a dried nut and different spices, laced with quick lime and wrapped in a leaf. It was said to be refreshing, and for all he knew it might be, but unfortunately when it ceased to give refreshment the residue had to be spat out, and few Indians cared where they spat it.

Other traditional Indian practices were unobjectionable, and if Indians knew what was good for them they would stick to them. Their adoption of Western practices only made them look ridiculous. This applied especially to things that the West was good at, like manufacture – although in all fairness it must be said that the fruit squash bottled in the Punjab was fruitier than anything on sale in Britain.

Leaving Indians alone to do things their own way called for broad-mindedness. We naturally thought our ways were preferable, but Indians just as naturally thought that theirs were. As a case in point, he took favouritism. Back home in Britain, when our younger brothers arrived as new boys at the same school, we cuffed them publicly to make it plain to them and to everybody else that they would get no favours from us. Indians found such conduct disgraceful. In their view if you did not do your second cousin a favour when you had it in your power to do so, you were failing in your duty. This applied to dependants too, so when one of our men asked us to approach the civil authorities on behalf of his family, it was not our job to inquire into the rights and wrongs of a dispute in a distant village. Our job was to throw our weight behind our chap.

He also cautioned us against misinterpreting physical expressions of affection between men. Indians did not find it odd to see two hulking chaps go wandering hand in hand. To us it might look mawkish, but that was just one point of view, so when we saw that sort of thing we must remember that men could behave like that and still be manly. Punjabi Moslems in particular, whom he had had the honour to command, were as tough as any soldiers in the world – including the British.

Everything he said, however, implied that these fighting qualities required British officers to elicit them, although he could not say so, and had instead to tell us things that he did not believe. Young Indians 'with a suitable family background' were invited to apply for King's Commissions nowadays. He spoke circumspectly, reminding us that some Indians attended English public schools and Sandhurst, and in any case India now had her own public schools and Military Academy, which were just as good. His manner implied, however, that when he said this he was repeating an official doctrine which he must not contradict but did not personally subscribe to. Strange as it might seem, Indian commissioned officers were now to be found in the Indian Army, and this was how one had to talk about them.

When he talked of *subedars* and *jemadars*, however, there was no doubting his sincerity. These officers held the Viceroy's, not the King's, commission. Unspoilt by western education, they had started at the bottom, as *sepoys*, and risen gradually through all the non-commissioned ranks. There could therefore be no doubt about their soldierly qualities, while they for their part knew their place. The judgement of a V.C.O., with twenty years' service, must yield to ours, the moment we had finished our training. Colonel Kelly did not find it necessary to justify this. He did, however, assure us that it was good to mix with Viceroy's commissioned officers off parade, now and then. They prized the honour of entertaining British officers at their mess.

His tips were not all military. He told us how to ensure that river water was fit to drink and how to build a field oven.

He advised us to stand the legs of our beds in small tins of kerosene, as a protection against bugs. He described the joy of sitting like a miner after a hard day, in a galvanised iron tub filled with hot water from a bucket, as only cold water was plumbed in. He warned us against sponges, Mugs were better. They were free of centipedes. He told us a Hindu legend of how the squirrel got its stripes.

As Morris and I could not bring ourselves to condemn him as an 'imperialist hireling' we dismissed him as a silly old buffer. Secretly, however, I was alarmed to think that I would soon be living in his world.

2: In the picture

When we docked in Bombay a few of us were allowed ashore immediately, as they had parents waiting on the quay to greet them. The rest of us had to wait until evening, staring at the port employees. Except for an Indian sentry, posted at the foot of the gangway, we were the only soldiers. We were also the only Europeans, except for an official dressed in white, who came out onto a balcony from time to time to take a look at us. Although they were civilians, the Indians nearly all wore uniforms. Even the sweepers were in uniform. The quay-side was spick and span. Whitewash has proved to be one of Britain's enduring legacies to India. The others are cricket, potatoes and tea.

I spent most of the day on deck, counting the hours until Morris and I could go ashore to meet my Bombay contact. A few days before our arrival we had heard on the BBC the news that the British Communist Party had at last been declared illegal. At last the government was taking us as seriously as we took ourselves. We found this bracing. When I opened Palme Dutt's book and folded it back under my shirt against my chest, I felt as if I was smuggling dynamite.

There were no taxis at the dock gates, so we took a victoria – a four-wheeled carriage with a double seat for passengers. Thanks to our Urdu lessons on the ship we knew that the driver's response to the address we gave him meant that we had a long way to go, and after ten minutes progress at a tired but remorseless plod we realised that this also meant a very long time, but there seemed to be no chance of changing to a taxi as we ambled through endless streets. To our surprise the apartment blocks looked habitable. We expected every Indian city to be a poverty-stricken slum.

Soon, with a rapidity to which we were now accustomed, the sun had dropped out of sight, and lights came on behind bars in open windows. As the one-speed horse plodded on, I began to feel less resolute. When we reached our destination, Yusuf Ahmed might very well be out, but even if he was in, what was the use of bursting in on a local party member in Bombay when we would be a thousand miles away next day? But this was the address the Party had provided. Ours not to reason why.

It had long been dark when the victoria came to a halt. Suddenly excited, we got briskly down into the street, telling the driver to wait, and entered a shabby doorway. The staircase was badly-lit, and stained half-way up its walls with scarlet stains, as Colonel Kelly had predicted. Our goal was several floors up. There was no bell, so we knocked – repeatedly, because at first nobody answered – until at last a man in a singlet and a *dhoti* (loin-cloth) appeared in the open doorway and suspiciously asked us what we wanted.

'Yusuf Ahmed?', we replied inquiringly. He shook his head, as if we had insulted him, and made to shut the door. 'Does he live here?' we persisted. 'Or perhaps you know where we can find him?'

'I am a Brahmin', was the answer. 'This Yusuf Ahmed, what caste is he?'

Concealing our shock, we asked whether he knew where we might find Mr Ahmed. 'I know no Ahmeds', he declared, as if we had insulted him, and closed the door.

According to our driver, my other Bombay address was on the other side of the city so we had to go straight back to the ship. We were to leave for Bangalore next morning, and I had been given no contact there, so this meant indefinitely postponing reporting to the Party. Meanwhile we had to digest a disagreeable impression. The Brahmin's evident anti-Moslem prejudice and the pride with which he had announced his caste were the sort of thing one heard about from imperialist apologists. It did not occur to us that the first concern of an Indian, at whose door two British soldiers arrived at night in search of somebody, would naturally be to establish the widest possible distance between their quarry and himself.

The coaches of the troop train in which we took our seats next morning, were designed for other ranks. They were open from end to end, divided into skeleton framework compartments of metal tubing, in which we sat in sixes, three facing three, on slatted wooden benches. The absence of partitions allowed air speeded by electric fans, to circulate throughout each coach from end to end. The sky outside was cloudless and the sunshine unremitting, but the really hot weather had not started yet. We made ourselves comfortable, and gazed out of the windows.

The only visible feature which had anything to do with Britain was the railway – built in late Victorian days at twice the real cost because the Government of India had guaranteed a five per cent return on the investment, to be met, if the railways did not earn it, from the taxes paid by the people we glimpsed far off in the fields, or saw at closer quarters as we trundled through railway stations or over level crossings, slowly enough to gaze at the halted wayfarers – and to be gazed at in return by them, as it was not every day they saw red faces in such large numbers.

Indeed, apart from the railway itself, the landscape presented no obvious signs of European intrusion. Throughout the journey, the only people we saw were Indians going about their business, in ways that were decidedly their own, against an exotic background of palm trees, cottages that seemed to have no real windows, and temples crowned by structures that were neither towers nor domes. As for their dress, hardly any of us had ever even seen a *sari* or a *dhoti* before the previous evening. Even western products were transformed. Shirts were worn hanging out of the trousers. Buses had ornamental coach-work, like fairground caravans. Bicycles were pushed along like wheel-barrows, loaded with furniture, or bundles of cloth, or metal vessels looped together with string. On railway station platforms wandering vendors served tea in glasses instead of cups. India seemed to be exactly as Colonel Kelly had represented it – a land where the only role of the British was to guard the frontiers and keep the peace, leaving the inhabitants free to go their own ways. The role which this superficially flattering view assigned to the British in practice was that of arresting India's development. In the nature of things, what might have been there if they had not been could not be seen.

Late at night on the third day we arrived at Bangalore Cantonment Station, to be received by the British staff sergeants who had been told to expect the cream of Britain's youth. As they told us later, the word went round that the cream had turned. With unpolished brass and battered pith helmets, we had been a shabby crew even when we boarded the train. Now we were also unshaven and grimy. Nevertheless, we were treated like arriving tourists as Indians were present. Just as in a school, teachers bolster adult authority by treating each other with exaggerated courtesy in the presence of pupils, so Europeans in India observed strict decorum in their behaviour to one another when Indians were present. There was therefore no crowding and no shouting as we emerged from the station, and military lorries rolled up like taxis to drive us off down smooth, well-lit cantonment roads.

We were about to be transformed. Next morning I awoke like a beggar in an Arabian Nights story, who wakes to find himself a prince. Instead of being roused by sailors giving the decks an early morning swabbing, I gradually became aware, through a haze of mosquito netting, of a murmuring bearer proffering tea and biscuits. My feet, once out of bed, were surprised to meet a rug, and looking around I saw furniture. The room was not all mine. On the other side of it, Morris was awaking to the same amenities, but what we had to share seemed too good to be true.

After a breakfast served by attentive uniformed waiters, at tables laid with cloths, our transformation was completed by the removal of every stitch of clothing that had been issued to us in England – a place where we had to polish our own boots. From now on we would be looked after as we had not been since infancy, by bearers who woke us every morning

*Morris Jones and the author, newly commissioned, in Srinagar,
Kashmir, 1941*

with cups of tea and every evening layed out freshly laundered uniforms for us to change into when we had bathed – and soon enough – like children, we took it all for granted.

Our officers were not as well trained as our bearers. A cavalry major, instructing us in motor vehicle maintenance set up an engine fault in a staff car for us to trace, but it began to rain, so he dismissed us, and by the time the rain stopped he had forgotten what he had done. In the end he had to summon a technician – as the technician, a British sergeant, did not hesitate to tell us later.

Another major had a way with mules. No matter how stubborn they might be, they were always pacified if he tickled their ears in the right place. Each time he approached a mule to demonstrate this skill, however, it threw back its head and bared its teeth, so in the end two *sepoys* had to hold its head and even then it showed no sign of gratification, when he had finished.

The saddest case was the captain who taught us map-reading. Repeatedly he warned us that as altitude was given in feet on Ordnance Survey maps, and distances in yards, we must convert yards into feet when calculating a gradient, until one morning he announced that he was taking back his warning. An idea had come to him the previous evening. What would happen if feet were converted into yards instead? He had made twenty different calculations both ways, to make sure, and got the same result both ways, every time, so now we were free to do it either way!

My happiest memory however, is of a demonstration of how not to communicate. Greatly to his credit (for he was the only one of our officers who did this) one morning an elegant captain from a crack Indian regiment visited our mess for breakfast, and attempted to protest on our behalf about the marmalade. 'Waiter. . . look here. . ..' (He had to speak in English because the Tamilian waiter would not have understood Urdu.) 'You don't call this marmalade?' He pointed to a blob of amber-coloured jelly on his plate. The waiter had learnt the English word for everything on the table and answered confidently. 'Yes, *sahib*, that *marmlet*.'

The captain sighed. 'What I mean to say is this, waiter. You can't *really* call this marmalade.'

The bearer had never tasted marmalade. He just knew the name *marmlet* and confusion between two European breakfast dishes – *marmlet* and *mormlet* ('omelet') – was all too easy, so he hurried off to consult the steward, before returning reassured and reassuring. 'Yes, *sahib* – that *marmlet*.'

The captain sighed, but now the thing had started he was going to see it through. 'Waiter,' he said crisply. 'This stuff is not what I call marmalade.' This made the question personal. The embarrassed waiter marched into the kitchen, to return apologetically, holding up a gleaming yellow can, for all to see the word MARMALADE stencilled on it in enormous letters.

'What can one do?' The captain did not reappear in the mess and there was no improvement in the marmalade.

The officers were there to teach the finer points of military science. Basic infantry skills were taught by British sergeants, seconded from regiments that had been posted for service in India before the outbreak of war. When they were directly in charge of us, they showed no mercy. I recall standing in a sealed room full of tear gas with the platoon sergeant. He was wearing a respirator. I was not. My task was to put one on correctly, and in my hurry to stop choking I kept ignoring the prescribed sequence of adjustments – so he kept making me take it off and try again, without telling me where I was going wrong. That taught me the value of a respirator.

The weapon training sergeant kept to his military manuals so closely that when he asked us to name one of the light machine-gun's stoppages the only answer he would accept was the subject of a sentence in the manual that ended - '... which is one of the stoppages'. The manual listed other stoppages, but none of the others was acceptable when he asked for 'one of them'.

He was not incapable of irony at the manual's expense,

however. 'Stamp! Stamp! Stamp!' he yelled at us one morning, as we advanced on sandbags with our bayonets fixed. 'It puts fear into the hearts of the enemy', he quoted from the manual. News of the fall of Crete had arrived that morning. 'It must have done, mustn't it?' he added.

On another occasion he informed us that when we heard him shout the words 'take cover!' we must not waste time looking for cover, but just fling ourselves flat on the ground in the firing position behind whatever happened to be in front of us, 'even if it was just a blade of grass'.

'Which means', he began his peroration, 'when you hear the words "Take cover...!"' The next thing I knew I was flat on the ground in the firing position, with the rest of the section gazing down at me. 'As you were!' he snapped, as I started to get up, and pointed down at me, as if displaying me for sale. 'That's what I like to see! Don't think when you receive an order!'

Their view of our officers was as low as ours. They felt no more loyalty to officers of the Indian Army than they felt for anything else connected with India – especially those who, but for the outbreak of war, would have been time-expired men on a troopship leaving Bombay.

One afternoon, when our platoon sergeant had lined us up at the end of a day's training, and handed us over to a captain, our platoon commander, to be told what we were going to do next day, the captain was just finishing his explanations when an eerie wail arose from somewhere in our ranks. He stopped speaking and the interruption died away. I stole a glance at the sergeant, expecting him to erupt, but he stood staring pebble-eyed into space. He had handed us over to the captain in good order, and now it was up to the captain to keep us in that state.

All the captain did, however, was stand a moment, wonderstruck, and then ask, 'What on earth was that?' 'It's only Harrap, sir', a warm, slow-speaking voice assured him, in a Mummerset accent.

'Harrap's mad', confided another voice – a feeble, bleating one, which was in fact the distorted voice of Harrap. The first speaker had been his room-mate, Comber. They were a comedy team.

The captain hesitated. Many a time, as a schoolboy, I had seen that weary expression on the face of a teacher, uncertain whether to ignore impertinence or accept it as a challenge. 'Carry on, sergeant!', he intoned, returned the salute of the sergeant with a wave of his swagger-stick, and strode away, in his baggy shorts, leaving us to face the music. But the pebble-eyed sergeant just dismissed us.

As long as it was staged when they were not in charge, the staff sergeants even appreciated the Harrap and Comber turn. Sometimes it included the leavening of military make-believe with private fantasy. On one occasion we were driven to a distant hill-top for a 'tactical exercise without troops', and viewing the landscape from this commanding height, were instructed to imagine we had certain forces at our disposal in occupation of various features down below, with which to resist an advancing enemy. Harrap and Comber, however, preferred to imagine that they were two charwomen on a picnic, eating potted shrimps. 'Oysters is amorous and winkles is lecherous, but shrimps, Mrs Rogers! I'm telling you. SHRIMPS!'

If they could do so without breaking regulations, the staff sergeants were even ready to contribute to the entertainment when an officer was in charge. The pebble-eyed platoon sergeant contrived a comic turn that Harrap and Comber could not have bettered. His victim was the least sympathetic of all our officers, our company commander – a florid, blond major, bursting with flesh the colour of raw sausage meat. Unlike our other officers, he belonged to the British Army, not the Indian. He had also been awarded the Military Cross – but received no credit for it from the staff sergeants. 'Awarded for firing Verey lights in Palestine', they said. The only time we saw him was when he was teaching us infantry tactics, and even then he did not see us in return. His eyes were fixed on the sand-table – an indoor expanse the size of a small swimming pool, arranged in miniature hills and valleys across which he manoeuvred counters, representing sections of infantry. We sat on benches round three sides of it while he crouched omnipotently at the far end with a pointer in his hand, disposing victory and defeat like a god on Mount Olympus.

Our two platoon sergeants did not normally attend when we were being instructed by an officer, but were required to do so on these occasions. The idea may have been that the tactical expertise they would acquire would make a difference after they returned to their regiments if they lost their platoon commanders in action. More probably, however, the Major wanted them there to enhance the solemnity of the occasion, like mutes at a funeral. While he was on his feet, expounding tactics, they sat behind him, one to the left and one to the right, on identical chairs, the three of them forming a triptych.

If solemnity was the object of this arrangement, on one occasion it misfired badly. Having first moved across in front of where the pebble-eyed sergeant sat, in order to get close to some new subject matter, the Major was as usual bending forward to point out features in the landscape, when suddenly it dawned on me that the eyes of the cadets facing me across the sand-table were not following his pointer but riveted by something just behind him – to wit the nose of the sergeant who by leaning forward, with an expression of devout attention on his face, had placed it just behind his commander's bulging shorts. In all apparent seriousness he somehow made it obvious that he was meticulously applying the Major's clipped account of hills and valleys, rising ground and dead ground, not to the contours of the miniature landscape but to those of the speaker's rump.

The most remarkable, because explicit, display of disrespect for officers, was made by the Company Sergeant Major. Addressing us on parade, the day after our arrival at the School – with no officer present – he denounced the sins committed in the army in the name of discipline. He was all for discipline, he said. An army could not last a day without it, but like every other good thing you could have too much of it, and when that happened you had bullshit – which was what they dished out in the British Army night and day. He wanted us to know from the start that he was against it, and if he had anything to do with it we were not going to find any in this company. True to his word, he exercised minimal control. The crisis came towards the end of our training when the Commandant – a brigadier who seized every opportunity to tell us that wars were still won with the bayonet – caught sight of us riding past his office on our bicycles in a disorderly fashion when we should have been 'riding to attention'. (This last meant sitting bolt-upright on the saddle in total silence, looking straight ahead, holding the handle-bars with both hands, and keeping both arms extended in parallel.)

He voiced his displeasure to his adjutant who passed it on to our pink company commander, who duly conveyed it to the company sergeant-major to be handed on to us that evening on parade.

'A certain gentleman has made remarks to me about your discipline and wants to know why none of you has been before him on a charge yet. That gentleman is telling me he wants to see some of you up there very soon. It's not something I'd like to see myself though. It wouldn't look well on your records. So I'm just warning you, a certain gentleman is looking forward to seeing some of you up before him on a charge.' Thanks to this moral giant, we all finished the course with clean records. '"They call this a war against German militarism', he scoffed, 'but if you ask my opinion, British militarism is the worst.' Commendable though this was, it was anachronistic, and the ignorance it revealed was not just political. Neither he nor the other N.C.O.s had any training, much less experience, of warfare in which tanks and aircraft played a part. The only preparation we received for modern war was a glimpse of a glorified elephant-gun, described as an anti-tank rifle – and instructions for turning a bottle into a petrol bomb, also for use against tanks. The Indian Army was fighting Mussolini in the Western Desert, but the only enemy we were trained to fight were tribesmen.

The endless war against the tribes was not confined to the North West Frontier. It was fought throughout India. Even in Bangalore, a thousand miles from the Khyber Pass, instead of lining up when it was turned out a guard took up firing positions, and troops on firing practice had to recover a percentage of the lead they had discharged into the butts, to ensure that it did not find its way to the tribesmen's cottage arms industry to be turned back into bullets. (Naturally, this rule did not apply to the cream of British youth. Our spent lead was harvested by *sepoys* after we had left the range.)

Lead was not the only metal tribesmen converted into bullets. A lecturer told us about a battalion stationed on the Frontier, whose officers improvised a nine-hole golf-course, and secured the holes with empty cocoa-tins. Early next morning, however, when the commanding officer and the adjutant went out to christen the course before the sun had risen uncomfortably high, they found that the tins had been removed in the night, to be beaten into bullets. This happened several times, but then the adjutant hit on the solution. Small earthenware pots were substituted for the tins, and sure enough, when the commanding officer and the adjutant played a round next morning before breakfast, they found the first eight holes intact – but when the triumphant C.O. stooped to recover his ball at the ninth he found it deep in human excrement.

It could have been something more lethal. Ruthlessness was normal – on both sides. Gleefully we were told how one tribe's greed for metal had been punished. They kept a close watch on what went on in the station, and one day they saw a funeral. Next morning the grave had been opened and the lead lining of the coffin had been removed. The battalion staged another funeral on completion of its tour of duty, but the coffin contained no lead this time – only explosives and a detonator.

These tales were spiced with admiration for the foe. Not so the stories of the Frontier told by the British Other Ranks with whom I shared a ward in the British Military Hospital for a few days. None of them spoke from personal experience of service on the Frontier, but all had tales to tell of atrocities inflicted there on British Other Ranks. A B.O.R. who fell into tribal hands was passed on to the women to be tortured unless he had red hair. In that case he was put to stud – the story went – because the Prophet's hair had been that colour. According to this lore, the most atrocious trick the tribesmen played on British soldiers was sneaking into barracks to castrate them on the loo – a place where, as I can vouch from personal experience, this operation could easily have been performed. In those days, few loos in India were plumbed in. Most were thunder-boxes, whose buckets were removed by sweepers. The sweeper entered the loo itself, through a back door, to get at the bucket in a private bungalow, but where loos were installed in large numbers in one building – as in a hospital or a barrack – there was a block of cubicles, each with a flap at floor level opening onto a back passage, which enabled a sweeper to remove the bucket through the wall without entering the premises. According to the story I was told in hospital, it also enabled a tribesman lurking in the back passage, to reach through when the loo was occupied and perform rapid surgery on the occupant.

When this was mentioned there was general confirmation, as of a well-known truth. I smiled smugly to myself when I left them to go to the loo, and almost laughed when, as I sat down, I heard the flap opening behind me. If I had been credulous, I said to myself, how this would alarmed me! Before I could laugh, however, I felt the pressure of cold steel on just the parts which would have felt it if the tales I had been listening to were true, and jumped to my feet, bellowing. The flap behind me banged shut and bare feet pounded away along the passage. They were not, however, the feet of a thwarted tribesman.

They belonged to a terrified sweeper who, unaware that the loo was occupied, had caught me in the handle as he started to remove the bucket.

The colonel who supervised our frontier warfare training, had lost an eye in battle and had no use for myths. He attributed the violence of frontier life ultimately to de-forestation and, more immediately, to eye-for-an-eye justice. Tribal territory was coloured pink on the map, Indian and British troops were garrisoned in it, and its inhabitants were recruited to the Indian Army, but the Government of India left its inhabitants to administer justice for themselves in their own way, according to which a criminal owed a debt to his victim, or his victim's family, not to society. Someone I know who lost a hand in a booby trap was accordingly awarded a sheep, and that settled the matter. In a case of murder, however, the aggrieved party was not the victim but his remaining family, and the only acceptable compensation demanded in many if not all such cases was blood for blood. The blood required, however, need not be that of the actual murderer. The blood of any member of his family sufficed.

Shortly after the war, having just seen Olivier's film of *Hamlet*, my Pathan bearer told me that he knew just how Hamlet felt. Doing what was called for had not come easily to him either, when at the age of eighteen he had joined a family team to avenge the murder of his cousin. They had cornered a brother of the guilty party in a hut, and as he was the youngest his uncle had instructed him to stick his knife in first.

Maintaining the authority of government against this background demanded a show of superior force, so the Indian Army periodically staged a march of a column of troops up and down a mountain pass, to demonstrate that it could go wherever it wanted to in tribal territory, in spite of any opposition that the tribes might care to offer. These columns were normally commanded by a brigadier, but although he did not tell us so himself, the one-eyed colonel had commanded one. Lovingly he took us through this operation step by step. The tribesmen regarded a column as a sporting fixture, according to him, and he may not have been altogether wrong. A few years after the war, when Karachi was still the capital of Pakistan, I watched a group of tribal leaders demonstrating outside the U.K. High Commission there. They had arrived from the Frontier to protest to the Pakistan government at the removal of their eldest sons from tribal territory – for the sake of their education, according to the Pakistan government, but to be exploited as hostages, the tribesmen said. 'Come back Britain!' was their cry. The Raj would never have done a thing like this! The Raj knew the rules, and had kept to them.

Pathans were sticklers for rules, the one-eyed colonel assured us. They were ruthless enemies but if they invited you to their village for a feast – as did sometimes happen – their code of hospitality not only ensured that there would be no treachery, but even guaranteed you cover during your journey to and from the feast. Even so, not all the practices he recommended were cricket. According to regulations, a column must not open fire until it had been fired on. 'But if something moves behind a rock, shoot before you're shot. If it turns out to have been some old woman, she had no business to be there behind a rock, and you can always say you thought you saw a gun.' He was the only officer for whom the staff sergeants expressed respect.

The enemy whose name was mentioned was neither Hitler nor Mussolini but the Fakir of Ipi.[4] This confirmed the belief in which I had volunteered for the Indian Army – that the Indian Army was engaged in a constant war against peasant guerrillas. A course on 'aid to the civil power' dealt with what I had pictured as their other activity – slaughtering demonstrators in city streets. The way in which this was presented on the course, however, was as a measure to prevent Indians from slaughtering one another, because they took religion so seriously. When their religious susceptibilities were offended, even when the offence was accidental, they were outraged, and to make matters worse Moslems and Hindus sometimes offended each other deliberately, provoking incidents which could develop into communal riots. Restoring law and order when that happened was in the first instance the duty of the magistracy and the police, but if things got out of hand they handed over to the military.

The resulting duty, it was stressed to us repeatedly and solemnly, was the most unpleasant that a soldier could be called on to perform, and I do not doubt that those who did perform it were repelled by it. On the other hand I also think there was a certain satisfaction in the fact that it was sometimes necessary to perform it. It seemed to justify the privileged position that the British had assumed for themselves – above the struggle. Far from agreeing with this view, Indian nationalists blamed a British policy of playing one community against another for communal riots. The Government of India may indeed have exploited communal suspicions, but as Nehru himself pointed out they could not have done so if communal tension had not been waiting there to be exploited. The real point is that Indians do not need help from foreigners to prevent one group from attacking another. They can do it for themselves.

More to the point, in view of what was to happen in the following year, was the fact that it was not only to protect one community from another that the civil power sometimes needed military assistance. We were being trained to deal with anti-British demonstrations too. The very example examined in detail in our Instruction was the anti-British demonstration at Amritsar in 1919 which led to the notorious massacre. The magnitude of this slaughter was the result of General Dyer's eagerness to 'teach Indians a lesson', but that was not how it was presented to us. It was presented simply as an object lesson in how not to do things. Dyer, we were told, had just disastrously failed to follow the correct procedures.

The matter-of-fact character of those procedures shocked us, but facing facts is an unavoidable preliminary to being practical, and one object of the routine was to minimise casualties. The other less commendable aim was to ensure that if we ever ordered fire to be opened to disperse a crowd, we could not later be accused of having acted without authority. To ensure this, a military detachment deployed in city streets on 'internal security duties' must always be accompanied by a magistrate. It was the magistrate's function to be the first to order a crowd to disperse when it was getting out of hand. The officer only entered the picture if the crowd did not obey the magistrate. In that event the magistrate handed him a signed statement – which the officer must insist upon receiving on the spot – to the effect that the situation was beyond his control so he was transferring responsibility for public order to the military. Only then did it become the officer's duty to disperse the crowd. That was where the commendable aim entered the picture. The crowd must be dispersed with minimum casualties. In other words, it must be frightened as quickly as possible.

For a start the order to disperse should be repeated, with the addition of a warning that they would be fired on if they did not do so, and – accompanied by the menacing rattle of rifle bolts – this in itself sometimes proved sufficient. General Dyer, however, had failed to give the crowd at Amritsar a warning. He had simply ordered his men to open fire.

His second so-called 'error' had been no less fatal. A crowd should only be ordered to disperse in a situation where there were exits allowing it to do so, but the crowd that Dyer had threatened was boxed in, as he and his men were stationed between them and their only exit.

The third rule was to fire as few rounds as possible. This did not mean firing into the air. If nobody was seen to suffer when the first shot was fired, the crowd would only grow more unruly, so that more shots would be needed to disperse it than would have been the case if the first had found a target. If a crowd refused to disperse, after receiving due warning, somebody had therefore to be shot.

With luck, however, only one shot would be necessary. That had been General Dyer's third 'mistake'. He had ordered his entire force to open fire, and continue firing at will.

On this point our instructions were precise. Not a single round should be fired without a specific command, and to start with only one shot should be fired – but it should be fired to kill. That too was to keep casualties to a minimum. Shots fired into the air or at knee level only served to increase the slaughter they were intended to avoid. They created an impression that bullets were nothing to be afraid of, so in the end more shots had to be fired than would other-wise have been necessary. One fatal shot at the beginning might well prove to be enough.

The officer in charge of the detachment should therefore ostentatiously point out a particular individual in the crowd, for everyone to see, and order the best shot in his detachment to shoot him dead, as wounds were less convincing. As soon as he confronted the crowd the unfortunate officer must therefore start looking for a target for this demonstration, in case it was going to prove necessary. There was always at least one noisy individual, urging on the others.

For Morris and me then this cold-blooded ruthlessness epitomised the brutality which underlay the whole procedure, but mobs have killed even more people than security forces have since then. The question remains – when does a crowd become a mob? – and if the answer has to be – 'When it refuses to obey a magistrate' – the decision is left with authorities who may wish to intimidate, especially when they are colonial authorities. Although independence has not brought a reduction in the numbers killed in the name of law and order.

No attempt was made to outline Indian politics to us, much less to justify the British presence. British rule was not perceived to require an explanation, and the existence of Indian opposition to it was ignored. We were, however, very clearly told that India was divided into two parts, and correspondingly there were two sorts of Indians – those who made good soldiers and those who did not. The favoured sort – known as 'the martial-classes' – lived in an area stretching south as far as Rajputana, and East as far as Lucknow. Indians from other areas might have their uses but were of no military interest. Our mess servants were a case in point. They were Tamils, and Tamils lacked the fighting spirit. Our lecturers really did believe this. They dismissed the existence of the Madras Sappers and Miners regiment as an anomaly, and the Tamil Tigers were yet to come. Another South Indian regiment, the Coorgis, escaped their attention altogether, but before the war was won a Coorgi – General Cariappa – was to be the first Indian to command an Indian Army brigade – including British troops – in battle. (In due course he went on to be independent India's first commander-in-chief). Similarly no mention was made of the fact that recruitment to the Royal Indian Navy and the Royal Indian Air Force completely ignored the distinction between martial and non-martial classes, and so too the Indian Army itself did in its selection of Indian officers.

The course, however, did all it could to perpetuate the myth. Accordingly our lectures on the peoples of India dealt only with those communities whose names, like the names of Highland clans, were also the names of regiments – Sikhs, Jats, Mahrattas, Rajputs and the rest – because recruitment to each regiment was confined to one community. As a colonial force the regular Indian Army benefited by this restriction because it made each regiment a focus for strong loyalties that stopped short of patriotism. When recruits joined regiments in which their fathers and grandfathers had served – sometimes under the fathers and grandfathers of their commanders – these loyalties were reinforced by family tradition. The *sepoy*, we were repeatedly assured, was *nimak-halal* (true to his salt).

Although the *sepoy*, as thus portrayed, was immune to patriotism, we were warned that he was deeply religious, so we would have to learn something about Indian religions. This sounded promising. We looked forward to having our horizons broadened. As it turned out, however, all that Indian Army officers needed to know about Indian religions was how to avoid offending religious susceptibilities. *Sepoys* ordered to do things that their religions forbade had been known to grow unruly. All that we were told about Hinduism, Islam and Sikhism, therefore, was a list of prohibitions together with a warning to take them seriously, as carelessness in this area had led to the Indian Mutiny. For fear of starting a riot, even the susceptibilities of Indian civilians had to be taken seriously. Visiting a holy place, for instance – should any of us take it into our heads to do so – we should be ready to remove our shoes. Other tricky situations might crop up unexpectedly in public places. Driving through a bazaar – which was sometimes unavoidable – we must restrain our natural impatience if a cow got in the way. A sacred cow was not just a figure of speech. As far as Hindus were concerned, all cows were sacred, so they let them loiter in the narrow streets, or even lie there placidly, blocking the thoroughfare for anything bigger than a bicycle.

Another Hindu belief that we must take seriously, preposterous though it might seem, was that we ourselves might defile them. This was not as offensive as it might sound, as it had nothing to do with hygiene – although Hindus did spend more time bathing than we did, and were revolted by our practice of sitting in our own dirty water. But that was not the point. A perfectly clean place could be defiled simply because somebody had gone there who was forbidden to. This might seem to be nonsense, but if you had Hindus under your command, it had to be respected so when you inspected the lines you must never set foot in a Hindu kitchen. If you did, the whole place would have to be ritually purified before it could be used again. In any case, there was never any need to inspect a Hindu kitchen. The floor was always clean enough to eat off.

Diet presented another problem. Hindus could not eat meat, but Moslems could, provided the animal had been slaughtered ritually and was not a pig. Fish, on the other hand, were no problem. (Towards the end of the war, however, a complication did arise when Indian troops were served with dehydrated whale-meat and the word went round that whales are mammals not fish, and so their flesh could only be eaten if they had been slaughtered ritually – which was unlikely. Fortunately the Grand Mufti in Cairo who was asked for a ruling was able to quote chapter and verse to prove that for ritual purposes whales, however they might breathe and no matter how warm their blood was, were fish.)

On the whole it was fortunate that the only place most British officers found for religion in their own lives was the public celebration of births, marriages and deaths, but a little more personal piety would have saved the life of one about whom I was later told a cautionary tale. In 1914, when Britain declared war on Germany, many Moslems in the Indian Army had misgivings because Germany was allied to Turkey, and the Turks were Moslems. 'What would you do, Sahib,' a trusty Moslem *subedar-major* asked his Commanding Officer, in an attempt to make him see the difficulty, 'if you were ordered to shoot Jesus Christ?'

'I'd shoot his father if it was an order', was the reply. The only use of blasphemy known to the colonel was as a form of emphasis.

Not so the *subedar-major*. As the subsequent court martial discovered, he was aware of the Christian view of Christ's paternity although he did not share it, and as Viceroy's Commissioned Officers wore side-arms he shot the colonel dead.

We were even given lectures about the martial class that we ourselves would belong to on completion of our training. I wish I could remember all the details. All I recall now is instruction in formal correspondence and a warning that on arrival in a cantonment on a posting we were to pay calls on the senior figures in the cantonment. I doubt whether many of us did so, unless they were specifically told to by their commanding officer, as later – once but once only – happened to me. Once a month an attempt was also made to instil us with a sense of privilege by investing our mess with as much dignity as its sparse furnishing and lack of funds permitted, when the cadet mess president – (appointed for that one month only, so that as many of us as possible could get the feel of it) – raised his glass to the equally temporary vice-president seated at the other end of the table, and intoned: 'Mister Vice, the King-Emperor!' The Vice-President then rose in his turn to repeat the *mantra*, and we all rose to murmur it after him and drink the imperial toast – in water, unless we had brought a drink in with us from the bar.

The purpose, if not invariably the effect, of this ceremony was to remind us that we belonged to an elite. We certainly belonged to a minority. Nobody else in India behaved like that.

The only Indians we met in Bangalore were employed to serve us. Presumably because instruction implies authority, our instruction was confined to British hands. The only exception was language teaching. We accorded due respect to the Indian *munshis* who taught us Urdu, but when we failed to prepare our lessons, they made no comment. Only fellow *sahibs* were entitled to criticize us to our faces. As Europeans we were entitled to deference, even as cadets.

Returning to our quarters one afternoon we found our bearer missing, and were told by other bearers that he had been arrested. Some item of equipment belonging to the contractor had been discovered in his kit. We asked where he had been taken, and went there to find him sitting in a one-roomed building, with a barred window. There was no policeman to be seen, and despite the bars through which we spoke to him the place did not appear to be a police station. He was undoubtedly a prisoner, however, so we asked him what we could do to help him.

He seemed unable to tell us, and yet our visit obviously cheered him up, as if this demonstration of support was all that was required to set him free. And so it proved. It might not have been so easy if he had been arrested on a warrant, and held in custody by the police, but the contractor had taken the law into his own hands and detained him arbitrarily, so next morning he was back at our bedsides with our tea.

In such conditions, safe in the certainty that one is not a bully, it is easy to become one. One night on a field exercise our company was defending an open area against infiltration by another company, whose task was to pass through our positions undetected, in the dark. Although this was an exercise in fieldcraft, our 'commander' (for the evening) posted a detachment to keep an eye on a public road that ran through the area, in case 'the enemy' tried to sneak through that way. It was late but bullock carts came creaking along the tarmac in twos and threes, and whenever they did so the detachment guarding the road stopped and searched them.

This was quite unnecessary. It was not inconceivable that 'the enemy' had borrowed carts and clothing from local villagers, but not their worn, unshaven faces and sinewy, spindly legs. Nevertheless, striplings in uniform ordered every cart to stop and searched it, in order to enjoy the unfamiliar pleasure of being obeyed.

Morris and I had no part in that, but on a map-making exercise we indulged in something just as nasty. Arriving sixty yards or so from the edge of a village, we sat down with our papers and pencils, on a bank beside a pond and set to work. In no time a couple of villagers had noticed us and stopped to watch. The unexpected arrival of uniformed Europeans was cause for concern, and they were quickly joined by others. There was no way in which we could assure them that we meant no harm. We knew no Tamil. But why did we act a pantomime of holding out our pencils at arm's length towards different places in the village, as if we were surveying it, and make such a show of taking notes? We told ourselves it was a joke, but the truth was that we were relishing an unaccustomed sense of power.

On one cadet the effect of privilege was different. It made him anxious. Realising that, despite appearances, we were at their mercy he grew afraid of the mess servants. Their subservience could not be genuine, so it must be a cloak. Who knew what they were thinking? They might well be in a plot to poison us. Soon something told him that they were, and had already started killing us – by slow poisoning, gradually day by day, so that nobody would realise what was being done to them. Even when he sounded a warning nobody believed him, so he was forced to take private measures to protect himself, leaving the food served in the mess untouched. He brought his own food in with him, from a store of biscuits and chutney, which at other times he kept carefully locked away in his quarters.

Soon his shirt and trousers dangled, his cheeks sank and his cheek-bones protruded. Then he disappeared into hospital. When it was my turn to be platoon sergeant for the week I visited him there. As he suspected – or, rather, knew – that hospital meals too were poisoned, he had turned into a bony framework wrapped in skin. His upper lip was so shrunk that the roots of his top teeth showed through. I asked whether there was anything he wanted. Nothing that India could provide was his reply. Eventually he was shipped off to South Africa.

It did occur to me that he might simply have been 'going dilally'. Deolali – was the place where homeward-bound British soldiers reported before embarking at Bombay, so 'going dilally' was the British soldier's term for feigning madness to procure release from service. Even if his mania was genuine, however, I would now commend it. He had done something that we were not encouraged to do and none of the rest of us did – imagined himself in the servile position imposed on every Indian employed at the college. They may well have hated us.

They were certainly afraid of us. So were the waiters at the cinemas. During the interval, at one of them, they toured the seats with menus, offering non-alcoholic drinks. Coca-cola was listed and at that time Coca-cola was still unknown in Britain, so Morris and I always ordered it. The waiters then solemnly repeated our orders, vanished and never came back. They felt it safer to disappoint us that way, rather than by telling us to our faces that the supply of Coca-cola had ceased on the outbreak of war. They were afraid of us just because we were British. We were not even officers yet.

Nevertheless, we were all supposed to be the Right Type, so we were offered access to the British United Services Club on application. I do not think many cadets applied, however. Bangalore offered pleasure in plenty without it.

In this it differed from other cantonments, where the European amenities available to the public amounted to no more than a cinema showing a different English language film each week, a second-class hotel, and the railway station restaurant. For British troops these were therefore the only amenities on offer outside the confines of the garrison. They might be Europeans, but membership of European clubs was barred to them as firmly as it was to Indians. Their function was to protect British residents, not to mingle with them.

In this their situation resembled that of 'Anglo-Indians' – the term by which, in 1900, residents of India of mixed racial descent had chosen to be known, disowning the term 'Eurasian' as pejorative, although 'Eurasian' itself had earlier been substituted for 'half-caste' for the same reason. The cause of this uneasiness was the refusal of Europeans to recognise an undeniable relationship beyond recruiting Anglo-Indians to the intermediate ranks of certain essential government services – the railways and the police for men and the medical services and education for women. (Even then, they were not recruited to the upper echelons of these services, while selected Indians were.) Nevertheless, although they had never been there, many

Anglo-Indians courted Indian derision by saying 'home' when they meant Britain. They also alienated the Right Type by speaking English with a characteristic accent and intonation, and employed locutions that were no longer fashionable. So too, of course, did the B.O.R.s, who were similarly barred from rising above what was regarded as their proper station, and whose existence too was ignored by their compatriots. The two groups therefore had much in common, and except for a minority who were prouder of their Indian than their European ancestry, Anglo-Indian families in cantonments relieved the barbarity of barrack life for B.O.R.s by welcoming them to their homes and inviting them to Railway Institute dances.

In Bangalore, however, a resident with European tastes did not have to be a member of the British United Services Club. So many of its citizens had a taste for western pleasures that compared with other cantonments it was a European holiday resort. Many of them had retired there after earning a living in another part of India. Although not high enough to be a hill station, it was high enough to enjoy a fairly temperate climate. There were already one or two factories there, but it was not yet a centre of industry. Retired professional and business people – Indians, Anglo-Indians and Europeans too – had settled down in peaceful suburbs named after past administrators – Richards Town, Cook Town, Fraser Town, Benson Town, Langford Town, Austin Town – where they dwelled in modestly priced bungalows, in quiet roads shaded by flowering trees.

It was also a happily mixed population. Most residents were Indian, but the proportion of Anglo-Indians was unusually high, as was also the number of residents from abroad. There were European managers of local businesses and factories, retired Indian Army officers who had decided that Britain was too expensive, or too chilly or too depressing, while other residents ranged from demobilised B.O.R.s who had married in India and stayed on, to European refugees, or people who had arrived somewhere else in India from as far away as South America to make a living, and then, instead of returning home when the time came for retirement, had moved contentedly to a place where, thanks to an efficient municipality, it was safe even to drink water from the tap. Not many of them qualified for membership of the British United Services Club, but they did not repine. They had their own clubs and institutes, and ample public entertainment – cinemas, restaurants and bars, prize-fights, circuses, and a fairground. All this made Bangalore a holiday posting for our staff-sergeants, which may have been why they treated us indulgently.

At week-ends, Morris and I cycled into the cantonment centre, where the two daughters of a retired Armenian businessman cycled in from a garden suburb to join us. We too found Bangalore relaxing – but we did not forget our Marxism. Witness our theory of the *tamasha-wallah*.

According to the Indian Army manual on 'Aid to the Civil Power', one reason for selecting the target carefully, if it became necessary to shoot someone in a rioting crowd, was to avoid killing a *tamasha-wallah. Tamasha-wallahs* composed nine tenths of any rioting crowd, according to the manual, so naturally we wondered who these revolutionary people were and, even more intriguing, why official care was taken to protect them when they were so prone to join in riots. Our Urdu vocabulary informed us that a *tamasha* was a public show, and we knew that a *chha-wallah* was a man who supplied tea (*chha*), a *pan-wallah* sold *pan*, and so on, so presumably a *tamasha-wallah* was a showman. Our *munshi* confirmed this. A *tamasha-wallah* was a vagabond, who wandered from place to place giving street shows and collecting money from the bystanders. What sort of shows? – we asked, expecting to hear about political street theatre. Snake-charming, juggling, dancing bears – things like that, he told us, disparagingly. Nothing daunted we imagined a tribe of bohemians, self-employed and therefore less class-conscious than the industrial proletariat but still rebellious. Nevertheless it was hard to believe that a shot fired at random into a typical rioting crowd would probably hit a vagabond bohemian. The final explanation was disappointing. *Tamasha-wallah*, in this context, meant an innocent bystander – someone who was only there to see the show.

The German invasion of the Soviet Union presented us with a problem that affected us more immediately. Its effect on communists all over the world was to turn them into jingoists, if their country was already at war with Germany, and war-mongers if it was not. If the Germans had invaded Canada but somehow left the Soviet Union alone the American communist leadership would have remained as indifferent as the British communist leadership contrived to be when the Germans reached Calais. As it was, however, their leader, Earl Browder, insisted that, as only a narrow strip of water separated Soviet territory from Alaska, by invading the Soviet Union Germany was threatening America, so America must rush to war! In exactly the same spirit, Morris and I could have decided that the struggle against British rule in India must be suspended for the duration of the war, but we decided to carry on with it.

3: Revolution rejoined

On receipt of our commissions we were posted to the Royal Indian Army Service Corps Officers Training School at Kakul, in the North-West Frontier Province, for further training. I had opted for the Service Corps because the range of training offered to me in India had not included my original choice of service, the artillery, and the pay in the Service Corps was higher. An officer's life in India, as I imagined it, required a private income which I did not have. Morris had made the same choice for the same reason. We both came of prudent, non-conformist stock.

We had ten days leave before reporting to Kakul. This gave us a spare week in which to contact the Communist Party, and I had two addresses left. One was an Englishman in Madras. I had personal information about only one of the contacts on my list and he was not the one. I did not even know that he belonged to the Indian Civil Service. As I was later to discover, I had only to speak the two words of the address I had been given – 'the Secretariat' – to a taxi-driver in Madras, to be driven straight to the offices of the provincial government, but the only application of the word 'secretariat' then known to me was to the committee responsible for the day-to-day running of the student branch of the Communist Party in Cambridge, and I had no means of locating its counterpart in Madras. Although I had been warned to do so only if I had no alternative, we therefore had to fall back on the only contact about whom I did have personal information, Jawaharlal Nehru's daughter, Indira. In Britain, just before the war, although not a communist herself she had Indian communist student friends who had now returned to India, and she would be able to tell me where to find them. Her address was in Bombay, and on our way North we could easily call in there.

We registered at a second-class hotel where there was no risk of meeting other officers, and changed into civilian costume. It did not deserve the name of mufti. No Indian Army officer worthy of his swagger stick would have allowed himself to be seen in the cheap hats and shirts that we had bought in Bangalore, and I can only guess what Indira Nehru would have made of our appearance if she had been at home! We rang the bell of her flat in vain, however, and when we inquired at the flat next door they told us that she had gone to Delhi but could not give us her address. The only difference between this and our previous Bombay expedition was the luxury of its surroundings. We would have to locate the Party without help.

We did not expect this to be easy. It was an illegal, underground organisation, but we might be able to detect its presence in reports of discontent organised under other auspices, so we searched an evening paper for reports of strikes and demonstrations. Our luck was in. Striking students had clashed with the police that very day, and their action committee was to meet next morning to plan their next move. Revolutionary student activity was bound to be spear-headed by the Party – or so we thought – and the report even included the time and place of the committee meeting.

It was in a cinema. Next morning, half an hour after the given time to ensure that the meeting would have started, feeling very professional we dismissed our taxi at the end of the street in which the cinema was situated, so that the driver could not say where we had gone if he was later questioned. On arrival at the cinema itself, however, we had to spoil this, by asking where the students' meeting was.

It was in an upstairs room. A dozen students, seated around a table, broke off their discussion immediately, and stared at us blankly as we went in. They looked hostile. Perhaps they took us for plain clothes police, or perhaps it was our white faces they distrusted. Guessing that they had had a bad experience with European bourgeois liberals, I decided it was worth the risk and told them we were communist party members.

But that was a mistake. 'Here we are all socialists', said one of them, so we decided to leave, before they telephoned the police. We had been told in Britain that the Congress Socialist Party was a 'social fascist' organization (a label also applied to the Labour Party).

But just as we were turning to leave, one of them shot from the table and stepping between us snapped, 'Come quickly!', hustling us away by our elbows into an empty passage. There he told us that he knew no communists in Bombay, but would give us a name and address in Lahore. He scribbled on a scrap of paper, handed it to us, and as we began to thank him said, 'Go quickly!' At least one of the people sitting round the table must have been a police informer, but we had introduced ourselves as students, and our civilian scruffiness would make it hard to place us.

We were astonished that it should have proved so easy. We had to visit Lahore in any case, to change trains on our way from Bombay to Kakul, so we went straight to the railway station and reserved places on the next day's express there. This left us the rest of the day to loiter in. We had no idea what to see or where to go, but we were in such good spirits that I still remember what we did for the rest of that day. We spent the rest of the morning exploring bookshops, astonished by the selection available. (I still have the anthology of symbolist verse, published in France, which I bought there.) In the afternoon we saw the first world blockbuster – *Gone with the Wind*.

Our hopes evaporated two mornings later, when we mounted the portico steps of a mansion in Lahore. No communist could be living in a place like this! But when we repeated the name the Bombay student had given us, the uniformed servant who answered our ring asked us to wait. This must be the home of our quarry's parents. Most Indian communist students in Cambridge were from rich families.

But how could we pretend to know their son when we did not even know who he was? We were still without an answer when the servant returned to lead us into the presence of a short, hunched little man, with lively dark eyes framed in horn-rimmed glasses, who received us reclining on his elbow on a bed. He apologised for this, explaining that he was ill, and then told us that the man we had asked for had left Lahore. Why had he invited us in to tell us this himself, when he was bed-ridden? We must have roused his curiosity. We waited, on guard. Was there anything he himself could do for us, he asked, but we had no wish to satisfy his curiosity, while for his part, although his communist sympathies were notorious, Mian Iftikar-ud-din – a major land-owner and at that time the President of the Congress Party in the Punjab – could not make his active commitment to the Party known. A humidor of State Express cigarettes was at his elbow, and we all three lit up to help our concentration. It was not until ten minutes later that a servant was despatched to send our taxi away.

All of that day – and the next – was spent in Iftikar's house but not always in his company. He was ill, and at the insistence of his wife Ismat he had to rest for much of the time. We had other company, however, starting with Peren Barucha, a Parsi girl student communist, who was already in the house. Luckily she had already been there when the police arrived at her parents' home that morning to arrest her, and she had been duly warned by telephone as soon as they left. She was in no hurry to go back there – not because she intended to evade arrest, but because before she went to jail she had friends to say goodbye to – especially Romesh Chandra, a young communist who turned up shortly afterwards. So too did two other young men, Mahmud Ali Khan and his younger brother Mazhar – nephews of Sir Sikander Hyat Khan, the pro-British, Unionist prime minister of the Punjab.

They were all communists, and sometimes as a group, sometimes in turn, the four of them spent that day and the next giving us a crash course on India which, in its approach to manners and customs was less sympathetic than the lectures on the same subject that we had listened to in Bangalore. All of them, except Iftikar, had been educated entirely in India, but their outlook on religion was distinctly secular. Their criticism of Indian religious life resembled an English view of Northern Irish bigotry. Their resentment at the way the British exploited differences between Hindus and Moslems was mild compared with their hostility to religious leaders for preserving the hostilities, especially as the harm religious differences did was not confined to public life. Their own happiness was threatened by hostility to inter-communal marriages. The prospect of a marriage between Romesh, a Hindu, and Peren, a Parsi, was opposed in both their communities. Mahmud and his Sikh wife had received death threats when they married. What our lecturers had regarded as administrative complications were experienced by our new friends as persecution. In addition to fighting for national independence they were therefore engaged in what to me appeared to be a 'bourgeois liberal' side-show. With the sad surprise of a member of the Clapham Sect[5] finding a French novel on the book-shelves of a fellow parishioner I was surprised to discover books by Lytton Strachey on Iftikar's shelves, and when he told us how a local worthy, introducing Aldous Huxley to a Lahore gathering, had announced:-'I have not read any of Mr Huxley's works, but I have read the complete works of Marie Correlli'[6] – I found Mazhar's derision snobbish.

The man of whom they were most scathing was Mahatma Gandhi. They were revolutionaries: he was not. Iftikar who was then a member of the Congress Party's Working Committee, knew him well, and Mahmud, a member of its All-India Committee, had observed him. At this juncture they both regarded 'the old man', as they called him, simply as a reactionary hypocrite. His puritanism and piety were not just undesirable in themselves. They were camouflage for cunning – witness the machinations by which he had toppled Subhas Chandra Bose[7] when Bose had run for a second term as President of the Congress Party and, against his declared wishes, had been elected. (Not that they backed Bose, they hastened to explain. Bose had not yet declared his support for Hitler, but they dismissed him as an 'opportunist careerist'.)

What they most deplored in Gandhi, however, was not his cunning but his non-violence. The only kind of force whose use he was prepared to countenance was 'soul force' (*ahimsa*), which sounded harmless but in practice, they insisted, meant counter-revolutionary sabotage. When the outbreak of war in Europe had offered an opportunity to promote a revolution he had promoted nothing more effective than innocuous civil disobedience, and now the war had been transformed by the entry of the Soviet Union he had continued with the same line, as if nothing had happened, although the war was now a revolutionary struggle. When the existence of the workers' state was threatened, its defence was the only issue for all the workers of the world, and the workers of India must join them in the battle – even if it meant supporting Britain.

In propounding this line so promptly, Iftikar and his friends were ahead of a large section of the Indian Communist Party. It was not until six months later that the Indian Party joined the other Communist parties in declaring that the war was the only issue in the world that mattered, because the defeat of Germany would make the Soviet Union irresistible.

Like all staunch party members Iftikar regarded religion as the opium of the people, but as a Moslem he had inherited a dignified sense that every human life is governed by a force, which, although incalculable, is significant. In other words, although he would never have admitted it, I would say that he believed in *kismet*. *Kismet* was eventually to reverse his attitude to Gandhi. In 1947 in the West Punjab, he made constant efforts to stop the killings of Hindus and Sikhs that came with independence, by intervening personally on the spot. At the same time Gandhi was halting massacres in Calcutta and Delhi by personal intervention, and believing that Gandhi's personal influence, even among Moslems, was still great enough for his presence to achieve a similar result in Pakistan, Iftikar flew to Delhi to persuade him to come there too. Gandhi replied that he was ready, but must first discuss the idea with Jinnah. Pakistan was now an independent state, and he would do nothing there against the wishes of its government.

Iftikar flew back to Pakistan full of hope. When he asked for an immediate interview with Jinnah, however, Jinnah replied that he had no time to spare, so he asked the Prime Minister, Liaquat Ali Khan, to put the idea to him. Two days later an embarrassed Liaquat gave him Jinnah's reply: 'I am the Governor-General of Pakistan. Who is Mr Gandhi that I should talk with him?'

Iftikar flew back to Delhi to report this. 'Gandhi chuckled', he told me, 'and said – "We really can't ask Mountbatten to resign so soon. We've only just persuaded him to stay." He was always calm', Iftikar concluded. 'In one thing Nature has been kind to us. She gave us Gandhiji'. (Like an enlightened eighteenth century European, when he was thinking in terms of God he spoke of 'Nature'.)

Kismet was to buffet his view of the Soviet Union as the years went by, but in 1941 a rational man could still believe that the Soviet Union was the Indian people's only reliable ally. From this it followed that as long as the Soviet Union was involved in the war, fighting for Indian independence meant supporting its allies – even including Britain.

This analysis simplified matters for Morris and me, but complicated them for Iftikar and his group. In the eyes of most Indian nationalists fighting for independence had to involve fighting against the British. The Government of India too found communist tactics difficult to keep pace with. The communist whose name Morris and I had been given in Bombay, had been imprisoned without trial, under 'Section 93' of the emergency regulations. Now Peren Barucha whom we had just met was about to follow him, and so, quite soon, as they were well aware, were both Mahmud and Mazhar.

Humbled by the way they all took it for granted that they would soon be either 'inside', or 'U.G.' (underground), Morris and I tried to console each other with the reflection that we too were U.G. in a way, and took pleasure in incriminating ourselves by giving them an outline of the internal security plan of Amritsar which had been confided to us as an example when we were being trained in 'aid to the civil power'. We also taught Ismat how to make a petrol bomb. More usefully, we also made a convincing contribution to party funds.

It was not only as party members, however, that I admired them. After war had been declared, a phrase that had become current among Cambridge communists was 'Bolshevik self-discipline', but what I admired about these two brothers was a more enviable, personal quality. When we spent our last evening, eating kebabs and drinking Scotch with them in a restaurant, I was astonished by their nonchalance. As a good Marxist, I attributed this to their class origin, and although I have long ceased to be one, I do not think that I was mistaken. They belonged to a landed aristocracy, the sort of people who demonstrated superiority by coolness at the guillotine. On a later occasion, Mahmud told me how he had paid an evening visit to the Lahore commissioner to clear up a misunderstanding about an incident at a student demonstration, before it led to violence. His visit was unannounced, and when he arrived at the house it was already dark. He entered without meeting anyone, and found the commissioner dining – in black tie but alone, as his wife was in the hills. The servants had been told to leave the food on the table, and go home, and the night-watchman had not yet come on duty, so the commissioner was entirely unprotected. 'Any *goonda* (ruffian) could have walked straight in and murdered him!', Mahmud snorted, 'and they'd have blamed us for his death!' But this indignation was only for the record. His admiration was obvious.

This meeting in Lahore, as well as the high civilization of Lahore itself, multi-cultural as the city and its university then were, transformed my commitment to Indian independence because it transformed my attitude to Indians. At Cambridge my only India acquaintance had been Arun Bose, whom I regarded as a disembodied intellect. (It was he who had put me right about 'revolutionary defenceism'.) Since then the little I had seen of India and Indians in Bangalore Cantonment had made me think of them as cringing. My Lahore comrades, however, were people to whom I simultaneously felt inferior but did not want to say goodbye to. They exposed the preposterous basis of British rule in India to ridicule without discussing it – the idea that Indians could not manage their affairs without supervision. I no longer needed Lenin's treatise on imperialism to make me an enemy of the Raj.

This shift of vision was just as well. My loss of faith in the Soviet Union was a prolonged process, but it had already started by the time we had finished our final training at Kakul. The training school was situated in sparsely populated country, among hills, at an altitude sufficient for autumn nights to be cold, crisp and clear, with only a few remote lights dotting the surrounding utter darkness after sunset – until one night we saw an extended scatter of lights where previously there had only been blackness. Next day we learned these were the campfires of a host of nomads, who had camped there with their flocks, after trekking all the way from Sinkiang, a region of North West China on the border of the Soviet Union, where the Red Army had moved in and – so they alleged – started to persecute them. The only explanation for this that Morris and I could think of was that they did not understand what the Red Army had been doing to them. It was not persecution. That was only how it had seemed to them – or, no doubt, been misrepresented to them by religious leaders. If they looked at it objectively, they would recognise it as liberation.

Less easily reprocessed was a lecture from an intelligence officer newly arrived from Teheran, where the Red Army and the British had co-operated to prevent a German sponsored *coup d'état.* In the course of praising our new allies, he told how, when he and his colleagues had failed to extract information from Iranian civilian prisoners who had been involved in the failed coup, the Russians had volunteered to extract it for them. 'So we handed them the prisoners and a list of questions and they handed back the answers, but we never saw the prisoners again – and didn't want to. They would not have been a pretty sight!'

In those days it was an accepted truth in the communist movement that the Chinese Red Army did not treat its prisoners as enemies but involved them in political seminars that converted them into revolutionary fighters. The Soviet Red Army's ways with prisoners must be the same. It would have been easier to think so if the lecturer had not sounded so like the happy owner of a savage dog. In the end we fell back on the reflection that there were occasions when humanitarian scruples were a bourgeois luxury.

The only Indian I spoke to during the course at Kakul – apart from my civilian driving instructor – was Bagga Khan, the bearer I shared with Morris. As cadets at Bangalore, we had only a quarter of a bearer each. We were now promoted to one between two, and instead of being allotted him were free to find him for ourselves. In the event, Bagga Khan found us when the train from Lahore stopped at Abbottabad, the nearest station to Kakul. The coolies waiting on the platform had been joined by unemployed bearers in search of new *sahibs* – some because their previous *sahibs* had just completed a course and left Kakul, and others, more desperate, because it was now two months since they had last been employed. Bagga Khan was one of the latter, and determined not to lose out. He was also big.

As soon as the train came to a halt, the coolies swarmed into the compartment, ascertained which bedding-roll went with which trunk, and soon had all our luggage out onto the platform, where Bagga Khan – a tall, lavishly moustached Pathan with a black waistcoat over his white shirt and one end of his turban spread out in a starched white fan, stood waiting to collar me as soon as I got out and ask me to point out the *cooly* who was handling my baggage.

Meanwhile Morris had been seized by another candidate, and as we were allowed only one bearer between us for a moment we seemed to have an insoluble problem. But it was only for that moment. Bagga Khan, who knew the school rules, asked me to identify 'his other *sahib*', and then waved his arm in a commanding gesture, at which his rival went away.

From then on, as long as we were at Kakul, he anticipated our every reasonable desire, and I had only to express an unreasonable one for him to satisfy it next day. This was my desire to imitate a detached-looking old man I had seen in Lahore reclining on a string bed and smoking a *hooka*. The morning after I asked him where I could buy one, Bagga Khan brought me a hubble-bubble from the local bazaar, together with a supply of country tobacco.

The hubble-bubble is the poor man's *hooka*. Its *chillum*, or bowl, although glazed and gaily painted, is made of earthenware, and instead of smoking a blend of rich tobacco with spices and molasses in it the poor man smokes coarse country stuff. The *hooka* smoker puffs his mixture through a delicate mouthpiece fixed at the end of a flexible, coiling tube: the poor man sucks at the end of a cane. My equipment was that of the poor man.

A further disincentive was that Bagga Khan could not bring glowing charcoal into our quarters, to place over the mixture in the chillum so that I could get it going, but only a bunch of smoldering rags. After a couple of days, in which this effort sent me reeling, I weakly asked him to get it going for me, but the stench of charred cloth still choked and impregnated me. Nevertheless, it was his gift (for he refused to let me pay for it) so I continued with it for a fortnight.

After a couple of months with us, Bagga Khan suggested that either Morris or I should take him to 'London' with us when we went home after the war. His 'London' swarmed with Indian bearers, because it was the place where *sahibs* came from, and he could not imagine *sahibs* cleaning their own shoes. When we told him that most *sahibs* managed without bearers, cooks and even sweepers it was clear that, although he did not say so, he was sure that we were lying. In his world *sahibs* could not survive unless they lived like lords.

Pouring out our bed-teas one morning he suddenly made a whinnying sound and then straightened up so suddenly that he cracked his head against the mantelpiece. Nevertheless, he went on laughing, so we asked him what the joke was. He was recalling a film, he said. He had seen it the previous evening. 'Laurel Sahib', he replied when we asked for details, 'and Hardy Sahib'. He shook his head in disbelief and wiped his eyes. He had seen the world turned upside down. How did Laurel and Hardy get past the censor in British India?

When the course ended we were advised not to take our bearers with us to our new postings, but wait until we arrived there, so that we could engage servants who knew the lie of the land at our new stations. Morris and I both feebly heeded this warning, so Bagga Khan had to be paid off. He gave us parting gifts – for me a good strap of his own to replace the inferior one on my bedding roll, to which, if I had accepted it, he would have added a fur-lined coat.

Morris and I too went our separate ways, each in the direction indicated by his performance in a written examination. Success in the examination in the organization of supplies called for the mastery of varied information by a logical mind, so Morris was posted to a supply depot. I was posted to a Mechanical Transport Training Battalion, as neither the hesitation I had shown in manoeuvring heavy vehicles on narrow mountain roads, nor my inability to trace engine faults, had revealed themselves on paper. What success in the mechanical transport examination demanded was an ability to draw diagrams.

On our ways to our new postings we both had to change

trains at Lahore, and spent the night there, but when we called on Iftikar he was out of town. We did not have the addresses of Mazhar and Mahmud, but even if we had they would have been no use to us. They were both in gaol.

4: Cantonment cool

The Mechanical Transport Training Battalion to which I was posted was stationed at Bareilly, a fair-sized city on the Ganges plain, between Delhi and Lucknow, but as it was located in the cantonment, all I saw of the city during my service there was a couple of glimpses caught driving through its outskirts when it was my turn to take charge of a convoy of recruits on night driving. Our learner drivers had been recruited straight from villages. The only wheeled vehicles that they were familiar with were powered by animals, so their instructors told them that lorries drank water, ate petrol, and had to be given regular doses of a medicine called 'mobiloil'. 'Without warning the vehicle dashed itself against the bridge', stated a driver's report of an accident.

Apart from those excursions, I lived and moved and had my being in the cantonment – an orderly world of broad roads, shaded by trees, with strips of tarmac down the middle for the convenience of the occasional motor-car. Much of the traffic, however – apart from bicycles – was still what it had been in the days of *Hobson-Jobson*. The conveyance most in evidence was the *tonga* – a light, two-wheeled vehicle, drawn by a pony. These ran for hire, usually carrying two passengers who sat back-to-back with the driver. *Tonga*-stands were scattered throughout the cantonment, with the drivers either sprawled dozing in the passenger seat, or squatting in a circle over a card game under a tree, while their ponies munched the contents of their nose-bags.

The roads were lined with long, low garden walls, behind which lawns and flower-beds led occasionally to a house but more usually to a thatched bungalow which was already approaching its centenary. With three other officers of the battalion, I shared a blindingly white-washed bungalow where every morning, as the birds came to life in the early freshness of the garden outside, our bearers woke us with bed tea and we shaved and dressed to meet the eye of our Commanding Officer. Then, still not prepared for conversation, we mounted our bicycles and rode off separately to the battalion lines. The sun was well up by the time we were driven in staff cars to the mess for breakfast, and then back to the lines to be driven to the mess again for lunch and back again to the lines to be on duty all through the afternoon without a *siesta* – 'because there was a war on'. At tea time we remounted our bicycles to ride home, where our bearers put the kettle on. Tea was the only meal we ate at home. Nevertheless, in addition to our four bearers we required the services of a sweeper, a gardener and a watchman, all of whom lived on the premises with their families – and probably their friends as well, as more than thirty people lived there. The extensive servant quarters were situated with a stable, out of sight behind a tall hedge, away to one side of the front garden. We did not investigate its occupants' right to be there. If anyone was inconvenienced by unauthorised occupants, it was our servants who had let them in. When one of us bought a pony, a room for his *syce* (groom) was found immediately.

The bungalow had been built in the mid nineteenth century. Its high roof, thick walls and deep thatch provided good protection against heat. Two identical sets of rooms, each with its own front door, ran side by side from the deep verandah at the front to the back. The front room of each set was a living-room, with a tall double door at the back, leading to a bedroom with two beds. Both rooms were at least thirty feet square, with very high ceilings, so that when the electric fans rotated the long rods on which they were suspended swayed. Even without the fans the temperature inside these rooms was tolerable, however, because they were protected from conditions outside by built-up spaces. The verandah that the living-rooms opened onto at the front was wide enough for itinerant carpet-sellers and Chinese cloth merchants to ignore our warnings that we would not buy anything and spread out their wares. Adjacent to each living-room on one side was a similar room, where two more officers occupied the other half of the bungalow, and on the other, outer side a work room where in the evening – after laying out freshly laundered uniforms for us to wear at dinner at the mess – our servants squatted ready to call on the sweeper to carry in hot water from a boiler for our evening baths, meanwhile polishing shoes or other leather, or sewing on buttons – or just chatting as it grew dark. The bedroom behind was flanked by a bathroom and backed onto a dressing room, so both main rooms were surrounded by built-up spaces, which insulated them.

As we moved further into 1942, the temperature rose to a hundred and twenty in the shade and opening the door onto the verandah was like opening the door of a furnace – even at night, for in the last months before the rains a scorching wind blows night and day in that part of India. *Tatties* were then installed in the battalion lines to protect offices from the heat. *Hobson-Jobson*'s description of a *tatti* cannot be improved. 'Tatty: A screen or mat made of the roots of fragrant grass with which doors or window openings are filled up in the season of hot winds. The screens being kept wet, their fragrant evaporation as the dry winds blow upon them cools and refreshes the house greatly, but they are only efficient when such winds are blowing.' The night air was full of powdery dust, through which the moon shone like a fog-light, and the verandah itself, lit by a bare electric bulb, was such a glaring white at night that one evening a multitude of ants which had sprouted wings were transfixed across it, while a browsing lizard picked them off with flicks of its tongue.

I was living in the world described by Colonel Kelly on the troop-ship. The garden teemed with birds that filled the air with cries that he had imitated, especially 'the brain-fever bird', whose name reproduces its exasperating cry: 'brain. . .feevah!', 'brain. . .fEEvah!', 'brain. . . FEEVAH!' – in a crescendo that starts reflectively but ends up in a screech. The hoopoo looked exactly as he had described it. The gardener even killed a cobra. There were also monkeys. He had not mentioned monkeys, as they did not flourish in the Punjab – but here they filled the trees that lined the roads, and chased me once when cycling past I pulled a face at one of them.

Bareilly had long been a military station, complete with Administrative Officer, Station Staff Officer, Garrison Engineer, Station Supply Officer, Garrison Church and Military Hospital. It was also a regimental centre. The arrival of a newly formed Service Corps battalion therefore disturbed an established pattern. One member of the Service Corps, the captain in charge of the Station Supply Depot, was an inevitable presence, like a chaplain, but more than one was excessive, and to make the battalion's intrusion worse, only our Commanding Officer, second-in-command and quartermaster were regulars. The rest were young civilians with emergency commissions.

When I reported for duty, those who had arrived before me were all the Right Type, and there were so few of them that they had all been appointed to posts of special responsibility. I was glad to have arrived too late for this to happen to me. In particular, I did not envy the four young men who, as a result of completing their training two months earlier, were majors in command of companies, each with five hundred recruits at various stages of training passing through their hands, They were all the Right Type. Only one, however, was a born leader.

Later, when I too found myself a company commander, the secret of leadership was confided to me by my *Subedar-Major* one trying afternoon when I lost my temper with him and then apologised. We were in the company office, and the door was open. He strode to shut it, so that nobody would overhear, and then congratulated me. It was as if he was a tennis coach and I was a beginner who had just produced a perfect stroke by accident. I must lose my temper with him regularly now I knew that I could do it, and he would pass the blast on to the *jemadars*, who would then excoriate the *havildars* and so down it would go until the very *sepoys* got the benefit. 'That way, surely,' he concluded, gracing his Urdu with an English technical expression, 'we will have a *good show*.'

Good shows came naturally to the born leader. He enjoyed keeping people on their toes. Whenever he burst out of his office he saw something being done the wrong way and exploded. Even when we were being driven to lunch at the mess, and the rest of us were glad to relax, he would stir things up by swearing at the driver for slipping the clutch when he took a corner, instead of changing down. Non-commissioned officers, who knew a real *sahib* when they saw one, delighted to salute him as he strode around the lines, tipping the brim of his pith helmet with his swagger stick in response. He alone among the emergency-commissioned officers possessed this gift, but those with whom the battalion started were all the Right Type. Six months later, however, when it had reached its full complement of forty odd officers, the Right Type were outnumbered by the Wrong. These had earned their commissions serving in the British Army, in the ranks, and the difference showed. For example, the Right Type spoke to *sepoys* in hesitant and mangled Urdu. The Wrong Type spoke to them in fluent English. They also had different notions of responsibility. When one batch of recruits persistently marked time as if something bulky in their trousers would not let them bring their knees together, the Wrong Type speculated merrily as to the cause. It was one of the Right Type who investigated, and discovered that – bereft for the first time in their lives of *dhotis* – they had tied their shirt tails together. The Right Type sometimes visited the lines in the evening, off duty, to see whether their men were comfortable. The Wrong Type scorned such gestures, but our gestures had powers like those conferred by hypnosis. They could even cure the sick. Every morning, instead of joining the rest of the battalion, that was marshalled in companies for morning parade, a miscellaneous two dozen recruits gathered in a huddle for sick parade. The Medical Officer – a civilian practitioner – did not visit the lines until well after breakfast, by which time they would already have avoided duty for half the morning, even if he refused to recognise their symptoms. As soon as the full parade was over and the hale and hearty had started training in platoons, the duty officer therefore carried out a preliminary check of the sick, in the knowledge that – for the sake of good order and military discipline – the claims of one or two must be rejected.

There was no questioning his decisions, but the procedure still demanded a display of judgement, exercised in every case in the same way – which was fair enough, as every invalid reported the same symptom. 'I have a fever.' If he had a fever he must have a temperature, and it was common ground that this could be established without the aid of a thermometer. The candidates lined up, in charge of a *naik* (corporal), and the duty officer then went along the line, looking each invalid in the eye, to see whether it was yellow or bloodshot, and then asking what was wrong with him. On receipt of the standard reply he ordered the applicant to hold out his hand – if he had not already done so in anticipation – lightly encircled the wrist with two fingers, checked whether it felt hot or cold, and – taking the colour of the eye into account – pronounced his verdict. It was a time-honoured process, so when an invalid was told that he was fit for duty he believed it and behaved accordingly.

The difference between the Right Type and the Wrong showed also in the ways in which they behaved off duty. The Right Type knew what the 'done thing' was and did it, even when he was letting rip. To take a case in point, a year after the war, at the stroke of midnight on New Year's Eve, a recently demobilised Right Type rode his Harley-Davidson motor-cycle round the dance floor of his club – in breach of its rules. The club secretary accordingly received a letter of complaint from a member, which the club committee had to consider at its next meeting. The first committee member to express a view could not see what the fuss was about. On New Year's Eve, 1919, he had ridden his Norton round the dance floor, on the stroke of midnight. That was nothing, an even older member told him. On New Year's Eve, 1907, he had ridden his polo pony round it. Both reported that a letter of apology to the club secretary had been all that was required, so when the secretary reported that one had been received already they proceeded to next business.

There would have been no saving precedents if it had been an Anglo-Indian partner that the reveller had taken onto the dance-floor. An apology would not have saved him, even if he had not broken a club rule. The *mem-sahibs* would have seen to that. (*Mem-sahib* is the feminine of *sahib*.)

Mem-sahibs were denied membership in some clubs, and even when they were allowed it their use of a club was confined by custom. Many male members were bachelors, and even when they were married they often went to the club without their wives. Even on dance nights, many men spent the night in the bar, where women never went. (Parties that included women had their drinks served at tables, on the verandah or in the lounge.) None of this, however, freed *sahibs* to behave in ways that *mem-sahibs* disapproved of.

When the British first arrived in India, simple prudence required them to show respect for the inhabitants, but it would seem that they also felt it. They were impressed by the splendour of its courts and grew accustomed to what at first was strange to them. Even later, when they had become a power in the land, it was not uncommon to find them wearing Indian clothes, relaxing with hookahs – and even chewing *pan*! One eighteenth century Englishman was an admired Bengali poet.

By the later Victorian period, however, the shock of the Mutiny and the brutality of its suppression made it impossible for either race to trust the other as they had previously. Other developments separating rulers from ruled, included the replacement of the East India Company by an administration answerable to Whitehall, the English public school system, and the evangelization of imperialism. Most damaging of all, however, was the Suez Canal. It swelled the *mem-sahibs'* numbers so that now the only admissible reason that a sahib could have for frequenting Indian company was the nature of his work. If he was known to mix with Indians off duty, he was suspected of a guilty secret. What respectable reason could he have?

Not all European – and American – women who came to India to stay were so provincial. Some mixed with Indians themselves, but these were artistic, intellectual, philanthropic or theosophist women, and therefore did not count, while the few who arrived as the wives of Indians were best forgotten. It was permissible – even admirable in the case of wives of high officials – to take a lady-of-the-manor interest in the lot of Indian women and children, regarded as victims of their own culture, but a *mem-sahib's* first duty was to convert a bungalow into an Englishman's castle. ('But there's something so English about a bungalow!', a *mem-sahib* protested, when I explained that 'bungalow' originally meant 'Bengali hut'.) At the club, if sprightly, she played tennis, if stately, she played bridge, but whatever else she did her duty was to inspire the chivalry that had inspired General Dyer to compel all Indians entering an Amritsar street to crawl along it, because a *memsahib* had been molested there.

In return for this protection, *mem-sahibs* protected *sahibs* – against themselves. European men had associated with Indian women freely, before *mem-sahibs* arrived in sufficient numbers to prevent it, and if their inter-racial unions were not invariably solemnised the barriers to marriage existed also on the Indian side – barriers that also forbade marriages between different categories of Indian. Sometimes the East India Company positively encouraged inter-racial marriages, but in any case relationships with Indian mistresses were enjoyed without concealment. The *ménage* of one East India Company official was reported by an early nineteenth century traveller to include – 'six or seven legitimate wives, but they all live together, some fifty leagues from Delhi and do as they like. He must have as many children as the King of Persia, but they are all Hindus or Moslems according to the religion of their mamas'.

A dug-out colonel I met during the war told me that Indian mistresses, or *biwis*, were still a regular feature of regimental life in the Indian Army in the days of *Hobson-Jobson* – despite its discreet omission of the word. Mourning a decline in mutual understanding between officers and *sepoys*, he recalled a similar lament which he had heard, as a subaltern, from a veteran *subedar* – a lament for the passing of *biwi-khana* – the *biwi*'s residence. The situation of a senior officer's *biwi*, he insisted, conferred distinction on her family, and she played an important regimental role as a link between officer and *sepoy*. *Sepoys* had felt sure of being understood when there was a *biwi* to whom they could explain their difficulties off the record. It could not last, however. The opening of the Suez Canal had released a flood of *mem-sahibs*, and the *biwis* had been swept away.

Anglo-Indian women, however, still posed a threat, and *mem-sahibs* were vigilant. An ostensibly European female newcomer to a European community was subjected to a searching scrutiny if none of its established members knew anything about her. Did she show signs of ignorance of life in Britain? Even 'domiciled Europeans' – as people who had been born in India to British parents were designated – incurred suspicions if they believed that nightingales really did sing in Berkeley Square, or had no idea of what happened at Henley. There were also more esoteric tests. I was told, 'under the *punkah*', that the shape of the half-moons on the finger-nails of the wife of a British officer in Bareilly were a proof of mixed parentage. Some Anglo-Indian women even posed a threat to *mem-sahibs* without concealing their mixed parentage. In Calcutta or Bombay, a clandestine affair between a young

European executive and an Anglo-Indian secretary could escape notice until it was too late to intervene. In that such a case it was up to the bridegroom's boss's wife – the *barra memsahib* – to make sure that they came to regret it. In a cantonment, however, things could not get so far unchecked. If a young officer started 'making a fool of himself' with an Anglo-Indian girl, his C.O.'s wife would hear of it in time to alert her husband, so that he could then make it plain to the delinquent that his behaviour was 'conduct unbecoming of an officer and a gentleman', before it was too late.

Such admonitions, however, were powerless, against officers with emergency commissions, who aspired to be civilians again, as soon as possible, unless they recognised the moral authority of the club, and to the Wrong Type the club was just a pub. Making use of it did not, therefore, rule out rubbing shoulders with Anglo-Indian railway employees, and their women folk, at the Railway Institute.

Although the Right Type heard about these lapses, they were spared the sight of them because they did not themselves go anywhere near such places, but there was one place where incompatible worlds sat under the same roof – the cinema. Except when affluent Indians came to see a film, however, there was *de facto* segregation even there, at least of rulers and ruled. The rulers sat at the back, in twos, on sofas, while the ruled sat packed on rows of tip-up seats, close to the screen. The two groups did not even leave at the same time. At the end of each night's programme the opening strains of the British National Anthem acted as a signal for the front rows to empty raucously, while the occupants of the sofas rose to stand to attention, staring at a line of warships plunging towards them, on the screen, through heavy seas.

In this display of patriotism the Right Type and the Wrong Type were united, and at first there was even a certain solidarity among the sofas during the interval. The Right Type, sometimes squiring *mem-sahibs* and the odd *miss-sahib*, acknowledged one another's presence with nods and smiles, and sometimes even visiting each other, as if the sofas were opera boxes. Even the presence of the Wrong Type might be acknowledged by a wave.

Not long after Japan entered the war, however, a number of Eurasian women refugees from Singapore arrived in the cantonment. The Right Thing to do was to take no notice of them, but the Wrong Type noticed them at once, went out of their way to get to know them, and installed them on the sofas in the cinema without a second thought. In these circumstances an officer of the Right Type who was there at the same time could only cut them although they might snicker - 'Nice little frippet that was I saw you with last night!' – at breakfast next morning, to show they were not prudes. It was all one to the Wrong Type. Wherever the war might take them, they were going to ignore local customs, and behave as far as possible as if they were at home.

The two types did, however, have one thing in common – an assumption that anything an Indian could do they could do better. If I parted company with them on this, it was not on principle. It was because I was so aware of counting on subordinates to do things that I could not do myself. Admittedly, the Right Type was more self-assured and the Wrong Type more skilful than I was, but that was not the complete explanation. When they set foot in India, the others had somehow received a revelation: Indians should be encouraged but must never be admired.

Once when I took a convoy into hilly country, one of the lorries broke a front axle, driving over rough ground. We were far away from any repair facilities, and it would be impossible to tow it back to Bareilly, unless its front wheels were hoisted securely off the ground. We had no lifting gear, however, so all I could think of doing was to leave it where it was, under guard, and arrange for a breakdown vehicle to be sent for it when we got back. At that time the battalion was still short of military vehicles, so the convoy included two hired civilian trucks, and their usual civilian drivers had been hired to go with them because they knew their idiosyncrasies. It was they who now dealt with the difficulty. Taking over, as if the *jemadar* and I were passers-by who had just stopped to watch, they told everybody else what to do. First they hacked a large branch off a tree and set it down in front of the damaged lorry, bushy end first. The lorry was then driven, shoved and heaved, well up onto the branches, and lashed onto them. Finally, in a strenuous combined effort – in which even the *jemadar* and I took part – this branch was hoisted high off the ground, while a roadworthy lorry backed up under its stock. The stock was then lashed onto the roadworthy lorry, so that the damaged lorry had its disabled front wheels clear off the ground and the roadworthy one could tow it.

To complete this demonstration of resource, one of the two civilian drivers then attended to a gash he had received in his hand. First he burned an old rag to ashes, thus disinfecting it, and then rendered the result more antiseptic still by urinating on it. He then applied this as a dressing, which was held in place by a bandage made by tearing a strip from his shirt. Back in Bareilly, when I invited the others to admire this they listened tolerantly, as if I was a fond parent, soliciting praise for a favourite child. I was believed to have a weakness for Indians. Nobody associated this with politics, and looking back I think they were right not to. It was their attitude, not mine, that was politically motivated. Without even considering the matter, most of the British in India realised that their presence there was only justifiable if they could do things for Indians that Indians could not do for themselves – and accordingly believed it. What was more, their behaviour made this belief so manifest that for a long time most Indians shared it.

People who would treat Indian visitors to Britain with the same courtesy that they extended to French ones, behaved condescendingly towards them in India, and while they rarely treated Indian servants barbarously the lordly tone in which they addressed them, together with the assumption of a twenty-four-hour claim on their time, implied that they belonged to different orders of being.

One morning I was chatting with a kindly member of the Right Type in the lines when a *naik* marched up with a message for me and saluted, so I broke off the conversation to attend to him. Years later, in a school corridor, I broke off a conversation with another teacher to attend to a child who came up to me with a note. The Right Type and the teacher both goggled at me in the same way. 'You'd do anything for one of these people, wouldn't you?' the Right Type said. But he would have behaved as I did if the *naik* had been a British corporal.

On the other hand both types readily credited Indians with powers to which they laid no claim themselves. A company commander of the Right Type hired a magician to give his men an evening's entertainment and the account he gave of this next morning was frankly baffled. Each time he had taken hold of a silver rupee in his pocket the magician had correctly told him the date on it – to be rewarded with the rupee. There was no possible explanation. If that was not genuine magic, he would like to know what was.

A junior officer of the Wrong Type was unsettled by what he took to be magic. It happened when he took a convoy of recruits on an exercise that involved spending a night at the roadside, and one of them was bitten in the hand by a scorpion. Not only the hand but the arm too had soon swollen alarmingly, all the way up, and they were in a place where western medical help was not available, but someone said there was a priest who healed people, so he had decided to try him. He had not liked what happened then at all. The swelling had got well above the elbow, but the priest had stroked it down with a big iron key until it was only in the fingers, and then made it disappear completely. And he had not just stroked it. He kept muttering spells. 'I didn't like it, I can tell you.'

Both witnesses had been impressed, but it occurred to neither of them that they had witnessed demonstrations of skill. They preferred to believe that they had witnessed exhibitions of occult powers, because occult powers do not command respect. The punter gives a gypsy no more personal credit for giving him a winner than he gives a cat for seeing in the dark.

Month by month, each of our four training companies enrolled a batch of recruits and passed out a batch of trained drivers – significantly heavier than they had been when they were recruited, thanks to regular meals and treatment for hookworm. (We weighed them in and out, and kept a record.)

There was also a permanent fifth company, much smaller than the others, whose ranks never changed. Composed of veteran *sepoys*, who had retired before the war but re-enlisted for its duration, it was known as 'Duty Company', because its function was to perform all the battalion's routine duties, so that the training companies were free to concentrate on training. Although a captaincy went with the post of O.C. Duty Company it was not coveted, and the C.O. was not doing me a favour in allotting it to me when it fell vacant.

The post of Battalion Welfare Officer, hitherto in abeyance, went with this appointment, and he told me that he had given me the post because he expected me to make this mean something, so I spent many evenings in the lines. The *sepoys* taught me to play *carrom*, a blend of billiards and shove-halfpenny, and how to smoke a cigarette without touching it with my mouth, so that it could be shared. A *subedar*, who was hoping to change his Viceroy's commission for a King's one, asked me to coach him in English. I remember the opening sentence of his essay on a subject set in an old exam paper – 'India'. 'India is a rich country where poor people live'. He volunteered for a part in a politically correct play I wrote. The action was set in Burma, where an Indian Army unit was forewarned of a Japanese night attack by villagers who were grateful for some sort of help they had been given. Mr Lal, my head clerk, translated this stuff into Urdu, and a group of volunteers rehearsed it once a week. Luckily I had left the battalion before it could be staged.

Most of my energies, however, went into supervising routine duties. Guard duties went like clock-work and fatigue duties too were automatically performed – except on one occasion, shortly after I had taken over. The battalion lines were on the edge of a wide open space, or *maidan*, one half of which served as a parade ground, where recruits drilled even in the heat of the day. The other half was used as a vehicle park. When I arrived in December, 1941, the vehicle park was still dotted with great ponds left by the monsoon, and the lorries could be driven to any one of these to be washed, but next year, as the hot weather intensified, the ponds shrank rapidly. There was no other water to wash the lorries in, so I hit on the idea of digging canals to drain all the rapidly emptying ponds into one specially prepared vehicle washing pond. It had to be dug much deeper than the existing ponds if it was going to drain off all their water, and if the lorries were going to drive down to such a depth there would have to be an easy slope down to it, so it was obviously going to take a lot of digging. The squad of Duty Company veterans detailed for the job downed tools almost as soon as they arrived on site. This was work for *coolies*, they protested.

The *jemadar* in charge of them immediately informed my *subedar-major*. I was lucky to have a *subedar-major*. My company was not entitled to one. It was the highest rank of Viceroy's Commissioned Officer, and there should have been only one in the battalion. It was the rank with which this V.C.O. had retired, however, so he had kept it when he returned to duty at the outbreak of war. There were therefore two of them in the battalion, with over sixty years service between them, and it was an awesome sight to see them standing side by side with their heads cocked towards each other in consultation, one grey-haired, the other white-haired, each with rows of campaign ribbons, and a grave, lined, confident face. It was he who had closed the door before instructing me to lose my temper with him, and he behaved with similar discretion now. He did not report the incident to me. That would have made it official, and every man concerned would have had to be put on a charge, with serious personal consequences for all of them and awkward consequences for the company. He reported it to my head clerk, Mr Lal, instead. Mr Lal, who was even wiser than the *subedar-major*, then came into my office and said I might be interested in a rumour he had heard. I went straight to the spot and found the fatigue party standing idle, but the ground had been marked out for digging. Remembering a tale I had read as a schoolboy, in which a captain of games on holiday halted a strike at his uncle's factory, I did what he had done and picked up one of the discarded spades. As soon as I started shovelling there were gasps and a second later, a *havildar* had seized my spade and started digging. The rest picked up their spades and followed suit. To complete my success, when it was completed my water system even worked for a time. It was not long, however, before the slope was hazardous because it had become slippery, while the water had become so shallow and filthy that it fouled the lorries it was meant to clean.

In appearance, Mr Lal and the *subedar-major* could not have differed more. The *subedar-major* was a big-made Sikh, robust, round, brisk and bouncy despite his white beard, and very smart. Mr Lal was slight, limp, hollow-chested, pot-bellied, and droopy. The overlapping folds of the *subedar-major*'s turban were as symmetrical as a geometrical diagram, and his Sam Browne belt shone like a fresh conker. The jacket that Mr Lal always put on before entering my office was baggy and his mouth was as red as Dracula's, from chewing *pan*. To complete the difference, one was a Sikh and the other a Hindu. The company provided ample opportunities for communal discrimination. All that its mixed personnel had in common was that they were all old soldiers, recruited from the 'martial classes'. They belonged to different religions and haled from different regions. The two *jemadars* were one a Punjabi Moslem and the other a Dogra Hindu. The non-commissioned officers included Hindus, Sikhs and Moslems, and all that the rank and file had in common was having re-enlisted for non-combatant duties for the duration of the war. Each separate platoon was also a miscellany. In short there were opportunities for Mr Lal and the *subedar-major* to take sides, but they never did so. As far as they were concerned, the only fact about a *sepoy* that counted was his subjection to Indian Army Regulations.

Whatever case came up in orderly room, they were always in possession of the facts, and as like as not had already discussed it. I almost always agreed with them. In short, they carried me. My middle-aged *sepoys* did not appear at orderly room accused of misdemeanors. They came to apply for leave or for assistance in difficulties reported by their families at home. Compassionate leave on account of the death of a parent was rarely asked for as their parents were already dead, but advances of pay were requested, when cash was needed to meet domestic or agricultural emergencies. The most interesting cases, however, arose when official intervention was requested to rectify alleged injustice at the hands of a minor official or oppression by a neighbour, especially land encroachment. By bringing such cases directly to the attention of officials who might otherwise have condoned an injustice or left it to be dealt with by subordinates, the Indian Army offered something like insurance against local injustice in return for a recruit, and once a family had benefited it took care to maintain its contribution, generation after generation.

An example of the operation of this system came to light when I was checking sheet-rolls. A *sepoy's* sheet-roll was a continuous record of his service, opened on the day he was recruited – before he even reported for duty – and maintained continuously thereafter until his discharge, when it was stored away with Military Records in Delhi. New sheet-rolls had been started for the veterans of Duty Company when they re-enlisted, and were kept up to date by us, in the company office, but Military Records eventually sent us their original sheet rolls – the ones which had been started when they first enlisted – to be filed with them. Before being filed, however, each old sheet roll was supposed to be checked against the *sepoy* it referred to, which meant interviewing the entire company, one man at a time. Mr Lal came to the rescue. They would present themselves to me one man at a time on pay day, so why not check their old sheet rolls with them then?

It was a neat idea, but it overlooked the fact that disbursing pay was already a lengthy business. Unpopularity rewarded the odd *sepoy* who slowed things down by signing his name, instead of allowing his thumb to be seized, squeezed onto an ink-pad, and then pressed onto the appropriate space on the roll. The additional business of checking odd details on each of the old sheet rolls against the man who answered to the name it bore doubled this time, even when it amounted to no more than asking him the name of his father and his place of birth.

Nevertheless, after dealing with some twenty of them in this way, I decided that duty demanded that in random cases I must investigate more thoroughly. Each sheet roll contained an entry under the heading 'distinguishing marks', and glancing at the entry for the man whose thumb-print Mr Lal was taking at that moment, I noted that the man whose details had been noted on the old sheet-roll had a long scar on his left thigh. Not knowing the Urdu for 'thigh', I explained to Mr Lal what I was after, and he told the veteran to show this to us.

The veteran made no move to obey. He just stared at us, dumbfounded, so the *subedar-major* moved to pull the hem of his shorts up. Before he could do so, the *sepoy* was on his knees, protesting that he had done no wrong. The man named on the original sheet-roll, whose scar had been recorded in it when he was recruited, was his elder brother, who after enlisting, in duty bound, in the regiment to which their family had already contributed two generations of *sepoys*, had been ordered to report to its training centre three months later. When the time came, however, he had informed their father that he was afraid to go, so their father, who had served with the regiment himself, sent his second son, with instructions to answer to his brother's name.

Although not the man described on the sheet roll, the man before me was therefore the man whose service it recorded so he was the one we wanted, and I told him to forget about it – and stopped entering into details.

Mr Lal shared my interest in the petitions *sepoys* submitted on behalf of their families, and did his skilful best to set wheels in motion to put things right. Dealing with them was the duty which he took greatest pride in, and it certainly enhanced his standing. The day before one of these cases came to my attention I had sometimes caught sight of the petitioner standing at Mr Lal's desk in the outer office, answering questions to which Mr Lal needed answers in order to frame a letter to be signed by me. He knew the ways and wiles of government offices – which sort of string to pull, which official to address and what terms the letter should be couched in. The two other junior civilian clerks stopped working to listen and learn.

Mr Lal did defer to me on questions of English usage, however, so to that extent at any rate we were a partnership. 'We might do this', he would say, when discussing a case. At the time I basked in our success, and when I came back from a month's leave I was conceitedly pleased to find that although my place had been taken by someone else during my absence, matters of this kind had been held over, pending my return. I should have asked myself why? If my services were preferred to those of my replacement, it can only have been because it was beneath him to take guidance from a *babu*.

I did deserve some credit for respecting Mr Lal. Most British officers despised and even execrated *babus*. In its original use, *babu* was a term of respect. Like *Bapu*, the affectionate title given to Gandhi, *babu* is derived from the Sanskrit word for 'father'. Its use was particularly characteristic of Bengal, and as that was the province where most of the East India Company's clerical staff had been recruited, the word in British mouths came simply to mean 'office worker', and 'babuese' was used contemptuously to refer to their distinctive use of English. The contempt was misplaced. Some usages pin-pointed significant features of a clerical transaction that might otherwise have escaped attention. For example, settling a troublesome piece of business by going through routine motions in the course of which it lost its power to cause trouble was known, not as 'disposing of it', but as 'disposing it off'.

Most British officers had more reasons than one for despising *babus*. They were not 'martial', for a start, and they usually wore *dhotis* instead of trousers or pyjamas. The *dhoti* is worn tucked in, without a belt, and its wearer leaves a length of material hanging loose, even when he has finished putting it on. More than once I heard a Right Type declare it to be 'no better than a skirt'.

The prime cause of a British officer's hostility to *babus*, however, was that once he had been given some responsibility, he could not cope with the office work without a *babu*'s guidance. I was told a cautionary tale about this.

A battalion commander was once summoned to Sub-Area Headquarters by the brigadier, who passed a letter across the desk to him. 'Is that your signature? It is? Good man! Now go ahead and read the letter.'

    'Dear Brigadier,
the colonel read

      'this is to inform you that I am always shouting at my head clerk, Mr Bose, calling him "bloody fool" and employing other such terms of abuse, but as this bears witness I sign everything he places on my desk without checking it,
      Yours faithfully,

To the credit of the Indian Army be it noted that this incident ended with the transfer of the colonel, not of Mr Bose.

The trickiest case Mr Lal and I had to deal with was that of a Pathan from the Frontier. He stood out among the other *sepoys* of Duty Company, being several inches taller than anyone else, and also straighter and younger. Indeed it was hard to imagine how he ever came to be in the company. A hulking man, with a melancholy face, he presented himself to explain that when he enlisted he had left his wife in the care of his brother, but now she had sent a letter asking him to come back home, as his brother had enlisted, so she was unprotected.

It was not in my power to grant a compassionate discharge, so I put his case up to the C.O., who decided to ask the local Political Officer to inquire into the circumstances and report whether they warranted discharge on 'very compassionate grounds'. The reply, when at last it came, was that they warranted discharge on compassionate grounds, but not on very compassionate ones. In retrospect I can see that such distinctions must be made, but then I was indignant. My indignation, however, was as nothing compared with the rage of the *sepoy*. He burst into ferocious speech, and when he disobeyed an order to be silent the C.O. gave him three days detention in the guard-house. Two feeble old Duty Company *sepoys*, who were posted outside the office, were then marched in to take him into custody. He looked them up and down contemptuously, and asked me what would happen if he refused to go – at which point the C.O. commendably pretended not to hear him by busying himself with papers. I told him that resistance would make things even worse, and he gave in.

Before the three days were up, Mr Lal had reminded me that the reason why the *sepoy*'s grounds for compassionate discharge had been checked by a Political Officer, and not by a District Magistrate, was that his home was in tribal territory, which meant that if he took leave and decided to stay there, nothing could be done to bring him back. This amounted to a suggestion. The *sepoy* need not be discharged. He had only to go home on leave to have everything he had asked for, and, thanks to his wife's letter, I could grant him a period of compassionate leave as soon as he applied for it.

The day after his release from detention he did apply for leave, but to my surprise it was not for compassionate but for privilege leave, which meant that he would have to wait his turn in a queue. For this, however, as Mr Lal, with whom he had evidently discussed it, pointed out to me, there was good reason. If he waited to go home on privilege leave, he would go with a month's earned pay in his pocket, together with the next month's pay in advance.

Even that, however, was less than he required when the time did come for him to go. He asked me for a personal loan. He had received another letter from his wife, telling him he had to bring money to buy timber to repair the house which had been damaged by heavy rain. Two months' pay, he told me, would not cover this. He named the additional sum required, and asked me to lend it to him. This struck me as cool. It was not a large sum, but he knew that I knew that he would not be coming back. On the other hand, the one-eyed colonel in Bangalore had told us how expensive timber was in tribal territory, as a result of deforestation, and there was no point in going to the lengths we had, only to send him home to live in misery, so I gave him what he had asked for.

The *subedar-major* had not been directly involved in these transactions but a month later the look on his face showed that he had been privy to them when, after duly closing my office door again, he told me that the *sepoy* had returned from leave. I summoned the man immediately and asked him angrily whether he realised that he would not be due leave again for another year. He said he did, but he had to earn the money to repay me. As it happened, he repaid me nothing, because even before he received his next month's pay I had left Bareilly for New Delhi, to join a newly formed section of the General Staff. After I had gone the C.O. let it be known this was because he had recommended me for any special duties that required 'an ability to mix with Indians'. My new duties did require something of that sort, but it was not to him that l owed my new appointment. I owed it to the Indian Communist Party.

5: Cloak and dagger

Some three month after my arrival in Bareilly, I had just sat down to breakfast when the mess *havildar* bent to murmur in my ear that a *babu*, who wished to speak to me, was waiting in the kitchen. Mystified, I left the table to follow him where I had never been before, and found Arun Bose, who had been my Marxist guru at Cambridge, sitting in a comer. I turned to ask the *havildar* why my friend had not been shown into the ante-room, but Arun stopped me with a sign, and we arranged to meet at my bungalow, after dinner.

Secrecy was impossible at the bungalow, so when he arrived I was waiting on the verandah with the light off, and went down the steps to meet him as he came up the drive. We walked out into the road together, and then around the cantonment in the dark, past name-plated gate-posts and long white garden walls. Arun was now a full-time party activist, one of those who had chosen – as Auden put it – 'to hunger, work illegally, and be anonymous', but I found him less impersonal than he had been as a student in Cambridge. Instead of confining our conversation to the revolution, as he had always done before, he opened it by asking how I liked India, what had I seen, where had I been, and even whether I had read any Indian philosophy. Before we parted he even expressed nostalgia for England, which surprisingly included memories of early mornings in the saddle on the Downs. But the purpose of his visit was to discuss what I could do for the Party in India. The sizable contribution to Party funds, that Morris and I had handed over in Lahore, had been taken as a proof of our commitment. I was gratified to hear this, but wondered what was coming next.

It turned out not to be alarming. The Central Committee had at last determined the Indian Party line in accordance with the views that Iftikar and his friends had voiced in Lahore. Thanks to the German invasion of the Soviet Union the war was now a 'people's war', fought in the interest not of Britain but of the workers of the world. By fighting to preserve 'the workers' state' British imperialism was therefore 'digging its own grave', and should be given every assistance.

It was not going to be easy to persuade 'the Indian masses' to support a war that the Government of India was involved in, but a start was going to be made with the students by pushing through a resolution in support of the war at the annual conference of the All India Students' Federation. This would be in Delhi in May, and I must be there if I could. Next day I arranged the dates of my annual leave to make it possible.

As it happened I was able to contact the Party in Delhi even earlier. I developed a relentless tooth-ache, an impacted wisdom tooth was discovered, and Delhi was the nearest place where it could be dealt with properly. The C.O. therefore sent me there to take delivery of a fleet of Chevrolet saloon cars which were waiting to replace our hired civilian staff cars. There would be no need to go to the vehicle depot to inspect them. I would not even have to sign for them. All that would be attended to by the battalion transport *subedar*, who would accompany me. While I was there my time would be all my own.

Just then Sir Stafford Cripps was in Delhi, trying to negotiate the support of Indian leaders for the war in return for a partial transfer of power, to be completed when the war was won. The city was so full of journalists that there were no vacant rooms at the hotel, and I was allotted one of a row of beds that had been installed beside the swimming pool. It was agreeably cool there, but it was not where I slept.

By this time Mazhar Ali Khan had been released from prison, and I spent the evening with him and a bunch of other young Indian communists. They were all euphoric. None of them expected anything good to come of the Cripps Mission, but they took it as a sign that the imperialists were on the run. Independence was in sight at last and we drank to it, although not every Indian nationalist would have approved.

Waking at dawn in my underwear, on a string bed in a sort of dormitory full of other string-beds – most of which were occupied, although nobody else seemed to be awake – I rushed back to the hotel just in time to smarten up before a convoy of gleaming Chevrolet saloons rolled up for me to take my seat in the leading one and be driven back to Bareilly, nominally in charge.

A few weeks later I was back in Delhi for the student conference. The proceedings were conducted in English. In Leeds in the spring of 1940 I had played a part in swinging the annual conference of the National Union of Students to condemn the war, and I could see that a reverse operation was now in full swing in Delhi. In both cases students had to be persuaded to move against public opinion. If Indian students adopted a pro-war policy they would have to oppose the mass civil disobedience movement which the Congress Party was threatening, now that it had rejected the Cripps's offer. I could not discuss the implications of this with Arun, because after emerging briefly from some back room to greet me on my arrival he had gone back behind the scenes, so I sat there on my own, until there was a break for refreshment, when a student swept me off to view an exhibition of 'student art'.

Another European was there already – a tall, middle-aged, balding man, with quizzical eyes, a high forehead and a small moustache above prim lips. His dress was sloppy and comfortable – a limp grey bush-shirt with unbuttoned, flapping sleeves, and floppy, baggy, unstarched shorts. The material of these loose garments was a coarse grey cotton cloth, called *mazri*, which until then I had only seen worn by *sepoys* on fatigue duty and sweepers, and I must have looked my surprise, because almost the first thing he said to me was – 'This is the stuff to sweat in'.

By that time we had been led speechless round the display – speechless because it took the form of scores of copies of the same originals – the standard portraits, executed in red chalk and charcoal, of 'the four great teachers' – Marx, Engels, Lenin and Stalin which were then displayed in every communist book-shop around the world. The only variety was provided by a few copies of Soviet posters.

An open book awaited visitors' comments at the exit, and the stranger was invited to record his first. 'Thank you very much', he wrote, and signed his name, to general disappointment. The disappointment was caused by his name, however, not the tepidity of his comment. Word had got around that this was Edgar Snow, whose *Red Star Over China* first brought Mao-Tse-Tung to the attention of the world. 'So you are not Snow?' one of the students asked, to make quite sure. The stranger apologised, and they left us alone together.

'My name's Bill Short'[8], the stranger said to me. The reason why 'Bill' or 'Billy' was the name he went by was a mystery. His first name was not William. 'Because he has eyes like a cat', an Indian acquaintance suggested. (*Billi* is the Urdu for 'cat'.) When I had introduced myself he asked what I was doing there – as if his own presence required no explanation. I said that I was visiting an old Cambridge friend. I did not ask what he was doing: he might not be Edgar Snow, but I was sure he was a journalist.

That evening, however, Arun told me that Short was a lieutenant-colonel from General Headquarters, attending the students' conference on duty. He had already worked out ways in which Indian students might assist the Indian Army, and a special military unit was about to be formed to organise this, with him in command. That was where I could come in. He would want a suitable junior officer. Obviously, he would not want a party member, but a party sympathiser whom communists trusted would suit his purposes admirably, so that was how we must try to make him see me.

Next day half way through an extended lunch, with conference delegates seated in rows at long tables, Arun rose to announce that an English student was going to sing the

Red Cavalry Song. I had chosen that particular Soviet song because it was the only communist song I knew that expressed naïf enthusiasm. Cambridge communist students sang a lot, but many of our songs were not even political, and those that were – like:

> *Wage the class war briskly,*
> *Put the thing through quickly,*
> *Hang the rich from the lamp-posts high but*
> *Don't. . . hang. . . me*
> *Stick to Marx my hearty,*
> *Damn the Labour Party,*
> *Keep the hell fires burning bright*
> *For the bour . .geois. . .ie!*

(sung to the tune of *Keep the Home Fires Burning*) – were not naïf. Although I only knew them because they featured an unintentionally comic rhyme:

> *With Voroshilov and Budyenny*
> *As of old once again we*
> *The Red Cavalry Army will ride. . ..*

The words of the *Red Cavalry Song* were suitably solemn and the tune was rousing. My solo went down well, and Short invited me to dine at his hotel.

There he explained what he was doing. It was something unheard of, but in his view inevitable because, as a result of mass recruitment, the Indian Army was filling up with a new kind of *sepoy*. As long as recruitment was confined to localities that had bred *sepoys* for generations, existing local traditions had taken care of morale. It was a question of simple *esprit de corps*. The *sepoys* of the 11th Sikhs, to take his own regiment as an example, believed in the honour of the regiment and believed that the good name of their community was in their keeping. No such traditions, however, stiffened the morale of the *sepoys* who were being recruited now, all over India. They simply saw their military service as a novel form of steady employment that had unexpectedly come their way, thanks to some war that the British had become involved in. No local loyalties bound them to service in the Indian Army. Some more widespread loyalty must be developed to enthuse them, and the only genuine one available was national feeling. The new recruit in the new Indian Army must be taught to see himself as fighting for India – and that had to mean an Indian India, not a British one.

It was a bold idea. It meant motivating Indians to fight the Japanese by presenting this as a way to get rid of the British. Short himself was in earnest about this. He believed that the granting of Indian independence would be the culmination of a process which had always been intended and was now coming to fruition. As soon as the war was won, arrangements would begin to make India an independent member of the Commonwealth.

But who was going to convince the recruits of this? Certainly not their officers, almost all of whom were then British and could not present a nationalist case convincingly even if they sympathised with Indian national aspirations – which was unlikely. Indians with anti-British credentials were needed. If Sir Stafford Cripps's proposals had been accepted, Nehru himself would have fired the troops, but as things were the Congress Party's approach to Indian involvement in the war was negative, whatever its view of the enemy might be. The Moslem League supported the war, but its appeal was sectarian. It would only appeal to Moslems, and in any case to bring it into direct contact with the army while denying the Congress Party the same access was out of the question. There was, however, another party.

Returning to India from early retirement when war broke out, Short had served initially as a Civil Liaison Officer in Lahore. As such it was his duty to protect the local interests of men who had enlisted, and giving this responsibility a wide interpretation he had mixed with political leaders and dignitaries of different communities and social groups. One family with which he was on friendly terms was that of Sir

Sikander Hyat Khan, the Prime Minister of the pro-British provincial government. Sir Sikander was also the uncle of Mahmud and Mazhar Ali Khan, the communists whom Morris and I had met in Lahore. They were not his favourite relatives, but Short did eventually meet them and when he got to know them found that their view of the war was just what he was looking for.

Most Indians regarded Germany as Britain's enemy, not India's, and were not displeased to see the British humbled when Germany gained a victory. 'He's a Hitler!' said a *tonga-wallah*, boasting about his pony. Mahmud and Mazhar, on the other hand, clearly hated Nazi Germany and Japan, and finding Mazhar keen to join the Indian Army, Short saw to it that, despite his spell in prison, his application for a commission succeeded.

Getting into uniform was not, however, the only way for men with views like Mazhar's to serve. The Communist Party line – that the war was now a 'people's war' – was just what new recruits needed to hear. Accordingly Short had proposed to G.H.Q. that every training unit should have two member of the All India Students Federation attached to it.

His plan had not yet gained final acceptance, but I was amazed that it had not been rejected out of hand, and according to Short it now looked like succeeding, if the All India Student Federation undertook to confine its propaganda to the issue of the war, and it seemed their leadership was prepared to agree to this. If the present conference supported the Communist Party's 'People's War' line – which seemed a foregone conclusion – he would soon be establishing militant students in military lines. But first he had to establish a special unit to supervise all this, and at G.H.Q. that sort of thing took time. Nevertheless, provision for the staff he had asked for was well on the way, and as soon as it arrived, if I was interested, he would arrange my appointment. He never asked whether I was, or had ever been, a member of the Communist

Party, but if he had, I would have lied. As it was, in the course of a wide-ranging conversation I did the next best thing by expressing doubts about the Soviet Union, which must have seemed incompatible with party membership – although oddly enough they were genuine. In short I deceived him.

At the same time, I liked him immediately and still remember him with astonished affection. He was continually winning friends because he was interested in people, and took pleasure in listening while they talked. Indians in particular found this unusual in a European – especially one to whom they could express themselves in their own language. Short's Indian roots went so deep that when India became independent he had difficulty in establishing British citizenship. Not only had he been born in India, but so too had his father, and his father's father.

What made him persuasive was a genuine interest in what anyone he met, however unimportant, had to say, backed by a readiness to help them, if they needed help, or to put them in touch with someone else who could. He also remembered them. Late one night, a few weeks later after I had joined his staff, we were sitting out on the lawn of the New Delhi Gymkhana Club when all the other members had gone home and a sweeper had already begun to clear away the litter. The lawn was only dimly lit from the lights inside the building but, happening to glance across it, he recognised the sweeper, greeted him by name, and called him over to ask how life had treated him since they had met last – more than ten years earlier. He even inquired about some ailment that the sweeper's wife had suffered from. To describe that as an impressive performance is not to question the genuineness of his sympathy but to indicate that it was also the demonstration of a gift that he was conscious of possessing. He exercised it deliberately every morning by gaining admission to G.H.Q. without showing his pass. When the *sepoy* sentry asked to see it he would reply by asking him what district he came from, and then go on to inquire familiarly about matters of general local interest there, as well as the wellbeing of the sentry's family. At last he would produce an elaborate farewell – and enter the building without having shown his pass.

As my bearer, Chhanga Ram, remarked to me after a long conversation with him – 'Short *Sahib* is a *purana sahib*.' (A *purana sahib* was mature: a *pukka* one was only ripe.) Chhanga was a qualified judge. He was a *purana bearer*. One of his testimonials, written by an officer whom, although he was a civilian, he had served in France during the 1914-18 war, described how, whatever the conditions might be, he would come walking up the trench at tea time, carrying a tray with a plate of excellent sandwiches together with cup, saucer, milk and tea-pot.

He had been in his teens then. Now he was a dignified figure, although diminutive. Our bearers waited in turn at dinner at the battalion mess table, and when it was Chhanga's turn, although a civilian, he wore campaign ribbons. The first time he appeared like this, an officer of the Wrong Type was so astounded by them that he made a derisive comment when Chhanga was serving him. I was on the point of intervening when Chhanga sharply caught my eye across the table and shook his head. *Sahibs* were not as *pukka* as they used to be. Propriety was no longer to be expected from them, and the decline in *mem-sahibs* had been even more regrettable!

His earliest memory was of assisting his father to attend their Edwardian *mem-sahib* on her way across a lawn into a carriage. It was night, and his father had walked beside her, carrying a lantern, while he walked behind, holding up the hem of her evening gown to keep it clear of the dew. But skirts no longer swept the lawn now, and gone were the great hats, decked with flowers and feathers.

Short returned Chhanga's admiration and shared his sense of the Raj's decline. Once, after the two of them had enjoyed a long chat, he told me approvingly that Chhanga had observed that the trouble with the Raj was that it had ears now but no eyes. I think what Chhanga meant by this was that British officials in India now relied on reports from prejudiced Indian subordinates instead of seeing things, impartially, for themselves, but Short interpreted the remark as an endorsement of his own constant complaint that district officers would rather sit in their offices nowadays than get out into the villages and see things for themselves. Admittedly they did have a lot to do on paper nowadays, but even when they had chances to break free they failed to take them. The British ought to feel at home in India, but no longer did. This saddened him, because in his view the British period of Indian history was a story of growing mutual understanding from which both parties had benefited.

Indians could teach the British a lot – not only about sensitivity, affection and selflessness but in fields more down-to-earth as well. One should always be ready to accept the guidance of an Indian subordinate. He had learnt this as an eighteen-year-old subaltern, when he was leading a night reconnaissance patrol up a slope towards the Turkish lines, and a Turkish officer, oblivious of his presence, had suddenly appeared above him, silhouetted against the sky. His patrol had only got back to base unharmed because his *jemadar* had gripped the pistol he had raised, and removed it from his grasp before he could steady it to fire.

Nevertheless, the British had something to impart to India that India needed but lacked. They might be unimaginative and narrow-minded, but thanks to a traditional wisdom that showed itself in their distrust of 'isms', they always ended up by doing what was best. His view of politics was patrician. The way to right a wrong was to bring it to the attention of someone in a position to right it. Common humanity and patience were all that was needed. (He did not seem to think that they were much to ask for.) Given common humanity and patience, people only had to listen to one another. Wisdom consisted in listening to one's dependants or opponents, as the case might be, and then giving them as much of what they wanted as seemed practicable. His watchword was 'consent'.

The nearest he came to cherishing an 'ism' was his enthusiasm for the views expressed by Lionel Curtis in *Civitas Dei* – a vision of the history of the world combined with a provincial vision of its future, that at that time was taken seriously in British imperial circles. In an initial summary of major civilizations of the past Curtis credited each with unearthing a different fragment of wisdom. He then asserted that all these fragments had been united in a unique English wisdom. Thanks to English wisdom, England had developed into an association of mutually supportive individuals, all different but all ready to assist one another – which must have been how he somehow saw English society in the nineteen thirties. The English, in their wisdom, had extended the same pattern to their relations with their neighbours by establishing a mutually supportive association of kingdoms – the aptly named United Kingdom. Finally the United Kingdom had started to incorporate its colonies into an even wider union of independent equals – the British Commonwealth of Nations – starting with Canada and with India now about to be the latest addition.

This had been of necessity a gradual process. (A characteristic feature of the English was refusal to be rushed.) Countries must not be admitted until they had acquired the necessary wisdom. African colonies therefore still had to wait their turn, which might well come after that of countries which had not even enjoyed the benefit of direct British rule. The U.S.A., for example, qualified already, and some European countries would soon be able to conduct themselves on British lines. When they saw the advantages they would inevitably want to join the Commonwealth, as membership involved no loss of independence. In the end every country in the world would join – but Curtis gave 'more difficult nations' fair warning that they would have to wait until they had been 'contained and moulded'. Meanwhile the fact that India was now qualified to join the British Commonwealth was greatly to the credit of British rule, as a self-governing community required the energetic participation of all its members, and India's climate enervated its inhabitants – witness the pessimism of its religions.

Short seemed to agree with Curtis about everything except Indian enervation. He did not doubt that India had needed to live under British tutelage for the past century and a half, and that the fact that it no longer needed a resident tutor was thanks to the tutelage it had received. In other words, Indians could not look after themselves until the British arrived to show them how. To understand how intelligent people of good will did honestly believe this, it has to be remembered that the alternative was to recognise that the British had no business to be in India at all.

Short's most immediately notable virtue was his courtesy. Two youthful American lieutenants in a jeep drove up to the New Delhi Gymkhana Club one Sunday morning before lunch, and joined the members who were sipping pre-prandial drinks on the verandah and at tables under umbrellas around the lawn. The Americans had no right to be there, as they were neither members nor the guests of members. Moreover they had brought two Anglo-Indian girls along with them, together with a portable gramophone and food and drink. The members watched incredulously as they settled down for a picnic, wound up the gramophone and put a record on.

Before anyone could inform them of their trespass, Short had left his table and joined them on the grass. Perhaps they did not know this was a club? He would be glad if they would spend the morning there as his guests. And now they did know that this was a club, if they would like to join it he would be happy to put their names up. They agreed, and when in due course their applications were considered nobody black-balled them. This story does not end entirely happily, however. Their Anglo-Indian companions were not seen again in the Gymkhana Club.

Short's behaviour at the club on that occasion, although unconventional, did not shock, but it did on another occasion.

We were dining with a guest, and had reached dessert when he expressed disappointment that there was no picture hanging on the wall for us to throw walnuts at. Throwing a walnut at a picture was, he said, the neatest way to crack it. His guest protested that the nut would break the glass. Only if there was a flaw in it, Short told him. The Bishop of Lahore had a portrait of a predecessor on the wall close to his dining table purely for that purpose. So saying he collected a walnut, rose and strolled off between tables to the only picture in the room.

He had to go some distance, as the picture was near the entrance, but his manner must have indicated that he was not just leaving but about to do something, because diners stopped eating and turned to watch him as he passed them on his way, halted before the picture and swung back his arm.

General silence followed the sound of splintering glass. It is impossible to explain to anyone who was not in India in those days the enormity of vandalising a portrait of the King-Emperor. All eyes were on him, but he made no effort to explain. He just called for a chit to sign for the cost of the damage. 'The glass was evidently flawed', was all he said when he rejoined us.

6: Glimpses of authority

'There could be an M.B.E in this for you'. One of the first things Short said to me when I joined his staff in New Delhi was a reminder that we belonged to different worlds – but also a sign that his idea had been accepted. He was now the regularly appointed head of 'Military Training 10', a newly formed section of the General Staff, whose concern was the morale of troops undergoing training. I had been posted to it, with the rank of major. This did not mean that I was a G.S.O. (General Staff Officer), he warned me. Nevertheless I was entitled to sport the red and black arm-band of a staff officer, and must always do so when in uniform, as it carried clout which I was going to need, because once we had started I would be on my own in Bangalore, supervising the activities of student activists attached to military units in Southern Army, and smoothing out the inevitable misunderstandings that would arise between them and the commanders of units to which they were attached. My headquarters would be in Bangalore because that was where Southern Army Headquarters had been transferred from Poona, but I must insist on my G.H.Q. affiliation at all times, making it clear that I was not responsible to Bangalore but directly to New Delhi. I must also stay in touch with the civil government and, as far as possible, with politicians, for which purpose I would employ two well-paid civilian subordinates with useful political contacts, one in Bombay and the other in Madras.

Matching my appointment in Southern India, another officer was to set up shop in Calcutta, where Eastern Army H.Q. was located. This was Lieutenant Colonel Kilroy, an old comrade of Short from the 11th Sikhs, who like him had returned to India from early retirement to become a Civil Liaison Officer in the Punjab. He was a soldier to his fingertips, a figure of unmistakably military authority whose word would carry weight with other soldiers. In brief, Kilroy was a good choice, but I cannot imagine what had led Short to choose me. I neither moved like a soldier nor looked like one, despite my uniform. If a dispute arose between a student activist and a commanding officer, neither party would have listened to me – unless the students knew I was a communist, and if they did know that it would be farewell to my arm-band, because the authorities would know it too.

Short warned me that success would depend on our ability to explain each party to the other. Commanding officers and student activists must be brought to see each other's point of view, he said – as if nothing could be easier. Amazingly, however, I had no qualms. Perhaps I just took it for granted that if Short thought I could do it, then I must be able to – or perhaps I thought that the clout of the arm-band would suffice.

An Indian Army order placed my astonishing appointment beyond doubt, but as yet no student activists had been selected, let alone sent to a battalion. Indeed, as yet no decision had been taken as to precisely what their duties and responsibilities were going to be. Short viewed these details as the final hurdle, bound to be cleared now that his proposal had been approved in principle, but in the event it was only when the execution of his plan began to be worked out in detail that it was realised how revolutionary it was – and therefore how unacceptable. In the eyes of practically every Indian Army officer Indian patriotism was seditious, and all the Indian Army needed to keep going was its own mystique. The moment a recruit joined up, he was proud of his regiment, and confining the membership of each regiment to a specific cultural group ensured that his regimental pride incorporated any other loyalties he might feel.

This belief was not misguided. Traditional regiments were still fired like that. Against this tradition, however, Short now proposed a mass army of patriotic citizens, because most of those now entering on the hardships of soldiering were doing so only to escape the even greater discomfort of poverty.

Embracing a *sepoy*'s life signified nothing to them, in itself, so it was essential to find a new and more accessible source of enthusiasm – the kind of stimulus supplied by orators and newspapers.

In the event he was proved wrong. The additional stimulus was not supplied, and the new recruits did well enough without it. Nevertheless, his scheme was based on a genuine perception. His lack of perception appeared in his belief that his scheme might be accepted.

When I joined him he had secured its acceptance in principle, his unit had been officially established and Kilroy and I had been appointed, so he was sanguine. It only remained to spell out the practical implications of his idea in a detailed proposal that would determine the precise responsibilities of the student activists attached to a battalion.

This proposal would have to satisfy both parties. He had made a start with the students. To make the presence of student activists acceptable in any unit of the Indian Army – under duress, for it would never be welcome – the Students Federation would have to consent to restrictions on their activities which at first to them seemed like surrender. Nevertheless, in negotiations which had already been completed when I joined him, Short had persuaded them to accept terms which he thought he could persuade the Army to agree to, and he was now converting the results into a draft directive for the approval of General Molesworth, the Deputy Chief of General Staff.

Its terms were a proof of his powers of persuasion. The students had agreed that appointment of the activists they proposed would be subject to approval by the Army which, as the police would be consulted, would in effect mean approval by the police. They were also prepared to warn their activists to confine themselves to denunciation of the enemy and explanation of the importance of a victory for India's independence, and refrain from making directly anti-British declarations. It had proved harder to persuade them to accept subjection of their members to military discipline – for example, to accept the condition that they must not disobey an order of the C.O. of the unit to which they were attached, even if it seemed to contravene the terms of their employment – but they agreed when it was conceded that after first consenting in such a case they could refer it to Short. It was also hard for them to grant that if recruits informed a student activist of a grievance his duty would not be to champion them, but only to notify their officers. In the end, however, they agreed even to that.

Nevertheless a soldier did not have to be a diehard to find the terms which Short had agreed with the students 'nothing short of lunacy'. General Molesworth, had so far only agreed to the proposal in principle, and when I joined him in New Delhi Short was still preparing a detailed directive for his approval. This was a very gradual process, because he drafted and re-drafted it, testing it step by step in detailed consultations. Somewhere he had acquired a tactic, which he explained to me. When a proposal had to be submitted to someone in authority it should first be shown to his subordinates for their comment, as that was the first thing the person in authority was going to do with it himself. The subordinates in question should therefore be identified and visited at their desks at every stage of the submission's preparation, at first to discuss its contents and later to get their comment on the wording of draft proposals. Drafting and redrafting his proposal he was therefore continually moving in and out of the rooms of staff officers concerned with Military Training. He took me with him a couple of times, and I was amazed to see how readily they helped him. (When I met him in London, shortly after the war, he was employing these same tactics in Whitehall, to secure funds for the Peckham Health Experiment[9].)

But it was not on General Molesworth's judgement that Short's success would depend. As the general himself smoothly declared when pressed for a decision, he had risen to be D.C.G.s. by dint of never taking one. In other words, when he circulated Short's proposal to other departments he was not going to back it, but just invite their comments.

Inserting political activists into training battalions was not Short's only responsibility. In the document setting out the Section's duties it was listed as 'category A work'. There was also 'category B work' – assisting other forms of co-operation with the Indian Communist Party. In this connection Short took me across the road from the imposing Military Secretariat building to its twin, the Civil Secretariat building, to be interviewed by Sir James Maxwell, the member of the Viceroy's Executive Council in charge of Home Affairs. In Indian newspaper editorials 'Maxwell' was a synonym for repression, so I watched him closely, and can still see him although he only gave me twenty minutes. He sported a neat bow-tie, but had removed his jacket, as if to demonstrate a readiness to sacrifice convention to efficiency. His moustache was neatly trimmed, his spectacles glinted, and he questioned me as if he was interviewing me for a job. In short, he personified bureaucracy – detached and cool – yet when Short told me afterwards that he had remarked on my 'honest blue eyes', and declared that he was 'glad they had me with them', I felt guilty.

Another Civil Secretariat interview that Short arranged for me, renewed my bolshevik zeal. It was with an officer of the Intelligence Bureau – the Indian equivalent of the Special Branch of the C.I.D. in Britain. Bailey, the man in question, was a specialist on communism. He agreed entirely with Short's policy of enlisting its services, and mocked agents of the Bureau who could not re-adjust themselves. His room was lofty, and an enormous map of India hung on the high wall facing his desk. Pointing to a bazaar centre somewhere in Bihar he said, with a merry grin: 'A fool of an informer there has just reported that the local communist declared in a public speech that an allied victory will make India independent – as if that was seditious.'

His tone was jocular. Taking it for granted that, as presumably I knew something about communism, I too must find it comic, he referred to Palme Dutt as 'Barmy Dutt'. I was amazed to hear a servant of imperialism treating its infallible accuser lightly, but obligingly laughed.

Shortly afterwards, however, my belief in the Soviet Union suffered another bruise. One morning over breakfast Short repeated something he had heard the previous evening from a brigadier. Delighted that we now had 'the Russians' as allies, and feeling it would be 'a good idea to get to know them', he had decided to spend his one month's leave in Soviet Tajikistan instead of making for an Indian hill station, and accordingly travelled to the border where he presented himself to the Red Army soldiers who manned the frontier post as an ally who had come to say 'Hello!'

The situation had not been foreseen. He had to wait on the Indian side of the barrier for several hours, while the officer in charge of the post waited for answers to telephone calls. Once through the barrier, however, he was treated handsomely. Only one thing was denied him. It was, however, what he had come for – contact with Red Army units. There was much wining and dining, accompanied by offers of girls – a detail which I found disturbing, as the girls must have been Soviet citizenesses, with rights. The final detail, however, was dumbfounding.

At the end of his stay the brigadier had been accompanied back to the frontier post by an English-speaking, Red Army colonel who, before bidding him farewell, said he trusted their visitor had experienced no difficulties on his arrival. To his subsequent regret, instead of lying the brigadier replied, 'Oh well, you know how it is. At first your chaps were naturally a bit suspicious'. Protesting, but still not anticipating the consequences, he then had to identify the soldier who had detained him, whereupon the Red Army colonel shot the offender through the head. 'When you get back,' he said, 'I hope you will tell all your comrades what you have just seen me do. We do not tolerate inefficiency in the Red Army.'

I knew from our lectures on military law that in time of war a Red Army officer of field rank could indeed shoot a soldier on the authority of his own signature, and I could not doubt that Short had heard this story from a reliable witness. Nastiest of all was the colonel's belief that his action would create a good impression.

While Short was busy with his drafts he sent me on errands to Bombay, in connection with 'Category A work'. I was off there only four or five days after I had joined him. Bombay was in my region, so in any case I had to make myself known to the Chief Secretary, and explain what we were going to do, but Bombay was also where the headquarters of the Indian Communist Party was located, so there were things that he could do as well. One was to assist in the publication of a weekly paper that the Party was about to publish – to be called *People's War*. The help the Party needed was not financial. As they saw it, financial help would turn them into 'imperialist hirelings' – like M.N. Roy, a rival Marxist whom they had cunningly incriminated in the course of explaining their scruples to officials.

Communists thrived on denunciations of 'hirelings' and 'deviationists', and in their eyes M.N. Roy was both. Like Satan, he had fallen from on high. Not only had he once himself been a Marxist-Leninist: he had even been a member of the executive committee of the Communist International for a time. Later, however, he had been blamed for the initial defeat of communism in China, denounced and expelled from the Party. M.N. Roy had already started an evening paper in Delhi when the Communists asked the Government of India for help in starting a weekly paper in Bombay, and suspecting that his paper was financed by the Government of India, when they informed officials that they did not expect a subsidy, they added – 'like the one you give to M.N. Roy'. Great was their jubilation when the imputation was not rejected.

I could not understand this at the time, but I can now. When one has been hurling accusations blindly, it must be a relief when one of them sticks.

Nevertheless, even the Communist Party of India could not start a weekly paper without government help. They needed newsprint, and newsprint was now a controlled commodity. Without an official quota it could only be obtained expensively on the black market. I told the Chief Secretary what they needed and he immediately released it. First of all, however, I had to explain how the Army came to be concerned. 'It isn't usual to find the Army ahead of us in these matters.' He was amused, and even agreed to release from gaol some Communist activists whose names I had been given. We wanted them to be free to work mischief, if the Japanese took India over for a time.

The possibility that they might do so was treated seriously. Hardly was I back in Delhi than I was on my way back to Bombay, to assist in setting up the underground that would be needed if they did – a duty so secret that the man I was to meet there was never named. He was a secret operations specialist, from Europe, who answered to the name 'Mackenzie', on the understanding that his name was something else. Recently arrived in New Delhi, he was staying at Viceregal Lodge.

Perhaps as a result of his European experience, the Communist Party featured prominently in Mackenzie's plans, and he had arranged a meeting in Bombay with P.C. Joshi, the Party Secretary. I attended the first of their discussions as a kind of ideological interpreter. Short had warned me to leave the talk entirely to the two of them, except when I thought that they were at cross purposes. This did happen once or twice. When Joshi spoke of the need for his party to keep its 'mass basis', for example, Mackenzie innocently assumed that this meant sharing secrets with the masses.

There was, however, no misunderstanding when Joshi broached the subject of guerrilla warfare in the event of a Japanese occupation. He claimed that the Party could muster fighters in Malabar and East Bengal, but Mackenzie had no intention of arming communist bands. The communists that he was interested in were strike-leaders and saboteurs, especially on the railways, and Joshi gave him details of more party members then in jail, to be released in readiness for this.

The most interesting discussion resulted from Mackenzie's advocacy of bribery as a weapon. Joshi reacted like a teetotaller offered a whisky. The support of men who could be bought, he said, was unreliable. Mackenzie agreed but remarked that unreliable men could still be useful and, without mentioning a name, spoke of a successful transaction of that kind made recently with a prominent person in occupied France. Gold could be buried in secret caches for the Party to employ in case of need. Joshi, however, refused to touch it.

After three or four hours' discussion they decided on another meeting. Mackenzie told me that my assistance was no longer needed, but later that day I went back for a private interview with Joshi. He was a vibrant, youngish man who shot out words like machine-gun bullets. After an artless inquiry about the military standing of Dogras – his own community – he discussed Short's plans for 'Category A' work. He was cock-a-whoop at the prospect of placing two student commissars in every training battalion, especially when he had an agent – namely me – right at the heart of things. There was a danger that I might attract suspicion by seeming too close to the students. It was not something I should do anything about myself. I must seem as sympathetic as I really was, but he would warn all party branches against confiding in me, and dispatch it by a channel that he knew was intercepted by the Intelligence Bureau, so it would serve to throw them off the scent as well. He had the message ready. It said that I was a well-meaning young bourgeois intellectual, who was genuinely sympathetic, but that did not mean that I could be trusted.

His anxieties about displays of sympathy were justified. The building which housed the Party's central office also accommodated a commune of devoted, full-time party activists. Few of them had ever met a European sympathiser, but they had always believed that they existed, and when I was introduced to them as a friend of Arun Bose, although they did not know that I was a party member they took me to their hearts. My memories of the ensuing evening are fragmentary, but I know that I invited a small crowd for a meal, and whatever the Party rules about full-time activists and alcohol may have been, we went from place to place, and drank at each in an atmosphere of growing bonhomie. Whereabouts in Bombay it was we went I have no idea, but the area was a working class one, and in the course of our wandering I was introduced to the heroic trade union organiser, S.K. Dange – recently released from prison because he was dying of consumption. He was polite, but it was clear that he found all this rejoicing, over one imperialist who had repented, excessive.

Next morning I was on my way back to New Delhi, where Lieutenant-Colonel Kilroy, who was to be my counterpart in Eastern India, had now arrived and was also staying with Short. I was off again next day, so I only caught a glimpse of him. He talked like a character in a John Buchan novel. The Government of India was contemplating some step – I don't remember what – which might cause offence to Moslems, and I can still see him jerking back his narrow head and saying, sternly as if administering a warning: 'We'll have *jehad* from Baghdad to Delhi!' (A *jehad* is a Moslem holy war.)

This time I was not off on a brief errand. Short was now confident that he was about to receive the go-ahead. Details of what was proposed had been sent to Southern Army H.Q. in Bangalore, and the time had come for me to set up shop there. On my way I was to introduce myself to the chief secretaries of the governments of the province of Orissa and Madras Presidency, in which I would be operating, in addition to Bombay Presidency. I was also to contact local student leaders.

My visit to Cuttack, which was then the capital of the province of Orissa, was short. I arrived in the early morning, left the same evening, and have completely forgotten my conversation with the Chief Secretary. The local student leaders, however, made a lasting impression. They had evidently not yet received P.C. Joshi's warning to be on their guard against me, and treated me as one of them, remaining with me all day, and giving me the clenched fist salute at the railway station late that evening when they saw me off on the train to Madras.

In the meantime, however, despite the brevity of my visit, they had arranged for me to meet local political leaders. What they had said to explain my visit I do not know, but they seemed to have conveyed the impression that the Indian Army was backing the demand for Indian independence. As a result, a dozen Orissan politicians had arranged a lunch, at which they all declared that they had never before talked with a soldier and how preferable they found this to talking to civil servants. They were only marginal figures, however. None of them was a member of the Moslem League, and only one was a member of the Congress Party. He was a dissident – a supporter of C. Rajagopalachari. Earlier, in accordance with the Congress Party's policy of non-co-operation, this judicious leader had resigned as prime minister of Madras Presidency, but now he was opposing the projected civil disobedience movement, and in its place proposed suspension of anti-British activity for the duration of the war. As a result, although deeply conservative, he nevertheless now enjoyed Communist approval.

Rajaji was a *brahmin*, and so was his follower in Cuttack. He was the only one present – and to embarrass him the others kept pressing dishes on him which he steadfastly refused. 'You see', they explained to me, loudly so that their victim would hear 'he regards you as unclean.'

'No, no!', he protested. 'Today I have a little indigestion.'

'He regards you as unclean,' they insisted, 'but do not be angry. We are unclean too.' Then, turning back to their victim: 'What would Gandhiji say to you?'

A silly incident on the next stage of my journey to Madras put me to shame. I was reading, still undressed, in my upper bunk when the train halted at a station for breakfast, so I was late in arriving at the restaurant, and the table I approached was practically full of officers. Spotting my red arm-band in the distance, one of them pushed back his chair, leaped to his feet and called everybody to attention, so they all put down their knives and forks and stood up as I arrived. I was not even in a position to tell them to sit down. I could only blush and let it dawn on them, as I saw it doing, that I was not some whizz-kid field officer but a boy wonder staff officer.

This was not the last time I was to experience this shame. I was even more prone to it later, surrounded by the 14th Army in Assam. For consolation I used to repeat to myself the words of Clausewitz, then so frequently on communist lips: 'War is the continuation of politics by other means'. The only difference between me and a fighting soldier was that I engaged in politics directly. Fortunately, however, I could not make myself believe this.

Sir George Boag, the Chief Secretary of the Madras Government, did however believe that politics came first. For him the class war took precedence above every other. In Madras a day or two later, when I was explaining to him that the Army wanted two leaders of the railway union to be released to organise strikes and blow up track in the event of a Japanese occupation, he replied severely: 'I cannot countenance any measure that might impair the rights of private property'. I saluted him, mentally.

My communist contact in Madras was an Old Etonian who had left Cambridge as President of the Cambridge Union – Mohan Kumaramangalam. He was one of the returned communist students whom Indira Nehru had known in England before the war, and later – when, as Mrs Gandhi, she was Prime Minister of India – he would become her trusted adviser, having meanwhile left the Party. At this time, however, he was a full-time Communist Party activist, recently released from gaol. Although I had never met him in Britain, I had met his sister Parvati, who was a communist too. They were now both living in Madras with their parents.

I spent two full days in their company, mainly for the pleasure of it, although they did have useful things to tell me about local politics, and suggested a man with useful contacts to be my local representative. He was not, they assured me, a secret communist. I was insistent on that point. I did not want what I was doing to Short to be done to me.

At the end of my second day with them, boarding the bus to go back to my hotel, I recognised the man who got on it behind me as the man who had got off it behind me when I arrived, and coming down to the hotel desk next morning to hand in my room key before going off to see Mohan and Parvati again, I noticed him in the foyer, apparently reading a newspaper. The clerk at the desk gave me a telephone number as he took my key, and when I phoned it I found myself talking to the local chief of the Intelligence Bureau. He wanted to see me, urgently.

His office was on the sea front, facing the Bay of Bengal. If a Japanese invasion ever came it would be by land, over India's North-eastern frontier, where their army was already poised. Nevertheless, the Intelligence Bureau chief gazed out of the window over the sea as if it was no-man's-land, and the first thing he said was that he had cleared out his secret files so drastically that if they looked like coming – here he nodded towards the window – it would take him less than two hours to destroy the lot. Then he asked me how I came to be consorting with communists.

Surprised that he had not yet been told about Military Training 10, I introduced myself, adding that I expected to employ a full-time representative in Madras and would be glad to know what he thought of one of the candidates. Without saying where I had got it, I then gave him the name that Mohan had suggested and he opened a drawer and produced a file. It might interest me to know, he said, after glancing through it, that three weeks ago the man in question had been one of the mourners at the funeral of a leader of the Forward Bloc. I was perplexed. A follower of Subhas Chandra

Bose was the last person I would have expected Mohan to recommend, but then came a smug footnote. The deceased was the cousin of my candidate's wife. I complimented him on the comprehensiveness of his information.

Not much happened in Madras that he didn't know about, he replied. Take the Kumaramangalams. Just then they were preening themselves because they had obtained a piece of information they were not supposed to have, but there was another piece of information which they lacked, and it so happened it made all the difference. He laughed. He knew that they knew.

As it happened he had already made the same boast in the presence of a member of his staff who was a secret Party sympathiser, so it had been passed on to Mohan and Parvati, who had joked about it to me. To state the situation in all its complexity – although he knew they knew, he did not know they knew that he knew they knew. He was sure to discover this in due course, however, and when he wondered who had told them I would be the obvious suspect. Presumably I had a police record in Britain, so if he took an interest in me I would be finished.

I had told Mohan and Parvati to expect me, but now I decided not to go to them. Luckily their house was watched and I was being followed, so if I stayed away the Intelligence Bureau would know that I had, and as their telephone was tapped, they would also know that I had not phoned them. They had told me all they had to tell me, so I had no need to see them again. I went back to the hotel and told Chhanga that we were leaving.

Salem, where Morris was posted in charge of a Supply Depot, was not too far from Madras for me to drop in on him before going on to Bangalore. I arrived at dawn to find him asleep in the open beneath a sheet riddled with cigarette burns, and sat there until he awoke. He was amazed to see me sitting there. I had left Delhi too abruptly to warn him to expect me. I had not even written to tell him about Short. I told him now. There was no hope of getting him into the same operation. The only remaining vacancy in Military Training 10 was for a staff captain. Nevertheless, public relations in general seemed a promising field for Party work in the Indian Army, and we thought of a way for him to gain an entry. Several months earlier, he had invited the citizens of Salem to his depot for a feast followed by an entertainment given by his *sepoys*. Guests and hosts had nothing in common – not even language – but it had gone well, and he had sent an account of the event to Southern Army Headquarters. There had been no response. Doubtless it was lying somewhere, filed away unread. I undertook to track it down and advertise its merits when I got to Bangalore.

7: Animation suspended

I arrived in Bangalore half-way through July 1942 to find new instructions from Short waiting for me. On the 8th August the working committee of the Congress Party was to meet to decide whether to launch a mass campaign of civil disobedience. If they did – and they almost certainly would – the introduction of student activists into army units would have to be postponed, and contact with Indian political figures would be difficult. For the time being all I had to do was make myself known to Southern Army Headquarters and wait to hear from him. In any case, his proposals had not yet been finally approved. They had been completed, and General Molesworth had circulated them for comment, but that was all.

This, the last hurdle, was to prove insurmountable, and he was also about to suffer temporary disgrace in Delhi on another account – his humane reaction to the use of excessive violence in the suppression of student demonstrations.

Nevertheless, the scheme might have been enough without that. By the time I arrived there, news of a crazy colonel's hare-brained scheme to let a pack of agitators loose among recruits had already reached Southern Army H.Q. General Beresford-Peirce, the G.O.C. Southern Army, expressed neither enthusiasm nor alarm at the project when I reported to him on arrival there – although when he showed me P.C. Joshi's warning to local branches of the Communist Party not to trust me I sensed that his intention was discouragement. 'So you see, you're not doing quite as well you may think you are. That's always a useful thing to know.' Childishly I felt challenged, so I failed to feign appropriate dismay.

I could not open an office of my own in Bangalore until I got Short's go-ahead, so the General offered me a desk in the office of the officer in charge of Southern Army's Public Relations – their D.A.D.P.R. (Deputy Assistant Director of Public Relations). I should have declined the offer. Short had stressed that I was responsible to him in New Delhi, not to Southern Army, and in any case until Short's plans received the final go-ahead I did not need an office at all. Least of all did I need an office where Indian civilians could not visit me without being first confronted by a sentry. Nevertheless, I feebly accepted – or, to be more precise, I obeyed.

After my meeting with the General I was passed on to the colonel in charge of Military Intelligence – a pointless interview, as our duties had nothing in common, but not surprisingly he wished to have a look at me. Seen from Southern Army Intelligence's point of view, I was a dubious interloper, who consorted openly with communists. There was more to it than that, however. Military Intelligence saw Short as a threat, and were bent on sabotaging him, so they tried to trap me.

Two days after my arrival, returning to my hotel for lunch, I found a young staff captain from Southern Army H.Q. Intelligence waiting for me at the door of my room. He said that he had something to tell me in strict secrecy, so I invited him in. He knew what Short was trying to do, he told me, and thought it was a great step forward. Unfortunately others did not agree with him, and that was why he had come to see me secretly. He thought I ought to know that Asian Communists had already proved that they could make a unique contribution to the war. They were the only people who were resisting the enemy in Malaya. Top secret intelligence reports that he had studied contained details of successful Communist guerrilla actions there, and I ought to see them, so he was going to smuggle them out of Headquarters and bring them to my room that evening. But they were top secret, he repeated, so I must not leave them lying about. If what he was going to do became known he would be in trouble.

I distrusted him. If he wanted me to read a top secret report, all he had to do was tell me that it existed and I could ask to see it officially. Or, without even revealing knowledge of the file's existence, I could simply ask Intelligence whether they had any information about anti-Japanese resistance by Asian communists. It was no business of mine in any case. I had finished with 'Category B' work. I therefore thanked him, but explained that Malayan communists had nothing to do with me. He left professing disappointment, and as soon as he had gone I felt remorse. I had no conception of inter-departmental hostilities, so I could think of no reason why Intelligence should set a trap for me – unless they knew I was a Party member.

I had not been there three week before my Party membership was suspected by two men. One was Brigadier Trappes-Lomax, the Brigadier General Staff – a brisk, clever staff officer. The other was Henry Solomon, a morose and witty lieutenant in Intelligence. They belonged to a regular bridge four, and at one of their weekly sessions the brigadier asked conversationally whether it had occurred to anyone else there that I might be a communist. 'If he's a communist,' said Henry Solomon, 'then I am'. In point of fact, he knew I was a communist – and yet he was not lying, because so was he.

We had hit it off from the day I heard him spelling his name out on the telephone: 'S for syphilis, O for osteoporosis, L for lockjaw, O for otorrhoea...', and so on through a dismal list. Before the war he had been a failed playwright and a successful solicitor – attributing the latter achievement to a sense of theatre which had inspired him to buy a third-hand Rolls Royce as soon as he opened his office. He only used the law books he had studied as stage props, and had never opened one since qualifying – or so he claimed. All that his clients wanted from him was common sense.

It never crossed my mind that he might be a Party member. He belonged to an earlier generation of revolutionaries. Mine was puritanical. He was a hedonist. Shocked by my admission that I had not read it he lent me his copy of *South Wind*. The pursuit of pleasure had not, however, prevented him from working as the legal representative of rent strikers, and one

Sunday afternoon, when I had just placed the stress on the second syllable in pronouncing the word 'Bolshevik', he said – 'All right! I'll risk it. I'm a party member. How about you?'

He had been practically sure about me, he told me, when he read a written explanation of what the Indian Communist Party 'thought that it was doing', which the General had asked me to write for him. The General had expected a straight answer to a simple question, written in plain English, but plain English was not suited to an exposition of the Party Line. Plain English would give a tortuous look to what was as direct as the flight path of a homing pigeon, rightly understood, but to understand this rightly the General must first be brought to see that history moved in a spiral. I had therefore begun my exposition by explaining why communists believed that the shortest distance between two points in history was not a straight line but a corkscrew.

The Marxist dialectic explains any development as an 'interpenetration of opposites'. At Cambridge I had revelled in doing this. My practised eye saw opposites interpenetrating everywhere I looked, and there was nothing I enjoyed more than disentangling them. The piece I wrote for the General may well have been a masterpiece. That was certainly Henry Solomon's opinion when it was passed on to him, although admittedly it had not been the General's. I had done my best to make it simple, completely omitting 'the negation of the negation'. Nevertheless, the General swiftly passed it to Intelligence, demanding to be told what it was meant to mean – and that was how Henry came to read it. He was the Intelligence dogsbody. Whenever Intelligence received a report with no immediate application it was passed on to him for summary.

For his generation of communists, politics had less to do with dogma than with indignation and contempt. My apparent mastery of convolutions that had never bothered him dazzled him. For my part I was overawed by his familiarity with Soho – although I drew the line at his admiration of Aneurin

Bevan, who had dined once a week at the same restaurant, after starving for days to be able to afford it. Bevan's one-man opposition to Churchill was objectively reactionary, I warned him, because no matter how reactionary Churchill's role might have been in the past, like it or not, objectively considered, he was now an agent of world revolution.

Disdaining the coffee served in the headquarters mess, a group of staff officers used to make unauthorised use of a military vehicle after dinner to drive into the city which was out of bounds to military personnel – to sip richly concentrated South Indian coffee. Henry was one of them and I joined them. None of them was a regular soldier. Before the war they had been practising in Britain as lawyers, doctors, engineers, accountants or civil servants. Unexpectedly now finding themselves in India, they were making the most of it. Some went in search of temples. When their leave came up, instead of fleeing to the hills two of them had even spent their leave on a cycling tour.

One of these cyclists, Abe Stewart – the only European I met in India during the war with a passion for Indian music – was a mystically minded amateur orientalist who had never settled down to one religion. For him they were all different versions of the same worship – with the exception of Roman Catholicism, as he had been born an Irish Protestant.

As an Irishman he also despised the English – especially the way they shunned bad taste and shut their eyes to the improbable. I was a case in point. When he asked for my opinion of a tawdry calendar, portraying the goddess Saraswati equipped with all her symbols, politeness held me tongue-tied. He had given it pride of place on the wall of his room. He even had an open mind on the Indian Rope Trick. Firmest of all, however, was his belief in absorption in the Absolute. It was much firmer than his belief in vaccination – so firm, indeed, that he admired and studied Saint John of the Cross although the saint was a Roman Catholic. He maintained, however, that mystic union was achieved more readily in India than anywhere else, and long before it became fashionable, practised meditation himself. He was the most unworldly man that I have met. He had never settled. Just old enough to be called up in 1918 he had served as an officer in the Indian Army, and then, already immersed in Theosophy and the 'Wisdom of the East', had entered the employment of the Irish Co-operative Movement because George Russell – the mystic Irish poet and painter 'AE' – belonged to it. A few years later he left it, disillusioned, and had not since then been permanently employed until he volunteered for military service in 1939, and was enrolled in the Pioneer Corps. In 1941 the Army circulated an appeal for officers with fluent German to volunteer for transfers to the Intelligence Corps. Abe had acquired his German from the lips of a German grandmother, so although he was about to be promoted to major he volunteered – which was how he came to be posted in the last place where his German might be useful. It was, however, the place where he most wished to be.

He quickened my sense of India's invisible presences. Empty spaces can feel fully occupied in India. I once passed a naked man, lying in the dust on his back in a public thoroughfare. Although his eyes were raised to the sky they were wide open, and he was chanting happily – 'Oh God, you see me!' – over and over again. It was impossible at that moment not to believe that he saw something which I could not – doubtless an effect like the illusion that the floor is heaving which results when bystanders sway in unison – but I still remember it.

I spent my first week or so at Southern Army Headquarters at a desk in the office of the D.A.D.P.R., looking for interesting material – such as the report on local recruitment that correlated an increase in the number of recruits with a rise in food prices. I also found Morris's account of the entertainment staged by his Supply Depot for the citizens of Salem and brought it to the attention of the D.A.D.P.R., who included it in his monthly report to the General. A few months later Morris had joined Public Relations there, and a year after that he was the D.A.D.P.R.

Another file I found was about a scheme to arrange a recital of Indian classical dance at a local cinema. I cannot remember how the Army had come to be involved in this. The proceeds were to go to some sort of war fund, but that cannot have been the reason. Perhaps it was because the willingness of Ram Gopal, a famous dancer, to perform in it amounted to a demonstration of support for the war. The Government welcomed gestures of this kind from eminent Indians. Recently it had given wide publicity to a donation to the war effort made by Sri Aurobindo, the renowned guru of Pondicherri. The Ram Gopal project, however, had stalled. For a reason which did not appear in the correspondence, the D.A.D.P.R. and the dancer had quarrelled. Having no other duty until I heard again from Short, I asked the D.A.D.P.R. if he had any objections to my re-starting the idea. He wished me joy of the attempt, but did not tell me what had gone wrong before, and sensing that it had been a personal matter, I did not ask him.

Soon I was visiting Ram Gopal almost every day. He lived in the cantonment, in a large house with deep verandah, and a summer-house in the garden, where he rehearsed. I was not officially attached to Southern Army Headquarters, so there was no need for me to spend any more time there than I wanted to, and after the first week I saw no point in spending any time at all there, beyond attending 'morning prayers' – the meeting of the General with all his staff at the start of each day. I dropped in after that only when I felt like it, flitting in and out at random, so I had plenty of time to spend with Ram Gopal.

Often I arrived early enough to catch him rehearsing in the summer house, sometimes under the direction of a teacher, with a musician rapping out on a *tabla* the complicated rhythm which the dancer's feet followed on the floor. At other times the speedy rhythm was called out vocally in coded syllables.

Afterwards there would be coffee in a long upstairs room where the light was dimmed by closed shutters. I was never the only visitor. He had an entourage, like a toreador's. Bronze gods and goddesses stood against the walls, rescued from temples when they would otherwise have been melted down for their metal because, as a result of being chipped or suffering a snapped finger, they were no longer sacred. He had bought them as so much metal for the value of their weight, and now they served as models for his dance postures.

As this was my first encounter with a performing artist, I was astonished by his vanity. One evening when I was there a friend brought him news of an offer of a certain sum for him to dance at the Mysore Palace. 'His father used to pay me three times that amount. Tell the Maharajah I will dance for nothing.' That was grand, but at other times his vanity was comic. When the final curtain had fallen on the performance we eventually succeeded in arranging, he told me that he was going to keep his make-up on all night, because he looked so wonderful in it. And yet this was the truth. When he danced, he had seemed superhuman.

On August 8th, the Congress Party launched its 'Quit India' movement. Its leaders' aims were muddled. In theory they did not support the Japanese, but in practice they rendered them more assistance than Subhas Chandra Bose's Forward Bloc, which backed them openly. Once the movement had started they had no control over it. In accordance with their usual practice, instead of going into hiding to continue the struggle underground they waited passively to be arrested, and found themselves in jail on the first day. As a consequence the initiative fell to impatient young men and women who campaigned locally and underground. Congress Socialists, or local patriots with no previous party affiliations, their idea of resistance was not passive. There was also an organised underground group – the Forward Bloc and its supporters – whose aim was positively to help the Japanese. Civil disobedience was therefore taken to lengths previously unknown, especially when even peaceful demonstrations suffered violence at the hands of the army or the police.

Viewed from an orthodox Congress Party standpoint the agitation got out of hand. Mobs set fire to police stations, railway stations and schools. On the railways, well-organised gangs removed lines and sleepers, smashed signals and wrecked signal boxes. Communications were disrupted by cutting telephone and telegraph wires. Some atrocities were also committed. Most of the bloodshed, however, was the work of the police and the military. In all over a thousand Indians were killed in over five hundred shootings, and more than sixty thousand were arrested.

For the first two or three days of this turmoil I remained in Bangalore, where there were demonstrations but no violent confrontations. Each day at 'morning prayers' a high-ranking member of the Indian Civil Service, seconded to the military for the duration of this emergency, reported on the previous day's developments in the internal security situation throughout India. On one occasion this included the casualty figures for street shootings in Delhi. The army had inflicted significantly more fatalities per round fired than the police, while wounding fewer. 'Which is how it should be!' the General commented, and appealed for confirmation to the I.C.S. official. 'Isn't it?' The civil servant cleared his throat and answered carefully that such was the agreed position.

I wondered how this development was affecting Short's relations with the communist students in New Delhi. The answer, had I known it, was to the credit of both parties. While the majority of their fellow students were defying the authorities in the streets, communist students were braving their contempt by attempting to dissuade them. They were still in touch with what was happening to them, however, and complained to Short, with circumstantial accounts, when undue violence had been used to disperse a demonstration. Forty years later Arun Bose told me how he had flared out at Short – 'Why should I speak to you at all when out there your people are murdering mine?' – and Short, who knew what it was costing them not to join in the demonstrations, had put his hands together, Indian fashion palm to palm, and begged his pardon. These cases of undue violence were reported to him in the expectation that he would do something about them, and when he was convinced they had a case he took it up. The Commissioner of Delhi promptly complained that he was unable to carry out his duties when 'G.H.Q. was 'trafficking with rebels'. Short was ordered to stop seeing students, and this was not forgotten when his plan for giving communist students access to the Indian Army was rejected.

Crediting me with courage like his own, he was afraid that I would be making myself unpopular with the authorities by behaving in the same way in Bangalore, so he ordered me to take an indefinite holiday in the southern hill station of Ootacamund. Henry Solomon was due some leave and came with me. We arrived at the Bangalore City railway station to find the entrance engulfed by demonstrating students who crowded round us, in the friendliest fashion, to discuss the issues.

That was all I saw of the civil disobedience movement of August 1942. I did not return to the plains until mass demonstrations had given place to occasional 'outbreaks of violence' and 'sporadic incidents'. Ootacamund itself was removed above the clash of armies on the plain. Throughout our stay there Henry and I behaved like convalescents in a sanatorium, reading the newspapers very thoroughly after breakfast and then taking a circular stroll – at a leisurely pace on account of the altitude, dropping in at the excellent public library or stopping at a cafe. To complete this detachment, we shared a table with an elderly lady, the principal of a ladies' college in Madras, who was given to unkind speculation about the other guests. Then Henry's leave was over and he went down the mountain, soon to be followed by the acid-tongued lady. I envied them both for knowing what they were going to do. I had heard nothing from Short.

8: A fresh beginning

In mid-September Southern Army H.Q. passed on a message from Short telling me to return to Bangalore and be standing by their teleprinter for a message at midnight in four days' time. I dashed back to Bangalore at once. There was no mistaking the coldness of some shoulders that were turned on me during the two days I spent waiting there. Henry could not tell me what had happened. The standard of his bridge qualified him to enjoy Brigadier Trappes-Lomax's speculations about my Communist Party membership, but not to learn that they had been officially confirmed.

Short's message on the teleprinter also left me in the dark. It was just that I must go back to New Delhi where he had things to tell me. Why had he not simply ordered me back there at the start? The question has only now occurred to me. The answer is probably that he kept me hanging about during those few days because my fate was in the balance. As part of their campaign against Short, Military Intelligence had obtained my police record from Britain, and used it to expose him as a communist dupe. My consolation has to be that I was not the only nail in his coffin. What had damned him was the Commissioner of Delhi's complaint that in his person G.H.Q. had been 'consorting with rebels' during a period of civil unrest. Even without that, his plan would not have been accepted, but thanks to that accusation he had to suffer the indignity of being sent back to Britain in renewed retirement, until in 1945 the general election in Britain produced a government that had a use for his originality. He returned to India in 1946 with a Cabinet Mission, as an adviser to Sir Stafford Cripps.

He said nothing to me by way of reproach, and I am ashamed to say that I said nothing to him by way of apology. The person I then was saw no need for one. As I saw it, I had been performing my duty.

'Some people are out to get you', Short warned me. Brigadier Trappes-Lomax, had suggested in a memo that I should be placed behind barbed wire or made a Station Staff Officer!

'They may try to do something irregular about you', Short told me, 'so I want you to dine with a friend of mine who can stop them if they do'. The friend was Sir Maurice Gwyer, an ex Chief Justice of India, who was then the Chancellor of Delhi University. In that capacity, while Short had been trafficking with rebels he had been harbouring them. Throughout the disturbances student hostels had been safe havens, because he had insisted on the University's chartered right to deny the police access to its premises without specific warrant. Even with the police in hot pursuit, student demonstrators had only to get back to their hostel to be safe.

Sir Maurice made no mention of my predicament when I dined with him. In a free-floating conversation that started before dinner and continued over brandies into early morning, we talked about nothing but books until it transpired that I had read *The Wrong Box* by Robert Louis Stevenson and Lloyd Osborne. For Sir Maurice the world contained two kinds of people – the benighted who had not experienced this illuminating pleasure and the elect who had. Fortunately for me Henry Solomon was one of the latter, and he never travelled without it, so I had read it less than a month before. Even so, I could not oblige Sir Maurice when after naming the first item on the menu of the dinner with which the story concludes, he invited me to continue – but as a member of the Wrong Box Society he had the additional advantage of having attended annual dinners, where that menu was ceremonially served.

Short had even secured a posting for me. Although his scheme had been rejected, G.H.Q. had decided to retain the unit that he had set up. His approach to revolutionaries might be irregular, but there was something to be said for his idea that the Army should communicate with the Indian public in person as well as on paper – at any rate in the province of Assam, which was then facing the prospect of a Japanese invasion. Much depended on the behaviour of the civilian population. Rumours might block a line of communication with panic-stricken refugees. Moreover, the civil disobedience movement started by the Congress Party was still sporadically active, and followers of Subhas Chandra Bose were out to maximise disruption. In a front-line province, this could have a direct effect on the outcome of war. Even without deliberate provocation, the possibilities of friction were enormous, when a population unaccustomed to a military presence suddenly found tens of thousands of soldiers of all nations in its midst. Hitherto the Indian Army's relations with the public had been restricted to the press and radio, but now it was decided that, at least in the war area, a team of military officers should establish reassuring contact with the civilian public directly.

What had been Military Training 10 had therefore been transferred to the Directorate of Public Relations and re-christened 'the Military Public Liaison Section'. The officer placed in charge of it was Lieutenant-Colonel Kilroy – the John Buchan character who had foretold *jehad* from Baghdad to Delhi, and although the only thing he knew about me was my membership of the communist party, at Short's request he had stipulated that he could not undertake the task without me. He might well have appointed me, however, even without Short's intervention. Nobody could have been more loyal to the Crown, but as an Irishman he had friends who did not share his loyalties and thought none the worse of them for that. My happiest memory of him is of later overhearing him interviewing an applicant for employment as one of our civilian assistants in Assam.

'Have you ever been a member of the Congress Party?'
'Oh, no sir!!'
'But haven't you even thought of joining it?'
'Sir, I never have, I swear!'
'Then you ought to be ashamed of yourself.'

He meant it. He might be a Protestant landowner, but he often repeated, with approval, a retort made by one of his tenants to an English visitor whom he was driving around the district in a jaunting car, to see the sights. After being shown the Devil's Dyke, the Devil's Corner, the Devil's Loop, The Devil's Well, etc., the visitor remarked, 'It seems the Devil owns a lot of property round there.' 'To be sure he does, sir', was the reply, 'and like all the other land-owners he lives in London'.

Sometimes of an evening he would sing songs of anti-British struggle, and when he sang

When Britannia's sons
With their long-range guns,
Came up through the foggy dew...

- his scorn for 'Britannia's sons' was palpable. When it came to politics, however, he believed that the Union of Ireland with England had been as providential as he also believed the British subjugation of India to have been. Considered as specimens of humanity, he found the populations of both these countries more amiable than the English, but in his view part of their amiability was an inability to distinguish fact from fiction. One had only to look at the condition of the country under De Valera, he insisted, to realise that the Irish could not organise their own affairs.

The first time he returned on leave from service in India to the newly created Irish Free State, two men in belted mackintoshes had closed in on him as he stepped off the gangway, produced identity cards, and curtly told him to get into a waiting car, which was driven by a third. With one sitting grimly silent at the back on either side of him he was then driven to an isolated house several miles out of Dublin and guided into a room where a man at a desk told him that there were some questions he must answer.

He replied that he was a tax-payer, and if he was dealing with the Irish Secret Service, before they went any further he had a complaint to make about their competence.

Why had he not been searched? He produced a revolver, laid it on the desk, and -'speaking as a taxpayer' – told them with genuine indignation that they were amateurs. During the past half hour he could have shot both of them.

According to him the Irish Republican Army was not a serious fighting force either, but just a band of murderous louts lurking behind hedges with guns. In a different mood, however, he could be more indulgent, as in a story he told about General Sullivan, an Indian Army general who retired to live in the Irish countryside with his invalid wife, at the height of the Troubles. The general preferred not to open the door at night, but had to do so every Thursday when the maid returned from her evenings off, and one Thursday three masked men with pistols followed her in, announcing that they had come to search the house.

They began in the main bedroom, and five minutes later, when the general crept upstairs, he found all three busy opening drawers and cupboards, with their backs to the doorway. 'Hands up the lot of you!', he snapped, and they obeyed. Then he ordered them to turn and face him.

'Now let this be a lesson to you, boys', he told them, when they had done so and seen that he had no gun. 'Wherever you may be, work out which way the enemy might come and post a sentry there. Right here that's the top of the stairs. Now remember that and carrying on searching – anywhere except the drawing-room because that's where my missis is, and she's got a bad heart, you know. And before you go, I hope you'll join me for a drop in the library.'

The intruders' leader, signing himself 'brigade-commander', wrote out a certificate before leaving, to the effect that General Sullivan was 'all right'. When on the death of his father Kilroy himself retired from the Indian Army and returned to Ireland to take over the family estate, the local newspaper greeted his arrival with a declaration that the presence of a British hireling was unwelcome, and he received anonymous threats. In reply he had issued an open invitation to an open-air feast, and from then on he was treated as a fixture, just as his father had been.

According to Kilroy, nothing could be more Irish than relenting, and he had other tales to illustrate it, most memorably one about a childless widow, who came to him in a rage, asking him to shoot a fox that had killed one of her hens. A few days later, however, sitting out in the evening on the hill-side, she saw the vixen playing with her cubs, and went home to kill a hen and throw it to them.

All this, however, he regarded as child-like, and there was similar condescension in his praise of virtues he attributed to Indians. When he declared that Sikhs were more generous than he was, or braver, he contrived to link their superiority with simplicity. In his view, Indians and Irish alike could no more manage their own affairs without the guidance of trained agents of the British Crown than adorable children could manage theirs without parental supervision. Nevertheless his Irish background did enable him to stomach revolutionaries, and the fact that I had a police record meant nothing to him. Many a good Irishman had one too. It was a sign that I should be taken seriously. Soon after I had joined him in New Delhi, he and the Section's newly appointed staff captain were taking an evening stroll, when they passed a scrum of brawling watchmen and felt called upon to calm them down. 'I wish you had been with us', he told me when they got back. 'I'd like to see you in action.'

Alas, it did not take him long to place me as a harmless crank! As he explained to me in due course, I was what he called 'an oddity'. There had to be oddities, he reassured me. His brother was another. An oddity, I gathered, was a reminder that – although it was important not to let this bother one – there was more to life than met the eye.

His reminiscences were usually of military service. Unlike Short, he had not seen active service in the Great War, but came under fire shortly after it, in what he referred to as 'the Arab rebellion' – the enforcement by the British, in the face of Arab resistance, of the carve-up of the Arab territories lost by Turkey after the Great War.

This had involved protecting the long desert railway line against Arab guerrillas, as previously the Turks had defended it against them. The defending Indian Army forces were disposed along the track in sand-bagged emplacements, and Kilroy had been a subaltern in charge of one of these detachments.

With baffled admiration he recalled how a band of Arabs on horseback had appeared on the horizon one day and approached until they came within range. At that point all of them had reined in except one, who continued cantering easily towards the emplacement, nearer and nearer, with Kilroy's platoon all shooting at him and missing, until they felt that he had magical protection. At last, on the crest of a sand-hill, absurdly close, the Arab had reined in his horse and sat there, viewing them at leisure from the saddle, while they redoubled their fire and still kept missing him, until at last he wheeled his horse and cantered back to his companions – to Kilroy's relief.

Kilroy himself, mounted, was an icon of the Raj. Later, in the Punjab, I saw peasants working in the fields raise respectful, almost reverential, eyes as he rode by, accompanied by his wife, in linen riding-skirt and sitting side-saddle. (The war was over by then, so she had come out to India to join him.) Whether he was talking to a couple of Indians or addressing an Indian crowd his tone was that of a patron, the result of being surrounded with dependants from his boyhood.

But he also had a gift with a crowd. He had already been once to Assam that year, to steady the morale of tired Punjabi *sepoy*s in retreat from Burma. Dismissing the sceptical expectation of their officers that he would want to have their men lined up to be harangued, he would wait until the evening when they were seated around in random groups, eating their suppers from mess-tins, and stroll up to the largest group to start a conversation about why, despite appearances, the Japanese could never win the war.

This would be a genuine conversation. He listened to the individuals he was with as well as talking to them, while paying no attention to the others who, as they finished eating, would gather round to listen, until those he was conversing with became fellow-performers in an act of which the others were the audience. On one of these occasions he had a brush with a young *jemadar* – one of a new, young, educated brand of Viceroy's Commissioned Officers that had been appointed directly, after war broke out, without first serving in the ranks. 'Why should we do anything for Britain?' he had interrupted Kilroy to object. 'Britain never does anything for us.' Invited to explain his particular grievance, he complained that in response to a circular inviting educated young V.C.O.s to apply for a King's commission he had done so, but received no reply.

'Aren't you going to try again?', Kilroy inquired.

'Why should I ask for another insult?' was the answer.

Kilroy's answer was another question. 'Are you married?'

'I am,' the young *jemadar* said scornfully, 'but what has that to do with it?'

'Any children?'

'No.'

'And aren't you going to try again?'

At this the battalion had fallen about laughing, while the objector had slunk away.

'But what if he had told you he had five?' I asked. But he dismissed the question. 'He didn't.'

Kilroy rarely spoke in public in Assam. In part this was because a few months after we arrived there, he found himself in charge of an expanded organization and spent most of his time in his office at headquarters. He regarded office work as the most arduous form of duty. It was he who warned me of the fate of the colonel who signed every piece of paper that his head clerk put on his desk. Production of his monthly report to G.H.Q. was an ordeal for him. No sooner had he sent one off than he was worrying about the next.

It was also an ordeal for his stenographer. Diffident with a pen, Kilroy never prepared a draft, but dictated. The real work began when he corrected what was read back to him – a painful process, because when dictating he felt constrained to speak an artificial language, using phrases picked up from official correspondence, and consciousness that his words were being recorded made him hesitate, so he got lost. The result was always a tangle. 'Where did you get that from? I never said that!'

'Sir, excuse me. These are your very words', the stenographer would say, and read the offending passage again to remove all doubt – at which Kilroy, red in the face, would start to thunder. The stenographer, supported by a sense of injustice and familiar with the situation as he had previously worked with Kilroy in the Punjab, would stand his ground until the dispute was abandoned and they started all over again. Sometimes the stenographer received a present next morning – but never an apology.

'Knowing the value of money' was a cardinal virtue in Kilroy's book, but he did not believe in hoarding it. Its value was the use it could be put to. In the early thirties he had been posted to a British possession in the Red Sea, between Saudi Arabia and the Sudan – a tiny island but significant for two different reasons. Ships carrying Muslim pilgrims to Mecca put in there for their passengers to undergo quarantine before sailing on to disembark at Jeddah, and Arab agents slipped across at night from the mainland with reports to be passed on by the Resident.

Kilroy, then a captain, was posted there for two years in charge of the island's garrison, a company of Sikhs. Having nothing else to do most of the time, he passed his first year following the Resident, taking such a detailed interest in everything he did that when the time came for the Resident to go on six months' leave he advised Whitehall that there was no need to send a replacement, as the garrison commander was fully apprised of all his duties and able to perform them in addition to his own.

Kilroy's first concern as acting Resident was to check the island's finances, and he found he had large sums at his disposal. For years, every pilgrim ship that called in at the island had paid dues, including a fee for every pilgrim who passed through quarantine, but the Resident had done nothing with the proceeds. Regarding his intelligence duties as his only serious responsibility, he had just let the money accumulate. If Kilroy had been miserly he would have done the same, but as he saw it this was money wasted. His first thought was for its source, so he built showers and other facilities for the use of the pilgrims. He also had a jetty built, so that coming ashore no longer meant disembarking into small boats. That done, however, he invested in facilities for the islanders themselves – including a troop of girl guides and another of boy scouts.

On his return the Resident refused at first to speak to him.

He was particularly proud of the girl guides because he was a champion of female emancipation. On his recall to India from retirement, to be a Civil Liaison Officer in the Punjab, he had been allotted a monthly sum with which to hire civilian assistants. It was understood, but not stipulated, that he would use this money to employ male assistants at one hundred and fifty rupees a month, which at that time was not a negligible salary. Instead he used the money to employ five times as many part-time women assistants at thirty rupees a month, together with imposing certificates of appointment as *Fawji Sewardanis* – a title of his own invention, which means 'Military Female Helper'.

Although working for so little pay, the *sewardanis* were astonished and delighted to find themselves important. Not only did they work more tirelessly than men would have done: they also did things that men could not do, because being women they had access to the illiterate wives of *sepoys* who needed help in approaching the authorities with their problems – or, if they had no other problems, needed somebody to write letters for them to their distant husbands. In his own way, Kilroy was as independent as Short.

He was eccentric, too. The crippling debts incurred by the Indian poor in paying for lavish wedding celebrations distressed him so much that I once heard him digress, in the course of a talk in a village, to boast that his own marriage expenses had amounted to less than twenty pounds. His talk was then supposed to be translated into Assamese, but listening closely he detected nothing that sounded like a reference to a wedding, so when the interpreter had finished he asked him: 'Did you tell them about my marriage?' The assistant was embarrassed. 'Oh, sir! I could not tell them such a shameful thing!'

We spent several weeks in New Delhi before we left for Assam, as – rejecting assurances that he would get everything he needed in due course and should meanwhile take himself off to Assam to reconnoitre – Kilroy somehow refused to move until his establishment was signed sealed and delivered – complete with office staff, staff cars, typewriters, filing-cabinets, and pistols (as we would be working in a war zone), together with financial sanction for the employment of civilian headquarters office staff and two civilian Assamese assistants. Even then we left New Delhi only to linger for a further week in Calcutta. Eastern Command Headquarters was there, and as we would be working in his area we had to explain to the General what we were going to do. For Kilroy, however, our really important business in Calcutta was making sure of our transport. Eastern Command had been instructed to supply us with a couple of staff cars, but the second-hand Fords they had allotted us were not yet fit for service. The vehicle depot assured us that they would be delivered to us in due course at our headquarters in Assam, but Kilroy insisted on waiting to take delivery on the spot in Calcutta, and as he was directly responsible to New Delhi nobody in Calcutta could prevent him. His obduracy, however, was dutiful. His only aim was to obtain the tools required to do the job he had been told to do. His not to reason why.

If Short had delayed, it would have been to ask his superiors why, if their object was to stiffen civilian morale in forward areas, his activities were not extended to East Bengal, as the Japanese were on its borders too. Conditions in Assam and Bengal were so similar that, when the war was over, it was theoretically possible to assess whether our presence in Assam had made a difference, and a study published a year or two later did indeed report that relations between the armed forces and the civilian population had been more stressful in Bengal, and attributed the difference to us.

Its author, Horace Alexander, a friend of Gandhi and a Quaker, happened to be in Calcutta with a Friends' ambulance unit when we arrived, and Short who knew him had advised Kilroy to consult him. He had just returned from China, and all I remember of him now is his account of the plight of a Swedish doctor he had met there. This unfortunate was one of a group of a dozen doctors, of various nationalities, who had volunteered to serve against Franco in the Spanish Civil War and moved on to China, when the Spanish government was defeated, to help in the war against Japan. In the view of Chiang Kai-Shek, however, Mao-Tse-Tung, not Emperor Hirohito, was the main enemy of China, and as these doctors had gone out of their way to fight Fascists he suspected them of being communists. On arrival in China they had therefore been imprisoned, and three years later were still living in captivity.

Chiang Kai-Shek's instinct had been sound. The imprisoned doctors were indeed all communists – except for one unfortunate, to whose political education the rest devoted all their energies, having nothing else to do. According to Horace Alexander, who had all this from the victim, although they had not succeeded in all that time they still rated him a promising contact, and refused to let him be. I was still a staunch enough communist, to commend these dogged comrades for continuing the struggle in the only way they could, but everybody else found the situation comic. Nobody saw the real horror of it. Brain-washing was in its infancy.

Kilroy, however, was shocked by the waste of medical personnel. Before we left Calcutta he had written to tell the right person in New Delhi about it, and within six months all twelve doctors were in India, attending to refugees.

We were to establish our Assam headquarters in Shillong. Situated high in the Khasi Hills between two valleys – the Brahmaputra Valley to the North and the Surma Valley to the South – Shillong was then the capital of Assam, a province in which more than a hundred languages were spoken. (The area it then covered has since been divided into separate smaller provinces.) The vehicle depot in Calcutta offered to arrange delivery of our staff cars in Shillong as soon as they were ready, but that was not good enough for Kilroy. The journey from Calcutta to Shillong was strewn with snags and snares, so he insisted on taking delivery in Calcutta so that we could protect them on their way.

At that time it was impossible to travel by rail directly from Calcutta to Assam. Shillong itself was thousands of feet above the valleys, so the last stage of the journey had to be made by road. The first part of the journey – from Calcutta to the foot of the mountains – was long, tortuous and trying by road so it was best made by rail. Even by rail, however, it was complicated. There were two routes, but both involved changing trains. The northern route involved changing from one railway gauge to another. This was a simple enough process for passengers. It merely involved stepping out of one train and across the platform into another. Transhipping our staff cars, however, would involve unloading them from one set of goods wagons and then re-loading them onto another – a problematic process that could result in indefinite delay. The southern route involved no transhipment, as both trains ran on the same gauge, so it was the route we chose for our cars.

It was less convenient for passengers, however, as it involved waiting twenty-three hours for the connection at the junction. Nevertheless, at least one of us had to travel with the cars to make sure that they were disconnected from the first train at the junction and coupled onto the on-carrying train when it arrived there twenty-three hours later. In addition to the possibility of negligence, as a result of the civil disobedience movement there was the practice of deliberate sabotage to contend with. One of us was all that was required, however, to go that way too and Kilroy decide that it should be me.

He was apologetic, but I welcomed the prospect of having three days to myself. I was already looking forward to the time when, as the Section's only field officer, I would be touring Assam on my own. The staff captain's bonhomie was as relentless as Kilroy's obsession with minutiae, and they for their part must both have found my company a trial. Neither had previously rubbed shoulders with a bolshy, and for some reason I felt constrained to make the experience memorable by startling them.

The countryside I passed through on the first stage of my journey with the cars was Mymensingh, a region where P.C. Joshi had claimed that the Communist Party could muster guerrillas. The fields looked more crowded than other Indian fields that I had seen from passing trains. Later I learned that the over-population of Mymensingh had consequences in Assam. Mymensinghis emigrated to the northern Brahmaputra Valley of Assam, to work as labourers, landless but hoarding enough from their scanty earnings for their children to buy a patch of land, after which there was no stopping their descendants. To increase the resulting tension, the Mymensinghis were Moslems and spoke Bengali while the indigenous inhabitants were Hindus and spoke Assamese. Outbreaks of violence resulted, and a few years before the war the provincial government had drawn a north-south line across the Brahmaputra Valley, east of which it was illegal for immigrants to acquire land – a measure duly denounced as one more instance of imperialist 'divide and rule'.

Everything went according to plan at the railway junction. My presence proved unnecessary – unless it concentrated minds. All I did in person was make sure the wagons carrying our cars were uncoupled and shunted to a siding when the train stopped, and return to the siding, a couple of times next day, to make sure that they were ready there waiting when the train for the southern valley of Assam arrived. I then watched them being hitched onto it, before entering my own compartment in the same train, and that was that.

The rest of my time at the junction was spent in the first-class waiting-room. I found it well occupied, but not with passengers. Although it was not important enough militarily to warrant the posting of a Railway Transport Officer, disruption of rail traffic through the junction could have serious military consequences, so a section of British infantry had been posted there, in charge of a sergeant, and the waiting room now served as their quarters. It was not their presence, however, that crowded it. The place had become a local rendezvous, where little Bengali boys played games or just watched the soldiers, old men dropped in for tea, and students came to practise their English. I remarked that they seemed to have made many friends. It had not been like that at first, the sergeant said. Insults had been shouted at them in the street, sometimes followed by stones. All they had done in response, however, was grab the lad who had thrown the stone and tell him they were there 'to do a job of work', and in the end the locals had got the message.

The Assistant Director of Public Relations at Eastern Command H.Q. had asked us to pass on any stories about good relations between soldiers and civilians, and the scene in the station waiting-room looked like suitable material. I did my best with it, and sent him something. If it was published it was not the most misleading news item he was responsible for that year. That must have been the story of the Bong of Wong.

I read it in the *Statesman* just before we left Calcutta. The Bong of Wong, described as a prominent tribal potentate on the Assam-Burma border, was reported to have pledged his support to the allies. Next day, however, Radio Saigon, which was now in the hands of the Japanese, was reported to have broadcast a statement from the Bong denying this story and rejoicing in his people's admission to the Japanese 'Co-prosperity Sphere'. The day after that, however, not satisfied with simply publishing the Bong's denial of this alleged denial, the *Statesman* illustrated it with a recent photograph of the Bong, in exotic regalia.

Nevertheless, the Bong of Wong did not exist. The Assistant Director of Public Relations was not to blame for issuing the story. He had learned of the Bong's declaration for the allied cause from a military intelligence report. Behind the intelligence report, however, lurked a story he was not aware of. The Intelligence Bureau officer in Assam, although a civilian, submitted regular reports to the local Military Intelligence officer, so that the civil administration's good relations with the tribal peoples on the frontier with Burma could be put to military use. On reading copies of subsequent Intelligence reports to the local military commander, however, he had found that they were unacknowledged repetitions of his own. He had invented the Bong of Wong to prove this for his own amusement, and sure enough his fiction had duly featured in the Intelligence Officer's next report. It did not remain there, however. The local commander passed the heartening misinformation to Eastern Army H.Q. in Calcutta, and then the joke got out of hand.

My railway journey ended at Sylhet in the Surma Valley, and the drive up to Shillong exhilarated me. The valley is completely flat and barely above sea level. A few weeks earlier it had been almost completely under water, because to add to the rain that falls directly into it every year during the monsoon, water crashes into it in a line of cataracts down the steep sides of the hills – on which Cherrapunji, the wettest place in the world, is situated. Survival in the flooded fields demands a special strain of rice that can grow fast enough to keep its tip above the rising flood, and roads are only passable because they run along embankments.

The monsoon had been over several weeks by the time I got there, but there were still a few white clouds in the sky, and the subsided flood had left everything that grew a shining, green. The hills, when I reached them, were well wooded. Sometimes, above the noise of the climbing car, I could hear the sound of falling water. The thought that I would soon be travelling alone like this around Assam made me as happy as a child when there are only ten more days to Christmas. When I was with the others I felt called upon to demonstrate that I was still a communist.

View from the Khasi Hills, Assam

9: Into Assam

At the end of the nineteenth century, when the Indian Civil Service settled down there, Shillong was just a Khasi hill village, and the only development after their arrival was that some of the richer tea-planters had built mock Tudor residences there. On the up-and-down roads that wound along the hill-sides, gable-ends and mullioned windows showed through flowering shrubs and trees. Many of the roads bore English women's first names – like Marjory Terrace or Dorothy Avenue bestowed on them by the first governor, who according to legend, had been a womaniser, so that the naming of each new road was an occasion for marital anxiety for husbands. There can have been few, if any, towns in India outside Simla where the British presence was so pervasive, and now that the war had come to Assam's borders this effect had been intensified by the arrival of British troops for whom it was a salubrious resting place.

Christian churches, schools and colleges abounded, as by this time most Khasis had been converted to Christianity – in defiance of a memorable prophecy in the late Victorian gazetteer which was our only source of local information. Reporting that Hindu, Muslim and Christian missions were competing for the Khasis' souls, it commented that none of them was likely to make headway, as each of them prohibited one of three prized Khasi pleasures – 'beef, alcohol and promiscuous sexual intercourse'. Fifty years later, however, Christian missionaries had somehow swept the board, and the only competition for souls was inter-denominational. 'But isn't he a Christian?', I inquired about one Khasi of another, about whom he had just said something damning. 'Oh no!' was the answer. 'He's a Catholic.' What the gazetteer had registered as promiscuity was matriarchy. Property was owned by mothers, not by fathers, so inheritance did not depend on who a child's father was. Husbands were accordingly irrelevant, and all a

Waterfall in the Khasi Hills

Khasi householder had to do to send her unsatisfactory spouse back to his mother was present him, in due form, with a torn betel-leaf.

In line with this state of affairs, Khasi mythology blamed the Fall on the first husband, not on the first wife. A tree was involved in this case too. It had its roots in the earth and its branches in heaven, like Yggdrasil. The first man had his eye on this great tree. Just like Khasi men still to be seen toiling on the hillsides, he was a wood-cutter, and every day he tried to fell it. Night always fell before he could chop right through its massive trunk, however, and next morning the gash he had made the day before had vanished, so he had to start all over again.

Then one evening, after hacking away all day, instead of going home to sleep he stayed by the tree in hiding and saw what had been undoing his work during the night. A tiger came and completely healed the gash in the tree, by licking it.

So now he knew what to do. The following evening, instead of lying down to sleep he lay in wait and killed the tiger. And that was the end of the tree. He felled it at his leisure, and it will never grow again.

The local Administration Officer could not find a house for us immediately so we stayed at the Pinewood Hotel and introduced ourselves to the officials of the civil administration. If half of what we learned from them was true, although the war was now on their doorstep, local politicians took no notice of it. Since the Government of India Act had established elected provincial governments, their only concern had been either to preserve or to unravel the majority in the provincial legislative assembly on which the ministry in power depended for survival.

In many Indian provinces there was no question which party commanded a majority: the Congress Party's position was unchallengeable. Such provinces had accordingly been governed by Congress ministries until in 1940 they had resigned, in protest at the refusal of the U.K. government to agree to their party's terms for support in the war. Their solid assembly majorities in such provinces remained, however, so there could be no question of setting up alternative ministries. In such provinces parliamentary government had accordingly been replaced by 'direct rule' by provincial governors. With the exception of the North West Frontier Province, these provinces had predominantly Hindu electorates. In provinces with more heterogeneous electorates, the Government of India Act had produced coalition governments which excluded the Congress Party. These coalitions could be solid, as in the Punjab, or they could be fragile, as in Assam where the only support in the Legislative Assembly that any ministry – Congress or anti-Congress – could depend on was that of the European Group.

The European Group held the next highest number of committed seats in the Legislative Assembly, after the Congress Party and the Moslem League, thanks to a special provision of the Government of India Act which reserved a block of seats in the Assam Assembly for representatives of the tea industry. (The important tea industry was then almost entirely European-owned and managed). The votes of the European members of the Legislative Assembly did not, however, affect the balance of parties. Instead they were sagaciously committed to the support of any party leader whom the Governor had invited to form a ministry – provided he did not interfere with the tea industry. Even with that guaranteed support, however, neither the Congress Party nor the Moslem League could command an assured majority because the only loyalty of many M.L.A.s was to their family and friends, in whose interest they were always ready to change sides. Setting aside the European Group, the votes in the Assembly were thus divided into three roughly equal groups – votes committed to the Congress Party, votes committed to the Moslem League, and uncommitted votes available to the highest bidder. The fundamental competition between the Congress Party and the Moslem League was therefore to devise a distribution of the fruits of office that would purchase more uncommitted votes than the one devised by their opponents. These fruits included ministries, so any government formed by either party had to be a coalition.

The first prime minister had been a member of the Moslem League, Sir Mohammed Syed Sa'adullah, but before long one of his supporters missed a crucial division – because he had been detained against his will, according to his story, but another version had it that he had been induced to absent himself voluntarily, and only pleaded kidnapping as an excuse. Whatever the reason, the result was that a Congress Ministry took office.

A day or two later a Congress party worker was involved in an incident with a police sub-inspector in Gauhati – a busy town in the Brahmaputra Valley which is now the provincial capital of Assam. Before witnesses, in a shop, he warned the sub-inspector that from now on British hirelings like him would have to watch their step. The sub-inspector ridiculed this notion, and a public row developed.

Next day the Superintendent of Police in Gauhati received a phone call from Shillong. It was from the Inspector-General of Police. After a quarter of a century's service, during which he had never been required to be more than civil to an Indian, the Government of India Act had now presented him with a Congress *wallah* as the head of government, and he was rattled. The Superintendent of Police in Gauhati at that time was a Bengali, called Gupta, but his mimicry when he told me this story conveyed his superior's anxiety with unsympathetic accuracy. 'I say, Gupta, it seems there's been a nonsense at your end, and the P.M.'s making a thing of it. The story is, one of your chaps. . . etcetera'

Gupta replied that he would immediately suspend the sub-inspector from all duties, pending the outcome of an official inquiry into his alleged misconduct. ' Oh no, sir!', he assured his superior, when the latter suggested that this might be going a bit too far. 'It has gone so far already, sir, it must go farther. Please leave this to me.'

Next morning when he came down the steps of his bungalow to drive to his office he found what he had been counting on – a group of petitioners, composed of all the sub-inspector's relatives who were of any consequence. 'Oh, sir! Why have you done this to us?'

He replied that while he sympathised there was nothing he personally could do for their. . . son, son-in-law, nephew, brother, cousin, or whatever the case might be. His hands were tied by regulations, and the Prime Minister himself was taking an interest. 'But you, Rai Sahib,' he went on, as if the idea had only at that moment struck him, 'you count for something across the river. Why don't you ask your local member of the Legislative Assembly to speak to the Prime Minister about this? And get other folk in your constituency to do the same. The Prime Minister is bound to listen to your local M.L.A. He does support the Ministry, doesn't he?'

'Yes, but he's not a member of the Congress Party.'

'All the better! Then the Prime Minister can't be sure of his vote. And you could do the same where you come from,' he said, turning to another petitioner, 'and get your friends to join in. And, turning to yet another petitioner, 'how about you?'

Two days later the Inspector General was on the phone again. 'Great news, Gupta! The P.M.'s had second thoughts. Wants to let bygones be bygones, and all that. Doesn't want to start on the wrong foot.'

'What splendid news, sir!'

'Yes. You can drop that inquiry now.'

'How I wish I could, sir! But, as you know, sir, once an official inquiry into the conduct of a police officer has been opened it must reach a finding. The rules are clear, sir. The charge against my sub-inspector has to be established or rejected.'

'You don't think that we could stretch a point?'

'Surely not, sir! The rule is categorical.'

A week later the Congress party worker confessed to the inquiry that his complaint had been unwarranted.

The Congress coalition government's demise was not caused by defection, however. It resigned in 1940, when all Congress provincial ministries throughout India resigned together as an act of common policy.

Sir Mohammed could not immediately stitch a new majority together, but Mr Rohini Choudhury, the leader of a party with only three votes in the assembly (his own included) thought that he could. He was an experienced democratic arithmetician. Although he commanded only three votes, he had already been Minister of Education in the previous ministry, because the Congress Party could not do without them. He was now aiming for the premiership.

As he explained to the bemused Governor, he could form a stable government without the support of either the Congress Party or the Moslem League. With the support of the European Group guaranteed, together with that of various unattached members in return for the offer of ministries or other benefits at a prime minister's disposal, he would command the constant support of one third of the house, and to make up the additional votes needed for an overall majority he could always count on Congress Party members to vote for measures that the Moslem League opposed, and vice versa. It was therefore the Governor's constitutional duty to invite him to proceed. The Governor, bewitched but not bewildered, did not agree.

By the time we arrived in 1942, however, Sir Mohammed Syed Sa'adullah was back in office with a solid majority, because the Congress members of the Assembly were either boycotting it or had been detained for participation in the recent Quit India movement.

I attended a debate in the Assembly, and was astonished to hear Victorian thinkers, T.H.Green and Bosanquet, quoted, but we decided not to bother with politicians. The people whose help we could not do without were the people with whom the population of Assam was actively engaged – the district officers. During the next two years the Indian Civil Service was to play an essential part in the war in that theatre by maintaining tolerable living conditions, despite the appalling famine in neighbouring Bengal and the disruption caused in Assam itself by the warfare on its Burma frontier. There were sudden and enormous demands for unskilled casual labour for urgent military construction projects, such as the construction of airfields, the building of new roads and the repair of old ones not designed for heavy traffic. The famine in Bengal required control of rice procurement and the movement of other foodstuffs. Rationing of essential commodities like salt and kerosene had to be introduced. Price control had to be imposed on vital commodities which were not manufactured locally but had to be imported from beyond the province. Meanwhile, as a result of the military presence, money started circulating in unprecedented quantities. (The paper one-rupee notes which had now replaced the traditional silver coins were so distrusted that they were sometimes exchanged for coins at the rate of two for one.)

When we arrived, however, the consequences of the presence of the Japanese on Assam's borders had not yet been completely grasped. 'I suppose the Japanese eat rice', observed one civil service *mem-sahib* to another, apparently expecting that she would soon be entertaining Japanese commanding officers, while her indispensable husband carried on with the administration. The only war-like measure the administration had so far taken in Shillong was to remove a small boat from an ornamental pond, thus forcing an invader who might want to pass from one side to the other to walk round it.

None of them saw a need for our arrival on the scene, but they were prepared to tolerate our presence, and enjoyed preparing us for what we were going to find by reminiscing about life down in the valleys below. A district officer carried a heavy responsibility even in peace time, collecting taxes and maintaining law and order. Villagers seemed to regard this as an ancient contract, in which the nationality of the parties was irrelevant. Whoever appointed him and whatever his nationality – Assamese, Siamese, Moghul, British, or maybe one day Japanese or the Indian National Congress – the district officer had a right to taxes and provided law and order in return. If he took unheard-of steps, however – such as controlling the movement of agricultural produce – the district officer exceeded his authority. At the same time it behoved the villager to minimise his own contribution. 'That would be a very good thing', one villager told me later, when I pointed out that but for the presence of the Indian Army the Japanese would be ruling over him. 'You people have been here so long now, it's no use telling the District Magistrate that the harvest will be poor this year, and so the tax must be reduced. He knows. It would take the Japanese two generations to get like that.'

Not all the inhabitants of Assam had their lives supervised from a distance by district officers, whom they might never see. There were two groups whose lives were subject to close supervision by Europeans. One of these was composed of workers employed in the oil and tea industries. Kilroy took it for granted that their morale could – and even should – be left to their employers. The other group was composed of various tribal peoples, and he made the same assumption about them. They could be left to the particular care of the political officers to whom they owed the preservation of their ways of life.

Political officers belonged to a different service from the district officers. Many of them devoted their entire careers to one tribe, publishing accounts of its customs and studying its language. Differences had been preserved because the various tribes lived in remote regions from which outsiders were banned. The relationship of these protected tribes with their political officers, like marriages, was marked by mutual understanding and misunderstanding. One morning in the early 'twenties – as I was told – the political officer in charge of the Kuki people awoke to find a cleft stick, containing a chilly and a feather, on his bedside table. He read this to mean – 'We will chop you and burn your house down with all speed'. (It is worth noting that they could have chopped him instead when they came to his bedside, but had observed the formality of declaring war instead.)

As the Kukis were so much more at home in the jungle, the only way for regular troops to deal with them was to enclose the region they inhabited with miles of barbed wire, and then gradually reduce the area enclosed, retreating to block-houses at night. It took two years for this tedious strategy to succeed. The Governor's Secretary (not the Chief Secretary) was responsible for tribal affairs, and at the end of the first year he visited the scene of operations. The campaign, if such it could be called, was proceeding satisfactorily, but there was nothing much for him to see. Nevertheless, when he got back to Shillong he had a tale to dine out on. He had beaten the Kukis at their own game in their own jungle. It went as follows.

He was being driven down a mountain road, when coming round a bend his driver barely had time to halt the car in front of a log that had been felled across it, and a second later a band of Kuki warriors rose from concealment on the lower side of the hill, some armed with antique firearms and others with bows and arrows. Without staying to parley with them, he flung open the door on the opposite side of the car and made off up the upper side of the hill, to the accompaniment of shots that sent musket-balls – or whatever ammunition was in use – ripping through the jungle to left and right of him, until he was hidden in the foliage.

And that was only the beginning. The musket-balls were followed by warriors, looking for him but, straining his ears in the undergrowth, he was always able to detect their approaches in time to get away. In addition to staying out of his pursuers' way, however, he had to find his own way to safety, and he had no notion of it. In any case, he had his work cut out just dodging his pursuers, who proved relentless. For three days, throughout each of which they were close enough for him to hear them – sometimes to the left, sometimes to the right, but always behind – the most he could do was avoid their pursuit. At night-fall he just lay down wherever he found himself.

Luckily, however, before he lay down he had always eaten. When they were all searching for him they left their camps unattended, with pots of cooked food just waiting to be eaten. Small wonder that he felt pleased with himself when at the end of the third day his story ended happily with him stumbling on a block-house – more, as he admitted, by good luck than by good management.

Discussing the recent hostilities with a group of Kuki chiefs a year later, when peace had been restored, the political officer agreed that neither side could accuse the other of serious misconduct, but felt compelled to question the propriety of ambushing his chief. One of the Kukis had played a part in this, and was glad, he declared, to have this chance to explain. 'We were disgraced. We were like beasts in a pen, not fighting you like men. So we resolved to send a raiding party, of which I was one, to harass you in your own lands.

'We pierced your wire and reached your road and set an ambush, but the very last thing we wanted was to catch the Governor Sahib's Secretary. We could not entertain him in a manner that befitted either his honour or our own. Luckily, he ran away from us off up the hill, so all we had to do was fire some shots to keep him going – being very careful to miss. But that was only the beginning. We could not leave him, defenceless in the forest and lost, so we protected him, and drove him towards your nearest block-house, without allowing him to see us. Some went behind him, making a noise to send him in the right direction. Others scouted ahead or moved beside him to protect him and make sure he was not moving into danger. The rest went very far ahead to cook some food – not suited to his dignity but the best that we could manage.

It was weary work, because he moved so slowly, but in the end we saw him safe. It was unbecoming but it was the best that we could do.'

I had no qualms about tribal peoples being left to political officers, but was less happy about abandoning the labour employed on the oil field and on tea gardens, to their managers. I cannot now imagine what responsibility I thought it was that we were abandoning. Our responsibility was for morale, not labour conditions, and in any case winning the war was all that should matter to a communist, until it had been won. According to a news story at that time, when London dockers were accused of lack of patriotism for going on strike and appealed for support to the Soviet Ambassador, he told them that in the Soviet Union they would have been be shot.

Unlike the tribal areas, the Digboi oil field fell within the jurisdiction of a district officer – who was responsible to the Labour Commissioner in Shillong for the application of industrial legislation there, as also in tea gardens. Our concern with all these labourers, however, was only that they should not panic, and in Kilroy's view, at the very most all this required was for us to remind their managers of their duty. I do not now see what other line he could have taken, and in the event there was no panic in the tea gardens or on the oil field.

The only difference between the two was that the oil company's management made a point of keeping in touch with us. The tea gardens were closed fiefdoms. They belonged to an earlier time. Half the coolies employed on them probably never knew there was a war on. I only once addressed a meeting in a garden. Our contact with the tea industry was mainly as guests of managers in areas where there were no government rest houses. Their control over their coolies' lives was almost total. The possibility of intervention by the Labour Commissioner in Shillong in a tea garden was largely theoretical. He was in touch with conditions in the oil field through the oil workers' trade union, but there were no trade union for tea-workers.

Tea estate factory

A private road to a tea estate, Assam

The isolation of the coolies was increased because they had nothing in common with the Assamese. They were indentured immigrants from other provinces, speaking their own languages and living in isolation with their families in housing provided by the owners on the estates on which they worked, and often many miles from the nearest village. The planters thus wielded wide powers over a large number of men, women and children in secluded worlds. The garden-manager was monarch of everything within many miles of his bungalow – usually a commodious, airy structure, well fly-proofed and raised high above the ground on pillars. The nearest fellow European was usually the manager of another estate. In such a situation it is easy to become a tyrant – even to another *sahib*.

On one big garden, whose manager had a younger compatriot as an assistant, the latter told me how he returned from his first home leave with a young wife, and duly installed her in the *chhota* (little) bungalow, which was next door to the *barra* (big) one. These two bungalows had no other European neighbours within half a day's journey by car, but for the first three days after his return the only contact between their occupants was between him and the manager when they were at work. He and his wife were not invited across to the *barra* bungalow in the evening, and received no visit from it.

On the fourth day, when the two men had gone to work, unable to face another day alone the newcomer went across to the *barra* bungalow at coffee time to pay a call, but got no further than the empty verandah, where a bearer appeared to tell her that the *barra mem-sahib* was 'not at home'. That evening, to make things clear, the *barra sahib* sent a note across, explaining that a *chhota mem-sahib* did not call on a *barra* one, before the *barra* one had called on her.

Offensive behaviour to Indian subordinates did not even merit an explanation. On one garden I visited, the Indian medical officer was not permitted to cycle past the manager's bungalow. He had to dismount, as a sign of respect, and wheel his machine until he was out of sight.

I only heard of one tea-garden riot. Once again my informant was Police Superintendent Gupta. After foiling the Congress Party in Gauhati he had been transferred to Silchar District, a hilly area at the Eastern end of Assam's southern valley, where tea estates abounded. Unusually, at one garden the coolies went on strike, and the manager vacated his bungalow. The coolies then threatened to burn the bungalow to the ground, and Gupta went there with a handful of police. He had not enough men to surround the threatened bungalow, but it was already surrounded by a hedge which the coolies inexplicably respected, so the only way they could reach the bungalow was through a gateway, over a cattle-grid. Although not a barrier this was a boundary mark, and standing there with a handful of men in uniform behind him, Gupta raised his hand to halt the advancing crowd and asked them what they wanted. Their business, they explained, was only with the manager. They were going to burn his bungalow down. What good did they think that would do them? – asked Gupta. None, they admitted, but that was what they felt like doing and nothing anyone might say was going to stop them. It was plain from the way he told it that the Superintendent Gupta found this sympathetic.

The monsoon had started a few days earlier, so he prolonged the argument, and as he had hoped while they were still talking rain came sluicing down. 'Look here,' he suggested, 'we haven't finished this discussion and there's no point in getting wet. Why don't we draw a line here on the ground between us?' He drew one with his cane. 'You're on that side, and I'm on this. Now why we don't all just go away until this rain stops, and then come back to stand where we are now – you on that side of the line and me on this side – and carry on where we left off.'

The rain lasted for days, and when it stopped nobody came back.

To an outsider the conditions of work on a tea estate seemed hard, and the coolies could certainly have won better ones with trade unions, but what had moved these coolies to riot, according to Superintendent Gupta, was not their pay and conditions. They objected to the manager's attitude and personal behaviour, and wanted to make him regret it. They regarded their pay and conditions as normal.

They may even have regarded them as acceptable. Shortly before the war, fresh from leading hunger marchers from Jarrow to Westminster, Ellen Wilkinson paid a visit to India which included the Assam tea gardens. For a time she stayed at a garden as the guest of a manager I knew, and convinced him that he could afford to pay his coolies more. He was sufficiently civilised to raise his rates of pay accordingly, but the result was not an increase in the coolies' take-home pay. They were paid piece rates, and stopped picking when they had weighed in enough tea to be paid as much under the new rates as they would have been paid under the old rates for more. The planter regretted not being as sane himself as they were.

Another insight into piece rates which he gave me was that they promoted female emancipation, because they did not discriminate between male and female labour. A woman had only to pick as much as a man to earn as much, so when a husband mistreated her his wife could show him the door. Neither of them owned the garden accommodation they had been sharing, but if the woman had children she stayed in it, and the husband was housed elsewhere with other men.

Kilroy was happy to leave the morale of tea garden labourers to their managers because his duty was simply to do what he could to ensure that the civilian population did not obstruct military operations, which it was unlikely to do when labour was under unified direction. Most villagers, on the other hand, had never even seen their district officer, and during the war, as he was burdened with additional duties, he had less time than ever to establish personal contact with them. It was in the rural areas that our duty lay. Information was still spread mainly by word of mouth, and our arrival in a village would be enough in itself to give people something to talk about. Our words would be repeated. Before making detailed plans, however, we must reconnoitre.

A tea estate manager's bungalow

154

10: Exploring

Our first excursion was to Sylhet, in the Surma Valley – the place where I had arrived with the two cars. A mass rally was to be held there by the National War Front – an organisation recently formed to rally Indians who approved of India's participation in the war. Even when they qualified, however, most prominent Indians shrank from it, as it was financed by the Government of India, but Sir Mohammed Syed Sa'adullah was less squeamish. His government embraced it, and one of his cronies had just been given the salaried post of the National War Front's provincial organiser. The mass rally at Sylhet launched both it and him. They then both disappeared from public view. Their launch, however, was a grand affair. Free transport brought in villagers from far and wide, to be marshalled by an army of police. The police were armed with *lathis* – quarter-staffs, like those that Robin Hood and Little John cracked pates with. The *lathi* is an accepted instrument for restoring order in an Indian crowd, even when its disorder is involuntary. Many Indian cities had seen police *lathi* charges during the previous six months, and civil disobedience was still smouldering in the other, predominantly Hindu, valley of the Brahmaputra, but their use was not found necessary on this occasion.

Seated for hours in and around a vast, brailed marquee, the crowd listened patiently to many speeches, one of which was given by Kilroy – in Urdu. His listeners all spoke a local Bengali dialect – Sylheti – but there were so many speakers that there was no time for interpretation. He was assured there was no need for it. His audience understood Urdu because they were mostly Moslems and therefore, thanks to their familiarity with the Koran, at home in Arabic. (Urdu has a strong Arabic component.) The two local assistants we were authorised to employ were clearly going to be indispensable, if only as interpreters.

Before we left Sylhet, Kilroy appointed our assistant for the Surma Valley. His choice surprised me. The composition of the population of the town of Sylhet differed from that of the interior in containing a considerable proportion of Hindus. Those who were solid citizens were supporters of Sir Mohammed, despite his membership of the Moslem League, and some of them had attended the official lunch before the meeting, where he set the table in a roar by warning one, whose family name was Roy, to beware of Colonel 'Kill-Roy'.

The leading Hindu dignitary of Sylhet – a merchant, land-owner and chairman of the municipal board – was too devout to attend the meal. Dietary restrictions prevented him. Nevertheless, he was a dutiful supporter of Sir Mohammed, and an influential figure, so we went to visit him. It was a waste of time. In answer to our questions he said nothing that he felt we would not like to hear.

Nevertheless, Kilroy asked him to name a suitable resident of Sylhet for us to employ as our assistant, and when unblushingly he named his son – at the same time indicating that the salary Kilroy had named was not sufficient – to my amazement Kilroy yielded on both points. Although he had swayed crowds himself in the Punjab, he did not believe that swaying crowds had anything to do with power. By raising major, national political issues the Congress Party and the Moslem League too had swayed crowds in the Punjab – but they had not gained majorities in the Punjab assembly. Barely ten per cent of the population had votes, and what had gained those votes was the pains-taking exercise of local pressures by local magnates. For all the enthusiasm their national policies might arouse, it was neither the Congress Party nor the Moslem League that ruled the Punjab but a coalition of self-interested Moslems and Hindus, united by their concern to preserve the status quo. The only Indians whose opinions counted were members of established families – in Kilroy's opinion. When he returned to the Punjab a year later, however, local influence no longer sufficed to secure the majorities on which power depended even there. To win votes, parties must now engage the major issues – the ending of British rule and the ensuing redistribution of power. But Kilroy refused to see this. The Government of India in its wisdom would decide what constitutional changes must be made, after consulting those few Indians whose opinions mattered. In Assam, in a modest way, the Chairman of the Sylhet Municipal Board was such an Indian, and it would be useful to employ his son.

As it turned out, his son proved no less useful than the assistant we soon afterwards appointed in the Brahmaputra valley on the advice of a deputy commissioner of Kamrup. The only difference was that the deputy commissioner offered us two candidates to choose between, but his recommendation of both must have been guided by a calculation of local obligations.

We got back to Shillong from Sylhet in time to spend a frosty Christmas there, but then set off to tour Assam's northern valley – the Brahmaputra Valley. As the mountain road was too narrow to carry two-way traffic safely down the hill, alternately at fixed times each half of it was closed to traffic in one direction, so that a queue of waiting buses, army lorries and cars built up at the half-way point. Over the next two and a half years I spent many hours waiting there, but never grew impatient to move on. There was always a mild bustle to watch. Indian civilian travellers found refreshment at a tea shop, while the military were catered for at a canteen, run by volunteer *mem-sahibs* and *miss-sahibs*. There was a small Khasi bazaar to stroll up and down, while tethered goats cropped the grass or banged their heads together.

Gauhati, at the foot of the hill, was the administrative centre of Kamrup – the only district which had seen serious violence during the recent civil disobedience movement. Bombs had been exploded north of the river, not far from the ferry which brought troops and supplies from Calcutta across the Brahmaputra on their way to the rail-head in Manipur, where 14th Army faced the Japanese. Our concern, however, was with the supporting forces in its rear, and the H.Q. of the military administrative area involved was just a few miles from Gauhati.

It was fortunate that we were answerable to G.H.Q. in Delhi and not to this Area command. When Kilroy asked them whether there were any local difficulties they would like him to look into, there was nothing they could think of. Their presence in Assam had caused no problems. In short, they saw no need for us. On the other hand, the deputy commissioner – a crisp Bengali intellectual with interesting contemporary Indian paintings on his walls – welcomed us as a sign of belated awareness in the army of the difficulties its presence was creating. The military presence in Kamrup, and in particular in Gauhati, was regarded as an unwelcome intrusion by everyone who did not profit from it, and he made it clear that he shared this point of view. What the army needed to do, however, was not explain itself more but to listen more. Nevertheless, we were welcome to explain its presence if we could, and he recommended two candidates for the post of our assistant in the Brahmaputra Valley.

Indian lawyers had played a major role in the struggle against British rule from its very beginning, and like other district centres Gauhati had its law court. Kilroy addressed the bar library. The questions put to him when he had finished were all hostile. Some questioned his presentation of the war situation, insisting that the Japanese halt on the border of Assam was only temporary. Others dismissed warnings about Japanese designs on India. It was only on the British that they had designs.

We also arranged to talk to students at the Bishop Cotton College. Kilroy attended, but left the talk to me. The role of Indian students in the national struggle was as traditional as that of Indian lawyers, but I fared better than he had, because my approach was the straight Communist one that victory would result in Indian independence, although in Kilroy's presence I could not push this line as far as I did later when touring on my own.

The college at Gauhati was then the only college in Assam that took its students all the way to a degree, but there were several other colleges taking matriculates half-way to one, and over the next two years I visited them all, presenting myself as a fellow student, eager for Indian independence, who happened to be in military uniform. I never went farther than British policy pronouncements justified, but that was farther than most *sahibs* then realised. A year later I addressed a joint meeting of the bar library and students, in Sylhet – an occasion which, to give Kilroy due credit, only the son of the Chairman of the Municipal Board, whom he had appointed, could have arranged. When I had finished, a lawyer quoted Churchill's declaration that he had not become prime minister to preside over the dissolution of the British Empire. Had he changed his mind, and if so how had I come to know? 'What Mr Churchill has to say on this subject is of no importance', I heard myself reply. The audience stared at me. I was startled too, but I went on. 'If the British people want India to be independent after the war, and Mr Churchill doesn't, then he will not be prime minister after the war.'

Silence was followed by hubbub, and report of my words spread so far that on a visit to Shillong, the Commander of 4 Corps – the troops actively engaging the Japanese in Manipur – asked Kilroy whether it was true that I had publicly foretold the fall of Churchill. I had merely been explaining the constitutional position, Kilroy told him. Churchill could not remain prime minister without a parliamentary majority.

'Nobody can quarrel with that,' the general reflected, 'but is he in fact a communist?' Kilroy lacked Henry Solomon's finesse. He simply lied. 'He's just concerned about the gap between the rich and poor.'

So are we all, of course. The General could not quarrel with that.

At Digboi, further still up the valley, we were guests of the Assam Oil Company. The Managing Director evidently thought it important to give the military nothing to complain about, as the entire management staff was mustered in the morning, during working hours, to hear an address from Kilroy about the military importance of civilian morale. He responded with an assurance that he and all his staff were well aware of the importance of morale, and asked the labour manager to describe in detail the happiness of everybody they employed. Self-respect demanded that one of us should add a grain of salt to all this. Before leaving Shillong I had consulted the Labour Commissioner about labour relations in Assam, and when I mentioned that we would be visiting the oil field he had told me that the company was in dispute with a particular group of workers. I can no longer remember who they were. The word 'donkeymen' comes floating towards me from some mental recess. It cannot be right, but I shall use it because I am writing these reminiscences strictly from memory. No sooner had the labour manager completed his assurances by declaring that, as we could see from what he had said nobody on the oil field had anything to complain about', than I asked, 'Does that include the donkeymen?'

The ranks of management must have been murmuring to one another until then, because the sudden silence was noticeable. The labour manager turned for help to the general manager, who nodded to me, as if we shared a secret. 'That business is as good as settled now', he said. All I could do was nod back, with agonised mental apologies to the donkeymen. Why had I not asked the Labour Commissioner to tell me more?

The managing director sought me out at the buffet lunch and I expected to be exposed, but he did not want to talk about the donkeymen. As he saw it, the incident was closed. I had just been indicating that before we came we had done our homework. Instead of talking about labour he talked about books. He had a good library, and whenever I visited Digboi afterwards I was his guest.

I addressed a large gathering of oil workers on a later visit, but the only proletarian employees with whom we came into direct contact on this first visit to Digboi were the Gurkha watchmen – ex-Servicemen who had only to catch a glimpse of Kilroy to stand to attention. The meeting took place in an open space outside their quarters, and although their wives remained indoors their sons were curious, and every now and then one of their fathers would leave the meeting to drive them further off with stones. These were not thrown in their direction, as a warning. Each stone was aimed directly at some particular boy – who always displayed indifference if it hit him.

Before returning to headquarters in Shillong we drove further East from Digboi to where the Americans were driving a road through the jungle into Burma. They had already gone a long way, and it took quite a time to reach the point where jungle was under clearance. Virgin forest stretched away darkly on either side, and the air was heavy with vegetable stench. Trees that had been growing there for ever were being felled, and heavy machines of a design and power that we had never seen before were performing impossible feats. The cheery friendliness of men who could so easily do what no one else could dream of doing seemed condescending.

The only fighting troops we saw were Chinese. There were no Indian troops, but there was a contingent of Indian civilian coolies, working on the road in the wake of the machinery, and the two nations had recently been involved in an incident. When a Chinese convoy, driving too fast along the stretch of road where the coolies were working, had run over one of them, the coolies had started throwing stones at it. The convoy had then halted and, descending from their jeeps, the Chinese had started firing in the general direction of the coolies with live ammunition but without hitting anyone. It was just their idea of fun, until the British officer in charge of the coolies tried to intervene. The Americans said that they had been only just in time to prevent a pointed stake from being driven through his stomach.

This behaviour was unusually spectacular, but otherwise not untypical in its callousness. Fortunately Chinese troops were not stationed in populous areas but only passed through them on their way to the front, but even so they earned a bad reputation. A year later, a junior Indian civil servant told me how a Chinese convoy, encamped near a village in his sub-division, had posted sentries and allowed nobody to enter it or leave the village for two days. At about the same time, when one of our assistants was curdling the blood of a bazaar crowd with an account of Japanese atrocities, one of his listeners told him that the people he was talking about had already been there. Investigation revealed that he was talking about a Chinese convoy.

On our way back to Shillong, we took the assistant whom we had appointed in Kamrup into a few villages. As we had expected, the appearance of a *sahib* in uniform was a notable occasion in a place where *sahibs* were seldom seen. Our assistant had a sufficient sense of the importance of his role as Kilroy's interpreter to speak as one assured of a respectful hearing. Questions were asked, but not about the war. The villagers were concerned with shortages and prices. We did not know the answers to such questions, so we undertook to pass them on the deputy commissioner and send our assistant back to them with his replies – thus discovering a useful form of liaison with the public that we had not bargained for.

We also discovered that how ill-equipped we were. Not only were we grotesquely thin on the ground, but even where we put in an appearance we lacked the means to make our presence felt. Beyond a very limited distance, people did not even know that we were there, and even when they did they had no inducement to come flocking to us. Bazaars where people from several neighbouring villages gathered once a week for market would offer larger audiences, but if we wanted them to pay attention to us we must somehow offer a *tamasha*. As we were, we could only nibble at the job.

Our luck turned as soon as we arrived back in Shillong. The Administrative Officer had found us a long L-shaped bungalow, with many rooms, only three or four years old, and earthquake-proof, half a mile up a hill on the outskirts of the town We all had separate bedrooms, Kilroy had a private office, so did the staff captain, and there was another office for Kilroy's secretary and a typist. Better still, hardly had we moved in than Kilroy was sent the minutes of a high-level conference between the U.S. forces and G.H.Q. that had just been held in New Delhi at American request. It was a belated response to the Japanese air attack on their air fields in Assam. The Americans were anxious about civilian panic that further raids might cause, and wanted to know how the British proposed to prevent it. In response they had been assured that three 'specially trained officers' were already on the job.

Kilroy saw his chance. 'They're so afraid of the Americans, they'll give me anything I ask for!' He wrote back at once protesting that he had not been allotted the resources he required, and asked permission to return to Delhi to explain. This was immediately granted, and he left without delay, leaving the staff officer to hold the fort at our new headquarters, while I went back to the Brahmaputra Valley, to tour alone.

I spent much of the next two years touring alone, in one or other of the valleys, usually visiting one or two villages or a bazaar in the morning and the same in the afternoon, rarely staying for more than three nights in the same centre and often for only one. At district centres I sometimes stayed at the Circuit House, the use of which was supposed to be reserved for judges, top civil servants and ministers, but more usually I stayed at a resting place designed for smaller fry – a *dak bungalow*. Circuit houses had flag-poles and were generally more dignified. They were taller, had loftier ceilings, and usually looked down on their surroundings from the highest point in the neighbourhood. They also contained framed photographs, sometimes of past viceroys, but more usually of Queen Victoria. Their accommodation was more spacious. They provided the traveller with a bed-room and a day-room. In the *dak bungalow* he only had a bedroom, and even that he might have to share.

The 'European' meals served in both, however, were identical: – soup – brown, clear or tomato – followed by fried or steamed river fish, and then the meat dish, which was almost invariably chicken, accompanied by vegetables which had been boiled to death. Caramel custard followed, and then a morsel of Welsh rarebit served in grandeur on a segment of fried bread, followed by a tiny cup of stewed coffee.

Even when the *dak bungalow* was in the middle of a town it was surrounded by an area of its own ground, full of the twitter of insects after sunset, an accompaniment without which I would often have dined in total silence, except for the padding of the bungalow servant in and out with dishes, through the fly-proofed door that banged behind him on its spring. There was always at least one other guest, however, so Chhanga kept me up to the mark. It was no use telling him that I would dine in my pyjamas. When I came out of the bathroom, tomorrow's fresh uniform would be laid out – together with a clean handkerchief in which he never failed to tie a knot, if the handkerchief it was replacing had a knot in it. The only time he offered me instruction, however, was when I asked him to produce a bottle of rum that had come my way, so that I could add some to my tea. Rum went with coffee, not tea, he told me. Only whisky went with tea.

He never contradicted me, but sometimes did allow himself to hint a doubt. Once, when a *dak bungalow* was unusually unsavoury, I asked him whether he was sure the water I was drinking had been boiled. 'Of course', he said. 'I know your caste rules.'

'Chhanga,' I said patiently, 'boiling water before one drinks it has nothing to do with religion. It is a question of medicine. Drinking unboiled water can make you ill.'

'Why?' he asked. 'Because the water is full of tiny. ..' I hesitated, searching for a word for 'organism', but the best I could come up with was *janwar*. This word does mean 'living being', viewed etymologically, but in general use it means 'animal', and Chhanga's reaction on being told that a glass of water was full of animals was what mine would have been. He held it to the light. 'Are you telling me, Sahib, that this glass is full of animals?'

'Yes', I answered desperately, 'but you can't see them. They're so small.'

'Very good, Sahib!', he replied without moving a muscle.

Two years later, in Bombay, he displayed the same politeness when he dashed into my room in the sea-front hotel where we were staying to warn me we must leave at once because the sea was rising. He had been standing outside, watching it 'Of course it's rising', I responded magisterially. 'It rises twice a day. There's no cause for alarm, though. It always goes back down again.'

This was the first time he had seen it rising, he replied, and we had now been there for months. Nevertheless, I assured him, it had risen regularly, and with equal regularity had then gone back to where it started.

He was almost convinced. 'Why?' he asked me. 'Why does it do that?'

'Because of the moon', I told him.

Dak bungalow guests dined when they felt like eating, and while they did not avoid one another, did not congregate for meals. The only exceptions I recall were two British civilians supervising local labour hired for work on military projects, who were quartered in the *dak bungalow* in Jorhat, from 1943. Whenever I stayed there they joined me for dinner because I was happy to listen to their reminiscences of Burma where, before the war turned them into refugees, they had been planters.

I remember one of them telling me how he had joined a miscellaneous group of Europeans, fleeing on foot from a burning town which the Japanese were already entering, when a burning building collapsed on one of the party in a narrow street. When it became obvious that they would not be able to free him from the wreckage before the Japanese arrived or the flames got to him, he begged to be shot. Their party included a young British subaltern and a sergeant, who had lost contact with their units. The subaltern drew his pistol and, standing several paces from his target, fired all six rounds. The head of the trapped man fell sideways. A moment later, however, it straightened up. 'You missed!'

'Give me that, sir!' The sergeant took the pistol, cleared the chambers, asked for one round, and loaded it. He then walked over to the man who had to die, put the muzzle into his mouth, and squeezed the trigger.

On all my later tours I had electric sound equipment to blare out Indian film music, but on this first tour my only means of attracting public attention was a portable gramophone, without an amplifier, and a couple of records of classical Indian music. With these I wandered from village to village, leaving the driver to wind up the gramophone and play the records, while I stood around with the assistant, making conversation with anybody whose curiosity had been aroused, until there were enough of them to be called 'a meeting'. I then made a ten-minute speech in a tongue which, to suit the community of my audience, was declared to be Hindi or Urdu, but was always the same. Indeed it was to vary very little for the next two years, during which I usually visited three villages in a day, so that eventually I probably spoke it in my sleep. Certainly the time quickly came when I spoke it without thinking. As it emerged from my mouth, my mind would wander off until – as when aircraft passengers are warned to fasten their seat-belts for a landing – my attention was somehow recalled to my surroundings. But although the words were flowing I had no idea where I had got to in my speech, until somehow – I do not know how – I managed to re-insert myself by listening to my words as they came out.

166

When I stopped, my assistant would make something acceptable in the language of my listeners out of what I had been saying, with additions he thought suited to the time and place. Questions would then be put to me through him. They were often to the point and I tried to answer them directly. The only questions I remember now, however, are unusual ones. On this first tour I was asked – 'What use would your pistol be to you if we all attacked you at once?' I answered that it was a special kind of pistol that shot many people at one go, but on reflection I did not find the question menacing. It was an expression of the kind of curiosity I felt as a small boy in the 'twenties, when I would ask a motorist getting into an impressive car, 'what it would do'. Carrying a pistol did imply menace, however, so I stopped doing so.

At the time of this my first tour on my own, the civil disturbances created by the August movement were recent, minor sabotage was still occasionally committed on the railway, and Gandhi, in captivity, was entering a thirty-day fast in protest against the brutality with which demonstrations had been repressed. At a village in Nowgong District I was presented with evidence of this brutality.

Only a handful of children arrived to see what was going on when we started up the gramophone, and the impression of turned backs was so unmistakable that I told the assistant, who was looking worried, to find out what was wrong. He went off and returned with the head man, who told me that during the recent troubles the village school had been burnt down, so a collective fine had been levied, and a platoon of Gurkhas, under the command of a young British officer, had been sent to collect it. Inexcusably, instead of supervising the operation personally, after they pitched camp, the officer retired to his tent and left it to his men to enter the village to impound valuables. The village had been looted, houses vandalised, and women molested.

The head man of the village stood silent while the assistant explained this to me. He obviously expected no good to result from my arrival, but I wrote it all down, repeating piece by piece what I had understood to be translated back to him, after which I asked to speak to other witnesses, whose statements I noted in the same way. I was then taken to see a house with carved wooden doors, which had been wantonly hacked. Last of all, two women with bowed heads, keeping their faces hidden in their *saris*, were brought out to declare what had been done to them.

Promising that all this would be officially investigated, I drove straight to Nowgong to see the deputy commissioner, who made it clear he thought I was out of my depth. 'Let me tell you something. I have served these people for twenty years now, and believe me, they are all swine.' I hope this was an expression of resentment at sometimes himself having to be a swine.

I replied that nevertheless the case I had brought to his attention called for investigation. He smiled. Investigations of the kind I was suggesting had to be initiated within six months of the alleged misconduct, so by a narrow margin this incident no longer qualified. Perhaps the villagers had expected the answer I brought back to them. The emotion they displayed was sympathy for me! Before I went away they told me that next time I came that way, instead of staying at a *dak bungalow*, I must be their guest.

This, my first tour on my own, lasted something over a month, but Kilroy had still not returned from New Delhi when I got back to headquarters in Shillong, so I could not consult him about an invitation to lunch at Government House that I found waiting for me there. In New Delhi Short had told me how the Viceroy had invited a varied selection of American officers to lunch, and just when the Vicereine was about to start post-prandial conversation with an American general who had been installed beside her on a sofa, a young lieutenant had squeezed between them and turned to her to ask brightly: 'Say, ma'am, how long have you been in this goddam country?' Short had commended the spontaneity of this behaviour, but I had no wish to emulate it, and the tips on decorum we had been given in Bangalore did not cover this.

On arrival at Government House, I joined a dozen guests standing around drinking sherry in a panelled room, under the eyes of two aides who, at the appointed hour, formed us up in two lines on either side of a wide double door, to be presented to His Excellency – at which point I realised that I did not know how to address a governor! It would be ridiculous to address him as 'your Excellency' if that was not the usual form. On the other hand I did not wish to be discourteous if it was, so I secured a position at the end of one of the two lines of guests that was farthest from the double door, so that I could hear what other people said to him before he came to me. Unfortunately he did not enter through the double door, but through a side door next to where I stood, so I was the first guest to be introduced to him. I called him 'Sir', and so, did all the others – perhaps because they had been listening to me.

After lunch we all went back to the panelled room to sit around while one by one – or in couples – we were approached by an aide murmuring, 'Sir John would like a word with you now', and led away to take the chair beside him which someone else had that minute been removed from, until this honour had been received by every guest but me. H.E. then rose, to take leave of his guests.

Trying to feel distinguished by being so pointedly ignored, I was joining the queue filing past him to shake his hand, when an aide intercepted me. H.E. was looking forward to a long talk with me when the rest had gone.

He knew that I had been on tour of the Brahmaputra Valley. How much more he knew about me I could only guess. A relative newcomer to Assam himself, he asked me for my impressions and shared his with me. When he told me about Rohini Choudhury's scheme for constructing a government I even felt that he was seeking sympathy for having to treat the schemer seriously. His seriousness was impressive. I was impressed by his knowledge of crops, price movements and scarcities.

Lt Col. Kilroy and his team.
Left to right Mazhar Ali Khan, Tahira (his wife), Alan Kilroy,
George Perry, S F R

170

11: Touring

A day or two later, Kilroy telephoned to tell us to join him in Calcutta at the Grand Hotel. On our previous stop-over in Calcutta we had stayed at the Great Eastern Hotel where there were many civilians and nearly all the guests were British. At the Grand Hotel the guests were all servicemen, half of them Americans, as they were whenever I stayed there during the next two years. I never saw it come to a fight, but there was always tension between the allies. If the allies found themselves at the same table they struck up reasonably amicable conversations, but each preferred the company of their own kind.

I can guess the kind of thing the Americans said to one another about us from the kind of thing we said about them – for example, the comments provoked by their after-dinner pastime of repairing to a room on the top floor, to see who was fastest on the draw. I sympathised with the derision, but abstained. Lenin himself had said that the revolution would call for 'American efficiency' as well as 'Bolshevik enthusiasm'. In the course of the next two years I saw enough to realise what he meant – and to be jealous. I had already seen what they were capable of on the road they were forcing through the jungle, but the way I saw them deal with smaller difficulties was impressive too – as when I shared a room in a *dak bungalow* with an American officer who, before getting into bed, shut the doors and windows and released D.D.T. from a canister to fill the room with a pungent mist which, he assured me, only insects had to fear. Sure enough, in the morning dead mosquitoes littered the floor at the foot of the door! Compared with this, the Indian Army's anti-mosquito weapon, the Flit-gun, ranked with the bow and arrow.

Their organization was up to their equipment. They even speeded up the railway in their area of Assam, with no change of equipment at all, but their most spectacular feat of organization came later that year – the building of an oil pipe-line all the way from Calcutta to their air-fields in Lakhimpur. During the weeks – not months – that it was under construction I drove two hundred miles along its route, and saw gangs of coolies digging a trench for it – simultaneously all the way from start to finish – while lorries cruised along dropping pipes to be joined up in a line that stretched to the foothills of the Himalayas from Calcutta, where the tankers docked.

It was fortunate that they were not our enemies, but it was humiliating to have them on our side. Like most Englishmen I fell back on seniority. 'You mean you people were in this thing before we were?' asked one American, surprised to infer from something I had said that Britain had been at war before Pearl Harbour. 'Well, yes, we were as a matter of fact', I replied, as British as could be. The truth is that we were all jealous – especially, in my case, because they were not implicated in the Raj. When I discovered that the Assamese referred to them as 'Naga sahibs' I was delighted. Nearly all my wartime recollections of Americans are tinged with envy – like the time when I was dining with an American officer in Calcutta, and the waiter asked me for the 'Americani sahib's order. Pleased by this recognition of his nationality, the sahib asked me to inquire what it was about him that revealed his nationality. 'His trousers are so tight behind', replied the waiter, when I put the question to him. I translated this: 'He says it is your friendly manner'.

On this visit to Calcutta, however, I had no time to talk to anyone but Kilroy. The concessions he had won in Delhi kept me busy running errands. He had been granted everything we had seen a need for on our tour – an assistant in every district, instead of one in each valley, together with loud-speaker equipment with record-players and battery-chargers, to make a tamasha and station-wagons instead of private cars to carry them. His officer staff had also been increased by two new Indian captains of his own choosing – both of them ex-prisoners. One, Mazhar Ali Khan, whom I had met in Lahore and drunk with in Delhi, was a communist. The other was an ex-terrorist, poet and novelist, Satchinanda Vatsyayana.

The duties in wait for Vatsal were as surprising as the facts of his appointment. ('Vatsal' is what he instructed me to call him when I began to call him 'Vatsy'.) Kilroy shared Short's belief in personal persuasion, and it was the only kind that he was good at, but he realised that we could tour the province until we died, even with our new outfit and still most villages in Assam would neither have seen nor have listened to us. He had therefore secured funds to publish a fortnightly, to be called *Our Assam*. Assamese, Bengali or English editions as appropriate were to be distributed, free, throughout the province, to schools and colleges, bar libraries, tea gardens and the Assam Oil Company. One job that kept us busy in Calcutta was therefore arranging for copies to be printed there and distributed by post every fortnight to addresses in Assam, as Calcutta was the only place from which this could be done. This ruled out news reports, as it involved a long delay between composition and distribution, but Kilroy saw that as an advantage. The aim of the paper, as he conceived it, was simply to make his readers feel in touch with a friendly army, not to keep them up to date. The more miscellaneous the contents, the better. From time to time it should even feature a story. Moreover, its readers should be spared intimidating blocks of print. Instead, lively illustrations should beguile them on every page, while multi-coloured pictorial front and back covers must tempt the semi-literate to pick it up. The inside pages must be coloured too.

A specially equipped printing press was therefore called for. Vatsal who understood such matters, would not be joining us for three months, so Kilroy got down to it himself, and if anyone in G.H.Q. had hesitated to entrust the running of a fortnightly to an infantry officer with no experience of publishing, he had no need to. After offering his project to a couple of printers who could not meet his requirements he grasped the technical difficulties and found a printer with a press that could mingle text and illustrations. Intense discussion of practicalities followed in detail, until he was satisfied. That done, as he had to keep within a budget, he haggled over costs – including the cost of wrapping and addressing and posting 20,000 copies. His experience of the Irish horse trade stood the Indian Army in good stead. He got what he wanted at the price the Army was prepared to pay. This was as nothing, however, compared with a project that took us into back streets to audition dancers and musicians. Playing film music over our new loud-speaker equipment might attract a hundred listeners in a village or three hundred in a bazaar, but he had thought of a *tamasha* to entice thousands. He had secured permission to form a troupe of dancers. The dancing must be classical, he insisted, because in addition to stiffening their morale he wanted to show the Assamese their cultural heritage. Once they had been selected and installed at a base in Shillong, the dancers were to tour the valleys in a bus he had purchased, supported by a military truck carrying costumes, stage equipment, sound equipment and lighting.

The dancers he auditioned in Calcutta were all Hindus. So was their art, apart from one Kathak dance, a couple of folk dances and occasionally a comic turn or a Bengali song, crooned over the microphone by one of the musicians. Otherwise their programmes concentrated on enactments of episodes from Hindu myth and legend, and some – like a dance of Shiva -were iconic. Nevertheless, his brainwave was justified in the event. For the next eighteen months, the gaudy costumes, seductive music and jingling dancing bells – not to mention the hypnotic brightness of the lighting in little market towns where electricity was still unknown – entranced Moslem and Hindu audiences alike, in both valleys. The entertainment was well worth the tedium of listening to a speech in the interval, half-way through the show.

The troupe's dance style was a promiscuous combination of movements drawn from the Hindu Bharat Natyam School[10], sometimes supplemented by rhythmic mime in time with the music, to enact a story. The orchestra's instruments were the classical flute, *tabla,* other drums, and stringed instruments – *sitar* and *sarode* – grouped on the stage around a harmonium and a microphone. We bought piles of glitzy saris and bedizened male costumes, not to mention paste jewellery and make-up. All this property, along with a set of curtains, stage lighting and other items, was placed on an inventory, maintained and periodically checked by the dependable *sarode* player, who had resigned an office job to join us.

Auditioning, like everything else, was something Kilroy did for himself, seated on the only chair in the room, as attentive as Diaghilev – although nobody could have looked less like Diaghilev than Kilroy with his tanned hatchet face, and he was looking out for signs of character, not art. The dancers he rejected were those he diagnosed as trouble-makers or weaklings. He took it for granted that anyone brought for audition by the manager he had appointed could perform. Lalit Coomar, the manager, was already in attendance when we joined Kilroy in Calcutta. He was perpetually apprehensive, partly because he could not believe his luck but also because the others all resented his position. He was the only Assamese in the troupe – a Sylheti Hindu. All the others were Bengali Hindus.

The dancers never set foot on a stage without first taking its dust to their foreheads, but it was not just because they were artists that they saw themselves as members of an elite. It was because they were Bengali artists. They admitted, frequently and proudly, to being temperamental. 'Just see our Bengali mentality!' they used to say to me, when a row broke out.

As soon as we were back in Shillong, Kilroy started interviewing local journalists and appointed one Bengali-speaker and one Assamese, together with an illustrator. Then Mazhar arrived, and Kilroy instructed the two of us to produce material for them to translate and illustrate, so that when Vatsal arrived he found that the fortnightly for which he was to be responsible already had a character in which he had been denied a say. The effect of exclusion was made worse because there was no room for him in the bungalow with the rest of us. He did not lack company, however. He was welcomed on his arrival by the intelligentsia of Shillong. He was quartered in a large rented property that also housed the dancers when they returned from touring in the valleys. They were allotted one wing, Vatsal and our Assam office were established in the other, and a large central hall was used for rehearsals.

For the next eighteen months the dancers went on exhausting tours down in the valleys from one small town to another, performing a couple of nights in each, and the audience at the second performance was always much larger than the one the night before. They were usually accommodated in a school, which had been vacated for their visit, and a stage was built in the open by local labour under their direction. The stage had to be high, because there were never less than a thousand spectators, and sometimes several thousands – all of them standing, unless a line of seats had been placed at the front for local dignitaries. Skill was required to improvise a temporary stage that was both high and firm. Usually low wooden platforms, made for sleeping on, were lashed together in layers, firmly enough to withstand the thud of the dancers' feet. Then bamboo poles were set up to form the skeleton of the proscenium, wings and rear, which were then draped with curtains. The company was usually housed in a local school, and if its grounds were wide enough to accommodate the expected audience this structure was built out from the school and a class-room leading into the stage served as a dressing-room. Otherwise a dressing-room tent, equipped with mirrors and benches, had to be erected at the side of the stage. Finally the bus-driver, who received extra pay as an electrician, installed the lighting and the sound equipment, which were supplied with electricity through a series of car batteries, charged by a portable dynamo. Once the show was under way I used to slip out and walk around on the edge of the crowd, to estimate the size of the audience. The effect of the brilliantly lit stage in the surrounding darkness was hypnotic.

As the principal touring officer I was involved in almost every tour the dancers made. After the first few shows on the first tour I knew that I could leave everything to them. While they were settling into their billet and erecting the stage, I would be away with the local assistant visiting a bazaar. The sarode player saw to everything that needed doing. When speaking to me confidentially, Rab Nawaz, the Afridi bus-driver, always referred to the Bengali artists as 'the black people', but even he accepted the *sarode* player's direction. So too did I. We also had serious discussions of wider issues. On one occasion the stage was being erected on the ruins of a school that had been set on fire during the disturbances. The walls had disappeared, but the iron framework remained for us to hang curtains on, and it had been built on a plinth, so it was an ideal site for a stage. Nevertheless, he shook his head. 'This is not the way to win our independence!' I suspected him of trying to please me, until he added – 'We must win it by a trick.'

On tour with the dancers I made a point of consulting Lalit Coomar, to make it clear that he was the manager. Six months later his need of such support became desperate. The first contracts we made with the artists were for a trial period of six months, and when the time came one or two did not want to renew them, so Kilroy took Lalit to Calcutta to find new ones. He wanted to expand the company in any case, and still had money to spend. This time, however, instead of leaving it to Lalit to select a bunch for him to choose from, he insisted on seeing a particular dancer whose fire dance – so other members of the troupe had told him – held audiences spellbound. What they had not told him was that this man was Lalit's personal enemy, and Lalit did not tell him this either.

Instead he pretended to have arranged an audition when he had not, and then reported that the fire-dancer had cancelled it. This only made Kilroy more determined, however, and at last he saw a performance given in total darkness, broken only by the flames from two brass plates which the dancer kept balanced flat on the palms of his hands – even when performing a back somersault.

It was more of an acrobatic turn accompanied by music than a piece of ballet, but Kilroy was hooked. In addition to demanding a higher salary than that of Lalit himself, the fire-dancer insisted that his performance must be distinct from the rest of the programme, that he would not take part in any other item, and would be free of direction by Lalit. Furthermore, although we already had a full-time stage-hand on the pay-roll, his personal assistant, who knew how to arrange the fire in the brass dishes, must also be taken on the pay-roll, solely for his service. Kilroy agreed to everything.

It was a mistake. He had no knowledge of the personal enmity between Lalit and the fire-dancer, but even without that the terms of this engagement would have weakened what little authority Lalit had ever had. Matters between the two came to a head one night, on an unusually prolonged tour, when everyone was tired. Suddenly, just before the interval, half-way through the show, the fire-dancer refused to go on as programmed. The practice was for his dance to bring down the curtain at this point. Now without warning he insisted that it must replace the usual last item on the programme, which featured the entire troupe – except him, as he only performed alone.

Lalit refused. The fire-dancer replied that he would not go on before the interval. Appealed to, I told the fire-dancer that the programme was Lalit's responsibility, and if he did not go on as programmed his contract was terminated. He did as he was told and by the time his contract expired, Kilroy had gone back to the Punjab, so it was not renewed.

That confrontation was the only time I recall when I acted decisively in dealing with the dancers. Their other quarrels died down as unpredictably as they arose. Jealousies, resentments and flirtations only served to keep the show on the road. Those who were not involved in them somehow absorbed and dissipated them, by the interaction of a complex web of personal relationships. First one interconnection would vibrate in response to an adjoining jangle and then another, until a temporary settlement resulted.

One hot night, however, just before the rains, when all the members of the company were at loggerheads, except for solitary Lalit who was out of touch with everybody, I made my own contribution to this process. Antagonism had never been so hectic. No sooner did a dancer come off the stage than he or she marched straight back to whoever they had been shouting at when they went on, and resumed the dispute where they had left it.

As soon as the final curtain had fallen they were all back at one another's throats, except for the *sarode* player and one of the male dancers, who were steadily collecting the costumes and jewellery, to be packed away. The *sarode* player calmly took no notice whatever, but the dancer, moving to and fro across the room, carrying costumes over one arm, stretched out his other arm whenever he passed behind his girl-friend, who was yelling at another woman, and calmly clapped his hand over her mouth. She did not turn to him to protest. She just stopped yelling, as if she had been corked, and then released the flow again as soon as he moved on.

Until then, I had always left them either to sort out their quarrels themselves or to exhaust themselves quarrelling, knowing that investigation would get me nowhere and settle nothing, and the scale of this melee rendered its investigation even more impracticable. Its scale, however, also made it impossible to ignore. Once again I saw the nonchalant dancer clap his hand over his quarrelling girl-friend's mouth, and once again she stopped quarrelling, as if upon her cue. It was all so theatrical! I decided that the way to deal with it was to play a role myself.

Silence fell around me as I drooped forwards with my elbows on my knees, and plunged my head in my hands, and I did not look up until a voice said, 'Sir, what is the matter?'

It was the voice of the nonchalant dancer. He had been the first to notice the change in me, but now others too were gathering round. 'I am a failure', I said, without looking up. 'I am responsible for you – and just look at you!'

There was silence. Then they all began to speak at once – ostensibly to one another, but entirely for my benefit. It can only have been for my benefit because nobody spoke in Bengali. The men all spoke in English. The women, lacking English, abandoned Bengali for Hindi for my benefit. It was they who took the lead. 'Look at him! See what you have done to him! And you are not worthy to clean his shoes.'

In no time everybody had joined in. People who had been yelling at each other presented themselves before me holding hands. I felt like applauding, but I had a part of my own to play, registering bewildered joy until peace reigned, and then making a pensive exit from the school-room to walk back to the *dak bungalow*.

As soon as Vatsal arrived in Shillong to take over *Our Assam*, Kilroy sent Mazhar and me off with the dancers on their first tour. It was in the Brahmaputra Valley. The only memorable event was our stay at the *dak bungalow* at Dibrugarh, which was occupied by three American enlisted men, absent from their base without leave. After a day spent quarrelling, they were hungry for fresh company when we got back in the evening, and one of them – whom the others called 'Red' – would wander uninvited into our room for a chat. His favourite topic was tropical disease. It was impossible to stay healthy in Assam. Americans who stayed more than a year there invariably died, with black spots on their livers – caused by the moist heat he assured us, but any spots on his own liver and those of his companions would have invited a different diagnosis. Prohibition had not long been repealed in America, and they thought the aim of drinking was to get drunk. Alcohol in any form would do, and they daily replenished their stock from shelf-loads of scintillating bottles on sale in a store close by, together with the ginger essence required to drown the flavour of their contents. These bottles were labelled 'whisky', 'brandy' or 'gin', and had their contents differently dyed to match resulting expectations, but all contained the same wood alcohol, distilled by an enterprising local firm which had started operation at a place called Dikhom when the Americans arrived. Their customers called it 'Dikhom Death'.

Red and his companions started on Dikhom Death before lunch, and had become quarrelsome long before dinner. Disagreement invariably mounted until it reached the point of challenges to 'come outside'. Nobody went outside. All three stayed seated, but they evidently felt that the affair had now reached a fitting climax, for silence fell, and when conversation was resumed its subject was entirely new.

'You want to know something, captain?' Red told Mazhar when we left. 'The Major here thinks you're inferior – just because you're black! But me – I think you're equal.'

Well, thanks, old boy!' drawled Mazhar.

That was our only tour together. Shortly before joining us he had eloped with his beautiful cousin Tahira, against the wishes of both their families. When he joined us, he had been uneasy at having left her in Lahore. The *fait accompli* had not softened the prime minister's disapproval of the marriage of his daughter with a communist jailbird, even though he was a nephew. Fearing that steps to separate them might be taken in his absence, Mazhar persuaded Kilroy to create a minor appointment for her, and she joined us in Shillong, but soon after our return from tour she had to go back to the Punjab because she was pregnant and Mazhar was posted back to his regiment at his own request.

Before leaving he told me that he intended to start an independent, radical periodical in Lahore after the war, but when the time came he worked instead as chief editor of *The Pakistan Times*, a daily newspaper started by Iftikar-ud-din in the newly formed state of Pakistan. Later, however, because of the early death of Iftikar and the suppression of free speech, he left that paper and did at last launch his own weekly – *Viewpoint* – to spend the rest of his life fighting bigotry, privilege and corruption, and doing it with style. In a personal tribute published in *The Guardian*, when Mazhar died in 1993, the actor Zia Mohyeddin recalled how he had been theatre critic of the *Pakistan Times*, when Mazhar was editor, and once severely criticised a production by an amateur society, who sent a deputation with alarmingly influential members to demand his dismissal. The response they got from Mazhar was that if they wanted reviews to be more favourable the thing to do was to stage better performances. 'It is a measure of the man's nobility,' Zia Mohyeddin concluded, 'that he never once mentioned this incident to me, and I heard it years later from a member of that deputation'. He might have been the original of some Moghul portrait.

His departure broke my last link with the Communist Party. As long as he was there I had felt obliged to restrict my view of Russia to admiration for the heroism of the Russian people, ignoring the brutality of their leaders, in line with the press and the BBC. Nevertheless, this became increasingly difficult, because although Soviet brutality never featured in the news it could not be excluded from reports of people whom the war had brought into direct contact with the Red Army.

The final blow to my faith was delivered by an executive of the Anglo-Iranian Oil Company, with whom I shared a railway compartment. He had just arrived from the Persian Gulf, where military supplies were being landed to be transported in heavy lorries through Iran to the Soviet Union, and as a result he was full of admiration for the way our allies managed labour. At first the lorries had arrived with tools and spares missing, but the Soviet authorities had soon put a stop to that! If any tools or spares were missing on arrival, the driver was shot. He was probably not the thief, but fear of sharing his fate made the other drivers keep a closer watch on their equipment. 'If only we could do things like that!'

12: Ups and downs

I did not inform the Party of my defection. I had already lost touch with it. As soon as I had left Shillong and was touring in the valleys I was even out of touch with Kilroy. He knew the date when I was due to return, but that was all. I was personally responsible for everything I did, and sometimes acted irresponsibly as a result. My most serious lapse was committed at a place on the north bank of the Brahmaputra in Kamrup District, called Barpeta, where during the civil disobedience movement anti-British demonstrations had been unusually persistent. It was also in the heart of the area where the immigration of land-hungry Mymensinghis from Bengal had been heaviest. In short it was the last place in Assam in which to take public peace for granted in late 1943, when I arrived there on tour there with the dancers.

I always stayed with the dancers from the time they arrived back-stage to put their make-up on until they had left the dressing-room to go to bed – except on this one occasion. As usual we were scheduled to give shows on two consecutive evenings, and the stage was erected in the compound of a school, and also as usual I was accommodated at the local *dak bungalow*. Unusually, however, this particular *dak bungalow* conveniently adjoined the school. This proximity was disastrous. After delivering my speech in the interval, leaving the artists to re-open the show I slipped away to the *dak bungalow* for a whisky. There was uproar next door as soon as I had poured it. I dashed back to find the school compound in darkness. The stage curtains were closed, the lighting had been switched off, and hundreds of outraged Assamese were tearing up the school railings.

The first item on the programme after the interval was not a dance but a one-act domestic comedy, popular in the Surma Valley but not here as it was played in Bengali, the language of the Mymensinghi immigrants. No sooner had the opening words been spoken than voices from the audience started ordering the actors to speak Assamese. The actors came to the footlights and retorted – in Bengali. The audience redoubled its interruptions. The actors threatened to close the show and – when the audience reacted with a general uproar carried out their threat, rounding everything off by switching off the lighting.

Before I could get to the stage I was confronted by a police inspector who told me that, in view of the situation we had provoked, we must leave Barpeta at once. My reaction was preposterous. I had no means of assessing the situation, but I told him that there could be no question of our leaving before we had staged the second show we had already announced. 'Then tomorrow we'll teach these bastards a lesson!' he said – in English. 'I'll send for the Assam Rifles.'

Smugly I replied that I had come to improve relations with the public, not to ruin them. His answer to this was that if I put on a public show while rejecting the protection he thought necessary he could not accept responsibility for public order, so if I went ahead I must give him a signed statement that I required no help from the police. Childishly accepting this, as if it was a dare, I immediately wrote out the disclaimer in his note-book, signed it, and went back-stage.

The *sarode* player, the drivers and the stage-hand were standing guard on our property. The orchestra had departed with their instruments, and the dancers too had fled, but luckily our local Assamese assistant was still there, so we could make an announcement in Assamese. We switched the lighting back on, the din of the crowd subsided, and switching on the microphone I took it out in front of the curtain to announce that there would be another show next day.

That done, I switched the lighting off again. I meant this as a signal to disperse, but the crowd held together and followed me back to the *dak bungalow* where, surrounding the compound on three sides, they stopped at the fence and stood there, waiting to see what would happen next. They had no programme of their own, but were not going to miss anything.

186

I decided to remain in view. If I disappeared into my room, leaving them with nothing to stare at, they would cross the fence and come up to the verandah to look at me through the windows, so telling Chhanga to move my bed on to the verandah, where everyone could see it, I slipped into my room and changed into pyjamas. Then I came out again, sent Chhanga away, and got into bed.

I have since read that sleep can serve as an alternative to hysteria in an unmanageable situation. On this occasion I fell asleep in no time, with the crowd still at the fence, and, the next thing I knew, Chhanga was waking me with morning tea, and the only people near the fence were walking past it, as they went about their morning business.

I was no sooner conscious than I was considering what I must do. The first thing was to find an unconfined public space to stage the show in. The audience was always bigger on the second night, and in this case, in view of what had happened the previous evening, a record crowd would be coming to see what happened next. Packing them back into the school compound would be asking for trouble, so with the help of our local assistant I got permission from its owner to use an area of untilled land on the outskirts of the town, and then left the usual team set about erecting a stage there as if nothing untoward had happened. But this time there would be no police so who was going to control the crowd? The answer came to me when I was on my way to address the students at the local college. I would ask them to do it.

No member of the teaching staff was present when I spoke to them, and luckily – as English was their medium of instruction – I was able to speak to them freely and directly. Citing the All India Students' Federation's declaration in my support, I spoke enthusiastically about the people's war, extolling the heroism of Tito and his partisans, before asking for volunteers to serve as stewards at the evening's show.

When I had finished, after a discussion conducted in Assamese, they replied that they would help me provided I did not address the crowd. I thanked them warmly, but explained that it was my duty to the united front against fascism to explain the situation to the masses. Perhaps they might reconsider? After all, there would be no police presence, and those who helped me would be joining forces with students throughout the world.

Again they conferred, and this time there was a split. One half still refused to help me if I spoke, but promised they would cause no trouble. The other half promised unconditional co-operation, and told me to leave everything to them. Rashly I took them at their word. I gave them no directions and arranged no rendezvous for volunteers to assemble before the show started – and, as it happened, I could not have done better. They turned up in plenty of time and, as a record crowd assembled, walked around arranging it in manageable groups, separated by open pathways. It was the best organised show we ever staged, and the crowd's behaviour was exemplary. I suppose that they were proving something. My speech was greeted with prolonged applause.

At the time I felt proud of myself, but it was not long before I realised that my behaviour could easily have led to a disaster. I had not been firm. I had been lucky. The complaint the civil authorities made against me was that my conduct had 'brought the police into disrepute'.

I feel less guilty about two other complaints made against me, although they were justified too. One was a breach of security. Passing through Gauhati on one of my tours, I visited Rohini Choudhury – the wily politician whose attempt to form a ministry had perplexed the Governor – and asked him about relations between the townsfolk and the troops. As luck would have it, he had just received a complaint from a widow about the behaviour of some *sepoys* who had broken into her house. They had done her no harm, and stolen nothing, but she had been frightened, and he was evidently going to make as much of the incident as he could. He warned me that he would be asking questions about it at the next session of the Assembly.

I asked whether he had reported it to Area H.Q and, as soon as he said that he had not, rushed him into my truck and drove him there, before he had time to think. Immediately on arrival, waving my G.H.Q. pass, I led him straight past the sentry into Area H.Q., and presented him to the Intelligence Section, where – mildly apprehensive – he made a statement which they duly promised to investigate. Whatever political use he might try to make of the matter in the Assembly, the Army could now reply that they were already in touch with him and the matter was under investigation.

In my excitement, I had forgotten that taking an unauthorised person into Area H.Q. was a breach of security – particularly serious in this case, as was pointed out, because the office I had taken him into had maps on the wall displaying troop positions. Nobody mentioned any of this to me directly. As I did not come under their command, Gauhati Area complained about my misdemeanour directly to G.H.Q. in New Delhi where at that very moment, as luck would have it, Kilroy had been recalled for consultations. My trespass, he told me on his return, had even been brought to the attention of the Member for Defence of the Viceroy's Executive Council! The latter, who was a civil servant, not a soldier, knew Rohini Choudhury of old. 'Just the way to deal with him', had been his verdict, and my error was dismissed as 'excess of zeal'.

My third offence was also a failure to give Area H.Q. their due. Without first consulting them I tried to arrange for them to make a major goodwill gesture to Assam, by bringing medical relief to Baniyachang – a 'village' in the Surma Valley, said to be 'the biggest village in the world.' This was not an enviable title. It meant that over forty thousand people were living without a proper water supply or a sewage system. But that was nothing new, so no one talked about it. Malaria was nothing new to the 'village' either. The 'villagers' had learnt to live with their local, Surma Valley brand of the disease. Away at the end of the Brahmaputra Valley, however, a different brand prevailed, and a gang of labourers, who had gone there from Baniyachang to work on the road that was being built through the jungle, brought it back with them when their contract expired. It spread fast. Precise medical statistics were not a feature of the village administration, but hundreds were credibly reported to be dying there every month, and in due course the outbreak was the subject of questions in the Assembly.

Asked what his government was doing to cope with the outbreak, Sir Syed Sa'adullah replied that death would come to every human being at the appointed time in Baniyachang, as elsewhere. He made this statement; he pointed out, because he was a Moslem and believed in *kismet*, but his questioner, although a Hindu, must agree with it because Hindus believed in *karma*, which came to the same thing in cases like this. The questioner responded by inquiring what the Prime Minister conceived to be the function of the Public Health Department, if this was so. The Public Health Department knew its duty, the Prime Minister assured him, and already had a medical officer on the spot.

Obviously a military anti-malarial squad could do a lot both for the villagers of Baniyachang and also for military-public relations, so I went there to see things for myself. The 'village' was a dozen miles away from Habiganj, a sub-divisional centre in Sylhet District already known to me. When I got there I was told that as yet the medical officer sent to the rescue of Baniyachang by the Public Health Department weeks before had got no further.

It was just after the monsoon, and Baniyachang was surrounded by miles of flood waters, but was easily reached from Habiganj by boat. Our course took us through miles of water hyacinth – 'the German flower' the boatman called them, because, as he explained when I inquired, they occupied fresh territory so quickly.

When I arrived I found the entire 'village' surrounded by stagnant water and enveloped by mosquitoes. The only medical services available were being rendered by three relief workers sent by a Hindu organization – the Ramakrishna Mission – which I already knew something about as I sometimes came across a copy of their monthly magazine – a publication so other-worldly that I was surprised to find their representatives so business-like and active. They told me that no less than fifteen hundred people had died during the two months they had been there. They were treating the sick with Ayurvedic remedies, but welcomed the possibility of assistance from a military anti-malarial squad.

I spent the night there on a string-bed, a few feet from a stretch of stagnant water. The mosquitoes were so thick in the evening air that they did not have to look for me. As long as I was in the open we just kept colliding. Chhanga set mosquito curtaining up on canes, around the bed, but when I retreated to it at an early hour I found them already inside, waiting for me.

Covered in bites, I left next morning and drove back up the Khasi Hills to Shillong and straight on down to Area Headquarters at Gauhati, in the other valley. The staff colonel I talked to pointed out that by offering the services of an army anti-malaria squad, without first ensuring that the Army was prepared to offer them, I had exceeded my authority. I saw at once that he was right and realised that the General was bound to share this view when the colonel reported my proposal to him. Sure enough, when he returned from doing so he told me that the General was not pleased. By broaching the possibility of military help in public I had made it impossible for the Army not to offer it. They would send a squad to Baniyachang as soon as the Assam Government's Director of Public Health officially requested them to do so.

Feeling very pleased with myself, I drove back up the mountain to the Secretariat in Shillong to give the Director of Public Health the good news – but that was not the way he saw it. He found the suggestion that he should ask the military for assistance preposterous. It would imply that he needed help to do his job, so there could be no question of it. In case this incident appears to be an instance of racial antipathy, like that expressed by the deputy commissioner of Nowgong, it should be noted that the Director of Public Health was a fellow-countryman of the people of Baniyachang.

13: Changing my mind

Mazhar was replaced by Abe Stewart, the mystically minded, Northern Irish Protestant captain whom I had met at Southern Army H.Q. Among the books that he brought with him was the sutra spoken by the Sixth Patriarch of Zen Buddhism. (He must have been one of the earliest western enthusiasts for Zen.) Teachers who sent their disciples away to make sense of a piece of nonsense without help attracted me and my conversion was completed when I equated the Patriarch's definition of enlightenment with absent-mindedness. Another *guru* of whom he thought highly maintained that the mind discarded its delusions, and was accordingly united with ultimate Reality, in dreamless sleep.

Although, as it was switched off, the mind was unconscious of its privilege on these occasions, this notion appealed to me. Falling asleep in the evening on tour became a deliberate enjoyment. Alone, in country places where life stopped at sunset, I would sit out on a *dak bungalow* verandah as light faded – which in India it does fast – while sounds in the foliage and the grass seemed to grow louder as it grew darker, and – in some places in the Surma Valley – women in a near-by village joined their voices to greet the approaching night with an undulating warble, like a lullaby. Its purpose was to drive away evil spirits I was told, when I inquired, but fear was the last response that it invited. In spite of the mosquitoes I would stay out there until dinner, after which I would go to bed and start to read, confident that, as the light cast by an oil lamp through the mosquito netting was not really strong enough to read by for long, I would soon have extinguished first it and then my mind.

In Habiganj I always spent the evening with the headmistress of the local girls' school. I was interested in Miss Thomas the minute I was warned against her by the head of a Welsh non-conformist mission. He had been toiling in the Surma

Valley for many years, and it was the first time I had toured there intensively, so I was keen to hear anything that he could tell me about it. All I now recall, however – apart from his disappointment when he realised I was not in search of spiritual advice – was his warning. If I ever went to Habiganj I must be on my guard against 'an evil woman' who lived there – by name Miss Thomas – who was headmistress of the girls' school. She had come out to India to be a missionary, but had given it up and was now so evil that recently when she fell ill not a single Christian had visited her! Only Moslems and Hindus had!

The details, when I pressed him for them, were disappointing. Miss Thomas had come out from Wales to join the Mission in the early 'twenties, and had duly spread the gospel for two years. Things only went wrong when she was temporarily transferred to a mission school for girls, to stand in for a teacher who had gone on leave. When the time came for her to return to evangelising, she had insisted on remaining a teacher, so stubbornly that in the end she had to be dismissed. As she had no personal income she should then have gone back to Wales, but instead of doing so she had stubbornly opened an elementary school for girls in Habiganj, somehow maintaining herself on the fees paid by the parents.

Had she been back to Wales at all since then, I asked. 'Oh no!' His tone suggested that God was not mocked. 'The fees she gets are just enough to keep her where she is.' Now in her forties, Miss Thomas had not seen Wales since she arrived in India in her twenties. The school fees, her only income, were just enough for her to live plainly in a small thatched house with a fenced garden. Thanks to local support and government grants, however, her school was now an extensive set of buildings in extensive grounds, with over seven hundred pupils. It had ceased to be an elementary school. The pupils were taught up to School Certificate level, and the teaching staff were all ex-pupils. Parents, who had at first sent their daughters only to learn to read and write, had been persuaded

A Surma Valley River ferry

A Surma Valley road bridge

in increasing numbers to allow them to stay on to matriculate. Some had then gone on to colleges.

She was locally admired and liked, but that did not stop her from feeling lonely. Over the long school holidays, during the hot weather, a local planter used to invite her to stay with him and relax in what to her was luxury. He too deserves commemoration. I met him once and cannot think he found her company congenial, but all I remember about him is that he was a bachelor with a big moustache – a fact that her ex-colleagues must have made a meal of.

As it was, however, all they could accuse her of was irreligion, and it was true that she had lost confidence in conversion, and had told them so. When they took her with them to show her how it was done, no matter what questions they were asked they were always sure they knew the answer. She was not. It wasn't that she was not a Christian, she explained – although the desirability of the crucifixion did sometimes escape her, and she envied Hindus their easy way of living on two planes at once.

She also envied Moslems their certainty that there was always an identifiable action waiting to be done, a belief I once saw in operation in another little town in the Surma Valley, called Karimganj. Two starving orphan children had somehow begged their way there from famine-stricken Bengal. Karimganj did not boast a school like Miss Thomas's, but two middle-aged British maiden ladies ran a mission there, and many people told me, admiringly, how the missionaries had taken the orphans in and fed and clothed them, tended their fevers and healed their sores. The next time I arrived there however, the missionaries were a source of discord. They had grown so attached to the orphans that they had made an application to the sub-divisional officer for their legal adoption, and the Moslem elders had protested. If they were adopted by Christian missionaries, the children, who must undoubtedly be of Moslem parentage, would be deprived of their true faith. The Sub-divisional Officer, who was himself a Moslem, had asked the missionaries whether, if they adopted them, they would undertake to bring the children up as Moslems, and they had refused. What was he to do? As he explained to me, as a Moslem he could not separate the children from their faith, but neither in all conscience could he deprive them of a home. What was my opinion?

I said I did not know, and went my way. A week later, however, when I was on my way back to Shillong through Karimganj, the Sub-divisional Officer told me that his problem had been solved. He had sat with the two children standing before him, and the two missionaries and the Moslem elders standing on either side of him, facing each other. It must have been a scene to match the judgement of Solomon – or Suleiman, as Moslems call him. First he had asked the elders which of them would take these children into his family and raise them as his own. None of them had responded. Then he put the same question to the missionaries. He did not ask me whether I approved. The elders had left him no alternative.

Rab Nawaz, the Afridi bus-driver, was deeply appreciative of the freedom conferred by having no alternative – what Iqbal called the 'the gold chain of the law'. Just before he joined us he had been a civilian driver with the Royal Indian Navy in Bombay, and naval regulations were so inflexible that he treasured the memory. No matter what you might have done, if you had not broken a specific regulation you knew for certain that you were in the clear, and if you had infringed one, no matter what the explanation, it was no use arguing. The law would take its course. The punishment prescribed would be inflicted. And as a result you always knew exactly where you were.

During his service in Bombay he had seen some Russians. Their faces were hairless, pale and sad – quite different from the faces of the Russians he had seen twenty years ago, just after the last war against the Germans, when he had been a driver at Baku with the British counter-revolutionary army of intervention. In those days Russians were jolly, red-faced men with whiskers. When I asked him why there should be such a difference now, and he told me it was because Russians did not now believe in God.

'Why not?' I asked. I remember his answer almost word-for-word.

'When the Communists came to power they made a law that all people must stop worshipping God immediately. Their leader, a man called Leninji, was very strict. Anyone who disobeyed his commands was put to death, no matter how important they might have been before the Revolution, so as soon as the Archbishop his Holiness learned of this order he fled from Moscow'. (He told his tale in Urdu, but every time he mentioned the Archbishop he referred to him as 'his Holiness', using the English words.)

'After many days his Holiness arrived in a village thousands of miles away from Moscow, and asked the villagers to hide him. The villagers still believed in God, but they also knew that Leninji had eyes everywhere and if he got to know that the village was sheltering his Holiness, he would put them all to death. On the other hand, however, if they surrendered his Holiness to Leninji the sky would fall. At any rate, so they thought then'.

'While they were still debating, a telegram arrived from Leninji. He had found out where his Holiness was staying and ordered them to kill him, so they had to make their minds up quickly. It was the oldest man in the village who worked out how to handle it'.

'First they took a length of rope, and tied one end of it to his Holiness while the other end was fastened to a stone. Then they rowed him out to where the lake was deepest, and the wise old man told them to lower his Holiness in, feet first, while someone kept a look-out on the sky. When the water came up to his Holiness's waist, the wise old man told those who held the rope to wait while the look-out scanned the sky, but he saw no sign of breakage, so the wise old man told them to go on lowering'.

'When the water reached his Holiness's shoulders, they stopped again to give the look-out time to see how things were in the sky, but still he could see nothing wrong there, so they lowered him in until the water came up to his chin, and still the sky showed no sign of falling, so – "Right, lads!" the wise old man cried. "Throw the stone in quick, and row back to the shore!"

'So that was the end of the Archbishop his Holiness and the sky stayed where it was – which is why nobody in Russia believes in God now.' Rab Nawaz paused. 'Some people believe in God,' he said reflectively, 'and some do not.'

'How about you?' I asked him. 'Without doubt', he answered placidly. 'Am I not a Moslem?'

Despite their reverence for the letter of the law, Moslems exempted poets and madmen from its strict operation because they had been 'touched' by God. This was first explained to me when I attended a recital by an Urdu poet. The listeners were served soft drinks, but the poet was supplied with a bottle of scotch. (His audience, however, were compensated. He repeated each line before speaking the next one, so that it could be sipped.)

The privilege of the insane was exercised by a citizen of Karimganj who believed himself to be the monarch of Assam. The first time I arrived there he paid me a visit, as he did to every visitor, to bid me welcome to the *dak bungalow*. On one occasion when I was there the Prime Minister also paid Karimganj a visit, and the Sub-Divisional Officer arranged a garden party for him to meet the local notables. Far from excluding the King he set him up in state with a private table on the verandah – as it would be improper for him to mix too freely with his subjects – and still arranged for him to descend to the lawn and mix informally with them for a while. Sir Mohammed consulted him with perfect gravity.

14: Personalities

Before the end of 1943 Kilroy had left Assam, taking the staff captain with him. Recruitment was flagging in the Punjab, and G.H.Q. had decided this was another public threat to the Army for the Section to attend to. He was glad to go. His heart was in the Punjab, but that was not the only reason. Although he had selected us himself, his officers in Assam were not congenial company for him. If he had made a boon companion of me, keeping his whisky ration in store with mine when I was away on tour, for us to drink together when I got back, that only showed how starved he was for company.

His successor was another Irishman, but unlike Kilroy a Catholic. 'You'll like him', he assured me. 'They hanged his uncle at the Castle'. This was true enough, but it would have been more helpful to tell me that, when he succeeded to his Irish title, Randal Plunkett, our new C.O. would be the twentieth of a line of Norman barons. Once we had seen him, however, there was no need to tell us that. With a head like a falcon and a body like a race horse he was clearly thoroughbred.

Kilroy's replacement had to be another Irishman, Abe commented, because only an Irishman could apologise for the English convincingly, but I doubt whether Colonel Plunkett saw the need for an apology. One evening during the hand-over he did join Kilroy in singing Irish rebel songs, but the way he did it reminded me of an officer from a Scottish regiment whom I had heard singing 'I belong to Glasgow'. He sang it in a way which made it clear that he did no such thing.

Out into the daylight marched our squadrons and platoons
Four-and-twenty fighting men and a couple of stout gossoons –
he sang, but then broke off to comment professionally that, well led, just such an outfit could do serious damage.

His father, Lord Dunsany, was a celebrated writer who wrote to suit himself and, to judge from one or two reminiscences his son let drop, he lived in the same way. I remember his son telling us that when in hospital during the early days of electricity the poet kept an air pistol under his pillow to shoot the light out when he wished to go to sleep. Plunkett himself, however, was such a flawless model officer and a gentleman that he had featured in a short propaganda film about the role of the Indian Army in the Western Desert, when he was serving there.

The courtesy that went with this conformity enabled him to settle down smoothly enough with a bolshy, a bohemian and a blue-stocking – all of us, that is, except Vatsal, who was still quartered where the dancers used to be, and only visited our bungalow on duty. The blue-stocking was our new staff captain – Muriel Da Costa, a junior-commander of the Women's Auxiliary Corps. Like Abe she came from Southern Army H.Q. in Bangalore. I had met her when I was there, but found her too formidable to get to know. She weighed her words so well, and spoke them so deliberately. Nevertheless, she laughed easily. Moreover the Tamilian *ayah* she had brought with her made genuine *milagu-tannir* – the South Indian begetter of 'mulligatawny' – to serve as a starter at every evening meal.

She was a Goan graduate of Oxford, and her taste in literature was irredeemably European, witness a whimsical piece she wrote for *Our Assam*, when Vatsal was away on leave. It told how, wandering on the hills one day, the writer had met a two-legged creature that was half man, half goat, playing a flute. Despite the helpful substitution of a flute for a syrinx, her Assamese readers must have found this report puzzling.

And yet, who knows? *Fauji Akbar*, an Indian Army monthly for *sepoys*, contained a regular feature in which a wise man called Socrates gave tips on agriculture and hygiene to a circle of Indian villagers. 'How many *sepoys* does the name of Socrates mean anything to?' I snorted to Vatsal.

The question was rhetorical, but he answered that in the Punjab the word 'Socrates' was still alive and well, after arriving there in the army of Alexander the Great. A *sokrat* was a pithy talker, who was worth listening to, as distinct from a wind-bag or *flatun* – otherwise Plato.

Evenings with Plunkett, when I was back in Shillong from tour, passed no more awkwardly than they had done with Kilroy, but he fell short of Kilroy in his conception of the Section's role. For him it was inconceivable that it mattered what the public – anywhere and of whatever race – thought. The only people whose opinions mattered were a select few who were in no need of instruction. They had the right opinions automatically.

Once Kilroy had left, instead of getting out into the villages, Plunkett took me with him on an extended tour of the Brahmaputra Valley to meet military commanders – first the Indian Army Area-Commander at Gauhati, then sub-area commanders, and finally the commanders of United States bases. Whenever he entered a U.S. base the sentry failed to salute him. He was and looked astounded every time. On the one occasion when an American sentry did give him a salute, however, he was even more astounded and failed to return it.

The only person who positively offended him, however, was one of the dignitaries he insisted on visiting – the Anglican bishop of Assam. At the end of our interview with him, he accompanied us onto his verandah to say goodbye, and raised his hand in blessing, when we stepped down onto the lawn to go. 'I call that a confounded liberty!' Plunkett said to me, as soon as we were out of ear-shot.

Whatever his rating of a Protestant blessing may have been, he was perfectly free of race prejudice, regarding it as vulgar. An American officer from the deep South, complaining that he and his kind were accused of colour prejudice unjustly, told us how well-disposed they really were to Afro-Americans, and then launched into a peroration: 'Let them worship in their own churches, study at their own schools, sit in their own cinemas and dance with their own whores. Who wants to stop them? We just don't want to have them worshipping at our churches, studying at our schools, sitting in our cinemas and …' He tailed off lamely, catching Plunkett's remorseless eye fixed on him sideways, like a bird's.

Not far from the bishop's bungalow was a tea-garden that I always visited when I was in the area, because the manager talked so freely about what was going on around him. I took care to visit him before lunch, when he was still half sober. Thanks to the German invasion of the Soviet Union, he was able to afford a limitless supply of gin. During the previous world war he had served in Russia with a detachment of the Royal Flying Corps before the Bolshevik revolution, and been awarded a czarist Russian decoration for gallantry. Before he could benefit from the generous pension that went with it, however, the Revolution had abolished it. In order to revive old-fashioned patriotism however Stalin had now re-instituted it, and unlike most of its other recipients this planter was still alive to receive the pension. He was already unsteady, although we visited him before lunch, and idiotically I found this amusing. Plunkett had a more just sense of merit. It saddened him.

Another planter, whose garden was situated on the edge of an American airfield, told us of an Indo-American culture clash, involving a miserable cow. A couple of officers he had got to know dropped in for a drink, and casually mentioned that on their way there they had used their pistols to put a sad-looking cow out of its misery, thus combining criminal damage with sacrilege. He could not conceal his alarm. His guests were startled and when they got back to base returned to the carcase with cans of petrol to immolate the evidence.

Throughout this lengthy tour we did not address a single gathering. We had not brought any sound equipment. Had we done so we would have been travelling in a fifteen-hundredweight truck, because the wear and tear of touring with a generator and public address system had already proved

The Brahmaputra River ferry

Ferry across the Brahmaputra

too much for our new station-wagons. On this tour, however, we travelled from place to place in comfort in the staff car, and in public kept our mouths shut.

It was as well we had nothing heavier than a car, because the next leg of Plunkett's tour involved being ferried across the Brahmaputra. It was often necessary to cross a minor river when travelling in Assam. Village roads passed over flexible bamboo bridges, which were stronger than they looked, bending under the weight of a truck without breaking – like the reed in the fable – and springing back to be as they had been before, when it had passed over. Sometimes, however, there was a ferry which was poled across – a stout wooden deck mounted athwart two country boats. Built to carry agricultural produce in bulk, the country-boats were buoyant enough for this contraption to carry a bus with all its passengers.

It was on a make-shift craft of this kind, but powered with the engine of a truck, that we crossed the Brahmaputra. The bank we had left was out of sight when we disembarked, because the monsoon had only just ended, and the river was in flood. Why Plunkett wished to visit the Eastern end of the North bank of the Brahmaputra he did not explain. There were no generals there for him to introduce himself to, and the North bank had no military significance East of Barpeta and the railway ferry. (There was no bridge). Perhaps it was the simple fact that none of us had been there yet that spurred him.

Tezpur, half-way along the North bank, where we landed, was the farthest east that I had been along it, and I had only gone there to appoint an assistant. Without bothering to take the assistant, we now set off further East. Plunkett had no use for an interpreter because he did not make a single speech.

In any case, there was no call for one. The sparse population of this area could panic endlessly without doing any military damage, and if one could forget the war the countryside was worth a visit. Crossing tributaries flowing down into the Brahmaputra from the mountains of Bhutan, we shared poled ferries with traders in huge felt hats, who – so we were told – were walking to Calcutta with uncut gems, for sale to diamond merchants.

On the first evening we stopped at a tea-estate. Then we crossed the boundary into the Sadiya Frontier Tract – a tribal area, supervised by a political officer. It was just the kind of region where Kilroy had decided that our services were not required, but the political officer was glad to turn his office into a tourist bureau. He was as much at home with the local people as he was in the Surrey atmosphere of his comfortable two-storey house where he lived with his wife and teen-age daughter, and could not stop talking about his tribes. Soon after his arrival in the early 'twenties, there had been a feud between two tribes inhabiting the same valley, involving violent deaths, so he had gone there and summoned the leading men of both tribes to a peace conference. So many who had every right to be heard desired to speak, and spoke so long, that this lasted a whole week. Every speaker had so much to say, even when it had been said already. The whole of the last day was taken up by the speech of just one very old man, who recounted every incident in detail, from the first disagreement up to that very morning, and finished by declaring: 'So there is only one way to bring peace back here. Despatch a runner to the Queen and ask her to send redcoats. Every member of the other tribe – men women and children – must be slain.'

I was not surprised at the trust in Queen Victoria evident in this appeal. She was a mythical figure in India. Listening once, while an assistant supposedly translated words I had just spoken, I had once been struck by the frequent appearance among unrecognisable words of one that sounded like her name and also by the reverence which it received when it was spoken. Later, I asked him whether he had brought Queen Victoria into what he had to say. 'Oh, yes. I told them that the British are of the same race as the great Queen,' he answered, 'and Japan is therefore sure to be defeated.'

The belief that the Great Queen was still alive when the political officer held his pow-wow was not surprising. The Great Queen had been dead for only twenty years, and the area was remote. What was surprising was that the tribesfolk imagined her to be installed somewhere so near that she could be reached by runner. The sense that Queen Victoria was closely involved in India's history was general. I was told more than once, as if it was a well-known fact, that she used to spend six months of every year in India, and presented portraits of herself to all the Circuit Houses she had stayed at, where they could still be seen. There were also innumerable statues of her. Shortly after India became independent some of these were sold to Caribbean islands to be installed in celebration of the centenary of the abolition of slavery. The Indian authorities concerned, were glad to see the last of them. Their presence in the cities of independent India was politically incorrect. Nevertheless, their removal was controversial. In Allahabad, the citadel of the Congress Party, removal of her statue was effected surreptitiously by night, with an armed force standing by in case of a riot.

The Political Officer's contact with tribal people still extended into northern areas of Burma, where the Japanese were not in total occupation. The commandant of a near-by U.S. fighter base invited all of us to dinner. His squadron was flying sorties to protect the transport planes that flew supplies to China over the Hump.[11] Half-way through the meal the Political Officer asked after one of the pilots who was not present. Silence fell, and then he was told that two days ago the missing man had been lost over Burma. His engine had failed and he had come down a long way from the border, so there was no hope for him. Angry because he had not been told before, the Political Officer immediately left the table, and two days later the missing man was on his way to rejoin the squadron.

This incident may have fired Plunkett's imagination, because no sooner were we back in Shillong than he decided to send me to the Naga hills to visit Miss Bower[12], a British anthropologist generally referred to as 'the Naga Queen'. Her influence with the Nagas, among whom she had lived many years, was legendary and contributed to the Japanese defeat, but it was hard to see how a visit from me would help her. Plunkett seemed to regard a visit as a good thing in itself. 'What do I say when I get there?', I inquired. 'Miss Bower, I presume?' 'Eventually he gave in.

When the Japanese invaded Manipur the hilly district of Cachar on the South-eastern border of Assam was under threat, so we went there with the dancers to steady civilian morale. Rumours of Japanese successes, many of them true, abounded, and our presence was undeniably useful. The performances were staged in the evening, and it would also have been even more useful to spend the daylight hours visiting bazaars, as this time we had a truck and sound equipment. Instead, Plunkett preferred visiting again, driving out in the direction of the fighting in a borrowed jeep, and taking me with him. I remember driving away after a chat with an outpost that had recently encountered soldiers of Subhas Chandra Bose's Indian National Army. With delighted horror he commented on the gaiety with which they had told us how easy it had been to shoot their would-be liberators as they rushed towards them through the trees, shouting, 'Don't shoot! We are brothers!' 'Did you notice how they showed their teeth?' he gloated, as we drove away. 'Murderous thugs!' So were the Japanese I reflected. Local people who had gone out into the jungle with a young civil servant I had met in Shillong had returned without him, reporting that he had been captured and decapitated.

Behind the northern sector of the Manipur battle-field, the Brahmaputra Valley was threatened too, so the dancers went there next. Abe Stewart and I both went with them. The Japanese invasion was reaching its climax, so it was a good time for military officers to show themselves in places where soldiers were not otherwise to be seen. Japanese successes were undeniable, so we spread the word that they had over-reached themselves. Our only source of military information was the public radio, but we spoke as people in the know because we were in uniform. The principal rumour we had to counter, however, had nothing to do with the military situation. It was a piece of sooth-saying. Word was spreading that the Mahabharata, the ancient Hindu epic, contained a prophecy that people who lived below the earth – which obviously meant the Japanese – would one day enter India from the East and conquer it.

Returning at last to Shillong I found Plunkett eager for another visit. He went off to the field of battle, leaving me behind to take his place at headquarters. A fortnight later, however, he returned with a plan for me to join in the campaign directly. The tide of battle was now turning, but instead of surrendering, or even retreating, the Japanese were staying put and fighting to the death. 'It's some sort of knightly code they have, apparently', someone had said. Plunkett clearly expected me to give full marks for his reply. 'Yes. I believe it's called *Bullshido*.' I did not grudge him them.

His plan for me to join the struggle was also to his credit. As the main obstacle to our advance was Japanese morale, a weapon to deal with morale had to be found, and on his way back to Shillong it had occurred to him that the answer was our sound equipment. It could broadcast spoken messages in Japanese loudly enough for them to be heard at a distance which would not be suicidal. I was therefore to report to 4 Corps H.Q., complete with sound equipment, and volunteer my services. The prospect of engaging the enemy directly made me tense but satisfied me. I got my pistol and ammunition out and two days later, when I reported at 4 Corps H.Q., and Plunkett's scheme appealed to them, I was agog. Before the day was over, however, they had rejected it. It would be too risky – for their Japanese-speakers. They had only two, and there was no equipment to record the message.

By the time the Japanese had been pushed back into Burma, Plunkett had left us, and Abe Stewart was promoted from captain to major, and appointed to replace him – to his embarrassment, although I saw it as a stroke of luck. In the event, the question of seniority never arose between us when he was in charge, and had only done so once when I was.

That happened on our tour of the Brahmaputra Valley with the dance troupe, when the threat of Japanese invasion was at its height. Abe's Urdu was better than mine, so he was the one who used to address the audience half-way through the show. On this occasion, however, someone started shouting that the Japanese were on their way and nothing was going to stop them. Other voices joined in. Abe's voice grew softer, as he tried to reason with them, but in response their tone grew more aggressive, and I sensed that the situation was about to explode. They felt that they could bully him, so I strode out from the wings to bully them instead and, asserting my rank, took the microphone from him, with the air of a man on the point of doing something terrible.

Silence fell. Perhaps, when I broke it with the assistance of the amplifier, they thought I was going to order them to disperse. Instead I thundered ridicule of anyone who dreamed the Japanese had any hope of victory. There was total silence when my bluster ceased. Then, after a pause while I remained standing there, as if challenging anyone to say something, the curtain went up behind me at Abe's prompting, the orchestra began to play, and the incident was forgotten in the entertainment.

Abe, who at the time had told me mildly that he thought my intervention had been mistaken, never did anything like that to me when our positions were reversed. Under his unassuming leadership the Section lost all semblance of a military unit. For the first time since we arrived in Shillong I would rather be there than be on tour. As no new officer had been appointed to replace Abe when Abe replaced Plunkett, there was now room for Vatsal to join us in the bungalow. We invited young Indian civil servants, whom we had previously met, if at all, only in their offices, and soon they were dropping in casually, inviting us to their homes or to the Indian club.

There were also unexpected European visitors. One was George Scurfield, who had been a fellow party member in Cambridge. I no longer remember how he found me. It was not thanks to the Party. He had never even tried to contact them. Each of us was reassured to find that the other had reneged, but there the resemblance between us ceased. He had been seconded to the Chin Levies – a force of irregulars that engaged the Japanese in close combat. 'What is it like?' It was a silly question but I could not help asking it. I had known him as the mildest of men. He replied that he had no idea what it was like. The last thing he could remember, until it was all over, was ordering the attack.

Michael Stratton,[13] another friend on leave from active service, had been a fellow cadet in Bangalore, whom Morris and I had known well enough to trust him with the secret of our Party membership. (When he was told he did not seem surprised.) Now he commanded a mule company on the Burma Front, where he had behaved with exemplary discipline. The campaign which ended in the Indian Army's disorderly retreat from Burma had opened with the despatch of reinforcements there, which included his company. The main body entered Burma by road, but Michael and his slow-moving mules were ordered to make their way on their own along hill tracks. As a result they did not receive the order to retreat when the others did. They did meet troops going back to India, whose officers kept urging him go back too, but he would not do so, continuing on towards the advancing enemy until an officer of field rank ordered him – in writing – to go back.

Michael, who was convalescing from infantile paralysis, told me nothing about this, but had a score of anecdotes about another ex-cadet – the anarchic Comber. Now a captain in charge of a supply depot, he was still an active satirist. Among a dozen Comber anecdotes was one about an inspection by a staff colonel, who found the depot unhygienic. Even when he was getting into his jeep to be driven away, he had to point to empty cans lying in a corner of the compound and explode: 'Good God, Comber! Look at that!'

'Good God sir, yes!' Comber drew his pistol and fired. 'Sorry, sir', he apologised, when his visitor asked whether he was mad. 'But you seemed so excited, I thought you must have seen a Jap.' None of us had ever met the intelligence officer who dropped in one afternoon and stayed for tea. He said that he had read about us in reports and felt a kinship, as he was a socialist too. We treated him politely – but he kept coming back. This seemed to us suspicious at the time, but it now occurs to me that we had taken to serving teas with whisky, as none of us cared for whisky drowned in soda. ('No *sahib*', Chhanga warned me, when I asked for rum in my tea. 'Rum is for coffee.')

Muriel Da Costa missed these tea parties. She had been posted away. The middle-aged Indian prince who had replaced her as staff captain missed them too. He had been welcomed on his arrival in Shillong into a poker-playing set. We saw little of him even in the morning, as his duties, as he conceived them, were completed as soon as he had opened the incoming mail with his handsome paper knife. After viewing each communication severely through his horn-rimmed spectacles, and reflecting on it, he would write the words – 'C. O. to see' on it, and place it in his out-tray, until at last he had given them all this treatment, and could bang his bell to have them taken away.

Free now until next morning he would stroll off, singing a snatch of song which I have never heard on other lips, but must have been popular in the 'twenties, when he was sowing wild oats in London in the company of Bertie Wooster. I heard this every day when I was back in Shillong from tour, and can still hear it. He had a rich, deep voice. It went like this -

Hello. . . mellow. . . .cello!
Mellow. . .cello . . .hello!

When we were notified that a Prince of Oudh had been posted to us, Abe had looked forward to extending his knowledge of Indian classical music. The royal family of Oudh had been famous patrons, and indeed the Prince complained that his father had bequeathed a sum to pay for his favourite *rag* to be played daily at his tomb at the appropriate hour.[14] The son's aesthetic tastes, however, were strictly Western. His favourite poet, he confided, was Omar Khayyam, but the original was not worth the bother. Fitzgerald was better: we could take his word for it. 'Oh, the brave music of a *distant* drum!' – he frequently repeated, with marked emphasis.

One part of his ancestral heritage did remain with him, however – a flair for chess. When he spent the evening in the bungalow with us, he sometimes gave me a game, drinking copiously, munching raw onions and winning effortlessly. If I pondered my move for any length of time he fell into a reverie, after which, when I reminded him that it was his move, he reviewed the position on the board with curiosity, as if what he saw there was unexpected.

One day it must have been, because during one of his reveries, instead of moving one of my pieces that was still on the board I moved a couple that he had taken back onto it. 'Good Lord!' he said, when I reminded him that it was his move – and made one that undid everything that I had done.

15: Race relations

In the spring of 1945 we were ordered to pack up. The 14th Army had entered Burma, so we no longer served any purpose. What purpose had we ever served? It was not thanks to us that Assamese civilians had stayed put, when the Japanese seemed on the point of invading. In retrospect I doubt whether there ever had been much likelihood of their abandoning their fields. The refugees who fled from Burma had been the immigrant Indian population, not the indigenous Burmese peasantry. Nor would I claim that we did much to prevent friction between soldiers and civilians, although sometimes we did do something to repair relations when an incident had soured them. The most effective protection against military harassment was the presence of the British Military Police. In 1944 I began to hear of incidents in which they had come to the rescue of civilians in the Brahmaputra Valley, and villagers started asking me to arrange for the white soldiers with red hats to be posted near them. Red-caps sometimes even intervened in cases involving troops of other nationalities. A notable example of this I came across occurred when a Chinese force, on its way to Burma, camped in the grounds of the historic Hindu temple at Sibsagar and cooked meat there. In vain the Hindu Sub-Divisional officer, who told me about this, had explained to the Chinese commander the offence which he and his men had unintentionally committed, and suggested a more suitable camp-site, but the Chinese commander took no notice, until the sub-divisional officer turned for help to a British Military Police sergeant, assisted by one private, who had been posted there,

What the Section might possibly claim to have done in Assam was personify the government in places where it lacked other personal representation. It may have been an alien government, but that was the kind of government the people were used to, and conditions would have been much worse if it had not enjoyed a reasonable degree of confidence at a critical time. The population may not have found the administration's performance satisfactory, but at least they believed that it was trying – and in areas remote from district centres this impression was due in some measure to us.

Administrative disasters did occur, but the agencies of government retained their credibility. Even before the war, as Short complained, the increase in the routine duties of district officers separated them from the people in their care. In Assam the presence of troops and the famine in neighbouring Bengal multiplied this burden, because in addition to their already heavy duties – which included judicial duties – district officers now had to organise rationing, assist in the procurement of local labour for military works, keep an eye on grain procurement, and prevent the illegal movement of foodstuffs.

These new duties did not merely increase the administrative burden. Their execution caused disquiet. Constraints which the administration had to impose, although beneficial, were resented because they were unheard of, and sometimes created new wrongs that might escape a district officer's attention. The information we brought back from our excursions can have done no more than supplement information that he already had, and our readiness to listen to a specific complaint did not inevitably remove its cause, but what we did do was still useful. We demonstrated official concern. In short, we were the government of India's *tamasha-wallah*s.

Our *tamasha* was at its most spectacular when, as happened several times, people at a village meeting accused the shopkeeper of falsely declaring that his supply of rationed produce had run out when the truth was that he had hidden it for sale on the black market. The invariable response of the shopkeeper to this was an invitation for me to search his premises, which – protesting that I had no authority for this – I would proceed to do. At first I undertook this in grim earnest, but it did not take me long to realise that these performances were theatre too. If the shopkeeper had indeed hidden stores somewhere, his shop was not where he had done so. Even so, I put a lot into these performances, sternly pointing to sacks and boxes and ordering them to be opened, while the suspicious crowd watched every movement eagerly. When the curtain fell the shopkeeper's customers were at least happy that he had been threatened, and felt that the government was on their side.

This last fact was by no means self-evident. Controls intended to preserve the supply of essential commodities sometimes seemed designed to make things worse. In the case of salt, for example, a government attempt to eliminate the black market by flooding the open market with all available supplies produced the opposite effect. The black market swallowed the lot. 'Why does the government do these things to us?', I was asked in one village. 'First they stopped opium and now they have stopped salt.' (Opium was freely available in the rest of India, but in Assam, where opium addiction had once been a serious problem, its supply had been gradually reduced to zero, bit by bit, year by year, during the years preceding the war.)

Villagers viewed attempts to control their own market operations as an abuse of power. When the Assam government banned the carriage of fruit and vegetables across the Bengal border – in order to prevent the importation of the Bengal shortage, the indignation in the Surma Valley at the arrest of boats defying this ban arose from a belief that in this instance the administration was exceeding its authority, and villagers I talked with made it clear to me that smuggling would continue. Looking back, and bearing in mind that I was an alien ruler, I am surprised by the frankness of these complaints. The good that we did was to listen, so if Short was correct in his belief that listening was half the battle, we half fulfilled our mission.

Besides listening, we explained. In addition to their legitimate complaints, the Assamese had some reasons to be thankful to the administration. It may not have protected them from the consequences of war completely, but it did mitigate them. Above all, it prevented the famine then raging next door in Bengal from spreading to Assam.

That life remained viable for the civilian population was due to unremitting and devoted effort by isolated officials. I often called on a recent Oxford graduate who had been posted to Assam on completion of his Indian Civil Service training. He was a Parsi with a passion for European classical music, named Rustomji. The crown prince of Sikkim had been his fellow student on the civil service course, and as India's emissary in the kingdom of Sikkim he later played an important role in securing India's north-eastern frontier, but when I knew him he was a novice, in charge of a sub-division of Sylhet District. Nevertheless he was responsible for the welfare of more than a million people. Although belonging to the other side of India, he already spoke Sylheti fluently, and I remember the disgust with which he told me how a minister of the provincial government, himself a Sylheti, had professed – in English – his inability to understand what 'these people' were 'trying to say', when they stopped to talk to labourers during an inspection tour of work on a new airfield. After a day spent on the move, deliberately sharpening his soft voice to inspect, direct and check, Rustomji would return in the evening to his bungalow, to play his violin and listen to his records. Measured against his responsibilities my activities were trivial, but people assumed that I must be somebody important because I was a *sahib* in uniform and – just because they did assume it – they were right up to a point.

Regrettably I must confess that I myself came to believe it too. Once, shortly after arriving in a remote rest house on the edge of jungle, I was visited by a burly Bengali in riding kit, who claimed to be a forestry official. With glowing eyes he announced that a tiger had just killed a villager, and he was going after it that evening. Would I care to join him after dinner? He had an elephant ready waiting, and two powerful electric torches.

With a show of regret I informed him that I had no gun – but he had already thought of that, and procured one for me. At that point I should have told him that he would do better without me as I had never as much as shot a rabbit, but I made my eyes light up instead, and thanked him warmly. As a *sahib* I felt that I had no choice. At the appointed time, however, he came back to tell me of a change in the arrangements. We would be going on foot. The elephant had fallen sick. The torches, however, were still in good order. At that point I did have enough sense to cry off – but it was not until years later that common sense made me to realise that the whole thing must have been a hoax. At the time I could not imagine that an Indian might pull my leg – unless he was a friend.

It was pulled often enough, however, by the young Indian civil servants whom I had got to know in Shillong. Their sense of the privilege they were conferring on Abe and me by inviting us to their club was quite as great as anything their British counterparts enjoyed when they invited Indian guests to the European club. I had often heard the phrase 'these people' applied derogatively to Indians. Now I heard it applied in the same way to the British.

Not that these bright young men spared their own people. In particular they were contemptuous of the puritanism that had accompanied the rise of national feeling. Film censorship ensured that, while the hero and heroine would never even kiss they might writhe with passion to music. My most memorable encounter with this handicap came in Gauhati when I was urgently summoned to the bar library to witness a military atrocity then in progress. The library overlooked the river bank, and taking me to a window the pleaders who had summoned me pointed, with noticeably trembling fingers, to *sepoy*s on the bank carrying laundry to help washerwomen.

This affliction, although widespread in India, had been imported from Britain. The two facts about Indian religions known to all Europeans were that Moslem men were allowed five wives each and that Hinduism sponsored child marriages. Observers on the spot in India, troubled by the presence in the public streets of unashamed eunuchs or the depiction of sex without shame in temple carvings, expressed their disturbance in print. There was still indignation in India in the forties at one such work that had been published twenty years previously – Katharine Mayo's *Mother India*. One response was to return such abuse by denunciation of the lascivious West, but the most natural one was to claim an unnatural purity.

Unique other-worldliness was the other feature in the national self-image that the young officials scoffed at. The last thing they wanted was to yield the prize for efficiency to the West. Unfortunately, however, Indian spirituality had been extolled in the West itself, as the sign of an enviable superiority. The early history of the Indian National Congress is intertwined with that of Theosophy, and Gandhi's chosen weapon was 'soul force'.

16: Peacetime

Away in the Punjab Kilroy was still in overall command of the Section. He had already sent for the dance troupe, and when we closed down in Assam he ordered us to join him there too. He had established his headquarters at Jullundur, not far from Amritsar, the site of the Golden Temple of the Sikhs. Vatsal and I drove there in a little convoy, with the staff car and the trucks. Both towns lie on the Grand Trunk Road, as did Kilroy's headquarters so, after arriving in Calcutta by rail, we had a straight drive of a thousand miles up it. Every night the sun set later by the clock, until one afternoon we drove into the imposing gateway of a mansion.

'Atma Niwas' – 'Abode of Bliss', as Abe freely translated it – had been built by a rich *seth* (Hindu merchant), just before the war. It was situated neither in the cantonment nor in the city, but a few miles to the west of the city among open fields. Some distance from the family house, but still within the high, spiked outer wall, was a guest-house, complete with its own kitchen and two tennis-courts. It was intended for the entertainment of Europeans, and the stables, garage and grooms' and gardeners' quarters too might have belonged to a European residence.

The family house was protected by a further inner wall, It had been designed to meet two sets of needs – one the needs of his immediate family and the other those of his extended one. Accommodation for himself and his immediate family was provided in an imposing citadel, where a flight of polished stone steps led up to a marble verandah – deeper than it was long. At the top of the steps, the verandah was protected by a sliding steel grille. Behind it was a living room, flanked by a dining-room and bedrooms with dressing-rooms and bathrooms – all with barred windows of stained glass.

Behind this citadel two rambling, shabby, plastered, larger buildings, had provided elastic accommodation for the *seth*'s dependant relatives and servants in two parallel wings that sprawled, facing each other across an unpaved yard. One, built out from the back of the citadel, had access to it through a single, lockable door. The other was one-storeyed, but otherwise they were identical, each consisting of a series of small rooms opening in and out of one another – sometimes so inter-linked that one small room would have three doors. This multiplicity of doors was necessary because the only way from one room to another was through the intervening rooms, unless one went out into the yard. There were no passages. Privacy was impossible. The doors had hasps, but padlocks were provided only on the outer ones. In short, precaution had been taken against molestation from without, and provision made for molestation from within. Years later, reading the opening chapters of V.S. Naipaul's *A House for Mister Biswas*, I knew where I was. Privacy was easily available in the citadel, however. The *seth* had only to lock the one door connecting it with the outer courts to be out of bounds to brothers, sisters, uncles, aunts, nephews, nieces and any other hangers-on. And who can blame him? It was generous of him to let them in!

The windows throughout the building were all barred and fitted with heavy shutters. The entire garden was protected by a high wall, with wrought iron gate to match, complete with a gate-house for a watchman. Within the garden, the citadel was protected by an additional, inner wall, which was also gated. Nevertheless the *seth* had no longer felt secure there when war broke out, so he had let it and returned to his old house in Jullundur City. That was how Kilroy now came to be living there – in the citadel, where he was joined by his wife and their two small sons after the surrender of Japan.

He belonged to a previous era. Believing that matters were still decided by local influence, not by national politics, and that the Punjab was still under the firm control of the Unionist Party, he could not grapple with the prospect of Indian independence. We argued once or twice about this, and also about what would be the still-awaited result of the British general election, concerning which he was equally mistaken. There was no question of returning to our previous relationship. Back where he belonged he had become a more conventional figure while I hardly rated as a *sahib*. Abe was quartered in the guest-house, with two other British majors who had been acquired. They had set up offices in other towns in the Punjab, but spent a week each month at Jullundur – to keep in touch, although what there was to stay in touch with was unclear. Vatsal and I were quartered a mile away down the Grand Trunk Road in a summer-house in a mango orchard which was part of the estate. I suppose that we were in the dog-house, but it suited us very well. Every morning we left our summer-house like schoolboys, to trudge down the Grand Trunk Road to our offices at Atma Niwas with heavy hearts, and every evening we strolled home with light ones.

There were more than enough rooms in the family quarters of Atma Niwas for every officer and every clerk to have an office to himself, more rooms to store equipment in, and even then still more left empty. For the first time since I had left Bareilly, I found myself sitting at a desk with an in-tray and an out-tray, but they rarely had anything in them that required anything more than to be noted as having been read. What we were supposed to be doing was clearly stated. We were supposed to be stimulating recruitment. But it was impossible to see how anything we did could serve as a stimulant. We rarely toured, and when we did it was only to assure the population that the war was drawing to a happy close. Malaya could be invaded any day now.

On tour I now addressed my audiences in English, to be translated into Punjabi by one of the local assistants Kilroy had appointed. It would have been ludicrous to address Punjabi audiences in Urdu like mine. The Urdu they were used to hearing from the lips of regular Indian Army officers was bad enough. I was taken to hear a comedian mimicking a *sahib* holding forth in Urdu. Even I could enjoy the mimicry of anglicised mis-pronunciation. It was as funny as Peter Sellers doing the same thing in reverse, but I missed the resulting doubles entendres. In the eyes of most *sahibs* it was undignified to contort the mouth in an effort to observe phonetic distinctions that English had no use for.

In over two and a half years on tour in Assam, I was only invited to dinner by Miss Thomas in Habiganj, regularly, and by a British official once. People were unused to the army there. Here in the Punjab, however, contact with military officers conferred prestige, and when on tour I was invited to dinner by strangers as soon as I met them. Luckily I was now entitled to sport three medals. Only one – the Burma Star – had any connection with a field of war, and all one had to do to merit that one was cross the Hooghly River – which one had to do merely to set foot in Calcutta. It was therefore known as 'the Chowringhee Star', after Calcutta's best-known street'.

On one occasion Kilroy sent me to tour the Sikh princely states of Nabha and Patiala with the dance troupe. On my first night in Nabha State I had barely arrived in a rest house, just inside the border, when a bus turned up, loaded with food and a fridge full of drinks, together with a *major domo*, a cook, a bearer and a man who informed me that his task was to provide me with conversation. It was a minor state, and wished to make a good impression. At Patiala, on the other hand, the only special consideration shown to me was that nobody laughed at me on an occasion when it must have been hard not to.

The day after our arrival we staged a show at a cinema, and the maharajah himself graced the occasion. He was a figure of national importance, so after making doubly sure that everything was ready behind the scenes I posted myself at the head of the cinema steps to welcome him on his arrival – only to realise, with just three minutes left to go, that I had left my hat somewhere. Without it I would not be able to salute him!

A search was instituted, but I was still bare-headed when the royal car drew up at the foot of the steps. Unable to salute I did the next best regulation thing. I snapped to attention, slamming my heels together.

Unfortunately I was standing directly over the groove, along which the grill slid when the cinema was shut, and my slammed heels jammed themselves into it together – and that was only the beginning! They were so close together that I could not keep my balance, and wavered, like a dynamited block of flats. His Highness, who was a keen cricketer, and well over six feet tall, sped lightly up the steps and fielded me before I reached the ground.

In the evening I was the guest of the cricket club. The walls were covered with photographs of touring teams that had played there – starting with Lord Tennyson's eleven. Not one of these teams had won, they told me. They all played two-day matches and no matter how well they had played on the first day on the second they collapsed, thanks to the hospitality they had received the previous evening. I found this easy to believe. The hospitality was memorable, but only through a haze…

All memory of how I wasted time in the office at Jullundur escapes me beyond the fact that we all began our day's work by reading the newspaper. I gave up hope of doing anything useful, and treated what remained of my military service as a holiday prior to release from service. All that news of the dropping of the atom bomb meant at the time was that release from service was now suddenly much closer. Those it had killed seemed to have been eliminated by an abstraction. There were no pictures, and so many had already died messily.

Abe Stewart's number for release came up quickly on account of his age. He had visited the summer-house regularly before his departure, but it was remote enough to deter any other evening visitor from Atma Niwas, and as Vatsal and I steered clear of Atma Niwas when we were not on duty our privacy was almost unbroken.

The summer-house was set in a mango orchard. Water from an electric pump was conducted down channels to the trees, but no electricity had been laid on in the house itself, so there were no fans to waft the air in its three rooms – two bedrooms, each with its own Indian bathroom, and a living-room. The flat roof absorbed the heat throughout the day and gradually passed it through to bake us. Nevertheless, I was never uncomfortable there. The place was fly-proofed, and if, lying naked in my bedroom on a Sunday afternoon, I found it grew too hot to read, I fell asleep and awoke to take an Indian-style bath, tippling water from an enamelled can over myself and down onto the cement floor.

We shared our accommodation with squirrels and lizards, which came in and out as they pleased, never interfering with one another, but ignoring each other's presence, even when in the course of climbing around on the metal gauze of the fly-proofed windows they came face to face. They seemed to be embarrassed when this happened, as if such meetings were taboo.

We only watched the squirrels, but we tampered with the ants. Ants are so repelled by sweat that they cannot bear to pass a line of it drawn by a finger on a wall, so whenever I saw a column marching across the wall of the dining room I drew a line of sweat to interrupt its course and then watched it dealing with the problem. Some who had been halted at the barrier, rushed back to alert the ones who were still far behind, while – after being temporarily halted and then spreading out – the rest of the vanguard re-grouped to march vertically up the wall beyond the barrier, and then resume their earlier direction. Meanwhile, instead of marching all the way to the barrier, the alerted rearguard struck out diagonally up the wall to rejoin the vanguard the shortest route.

When ants kept climbing into jam jars that were on the table and contaminating the contents with their corpses, Vatsal hung a jar half full of jam from the ceiling on a string. Their response was to walk upside down across the ceiling to the hook from which the jar was hung and drop straight into it, to die in bliss.

Birds never came right into the summer house, but they walked around on the brick platform that ran in front of it, along its entire length. As this was unroofed, we could not use this as a verandah during the day, but during the hot weather, when the sun began to set, we had our beds brought out onto it, and eventually fell asleep there in the middle of drifting conversations.

From the time when he first arrived in Shillong, I had been in closer touch with Vatsal than the others had. His isolation in separate quarters there was not in itself disagreeable to him. It placed him nearer to people in Shillong, who in any case would never have visited him at all if he had been living at headquarters with Kilroy. Nevertheless, he felt that despite his captaincy the separation indicated a difference in status, especially when Kilroy told him that his duties did not include touring, and worse still, refused him a pistol. According to Kilroy, when I protested about this, the reason was that Vatsal's duties did not require the use of one – but then neither did ours. We had only been issued with pistols because regulations required us to be armed when serving in a field of war, and the same regulations applied to Vatsal. The truth was that Kilroy distrusted him because he had been a terrorist. He reminded me that Vatsal had once made bombs to be used against public servants. Mazhar, for his part, kept his distance too, because Vatsal was a supporter of M.N. Roy.

The dancers were quartered in the same large house as Vatsal, and when I was back in Shillong and they were not on tour I sometimes called in to watch them rehearsing, or to borrow one of Vatsal's books – Expressionist and Psychoanalytical works by German and Austrian writers whom I only knew by name. For a long time, his name was also all I knew of Vatsal. He preferred not to be known in person.

Decades later, when he was nominated for the Nobel Prize for Literature and invited to teach and lecture on both sides of the Iron Curtain, he was still reclusive, and often seemed morose. He hardly ever laughed, and smiled as rarely and superciliously as Cassius. His favourite expressions were one of bemusement and pained surprise. When I first knew him I kept catching myself babbling to stave off the silence, but as time went by he began to talk as well. Although a nationalist, he had no illusions about the kind of society that independence would produce – especially in Assam.

The ban that Kilroy had placed on Vatsal's touring was removed when Abe took over, and we toured together a couple of times. He was already concerned about the probable effect of national independence on the welfare of Assamese minorities, and later, when that time did come, he consistently sympathised with their cause and supported it. He also foresaw the excessive exploitation of forests that national independence would permit. For the first time in my life I listened to an environmentalist, although I was too ignorant to take his forebodings seriously.

As I got to know him better I was surprised to find that he had a love of play and enjoyed leading people on. One day he took me to a gathering of novelists and short-story writers in Delhi, introducing me as an English poet. (For me at least this was not a joke. I did write poems then, and he had arranged for their publication, as a reward for improving a series of translations of Hindi novels that he was editing.) They were meeting to reminisce on the theme – 'How I became a writer'.

The contributions of the others made it clear that none of them had started writing fiction frivolously. One after another rose to describe an instance of oppression, cruelty or injustice witnessed in childhood, that had led to a resolve to expose man's inhumanity to man. (There were no women present.)

Vatsal spoke last. He was the most celebrated person there. His vocation too, he told them, had come early. He was still a school-boy when it happened, and he owed it to his mother. So far, so good. That was exemplary. What followed, however, was not. He owed it to her as a result of her insistence that he must always come straight home from school. Instead of obeying he used to stay back to play with friends, so that when at last he started on his homeward way he had to invent an excuse for being late. As the previous day's excuse would not be accepted, he had to think of a new one every day, and in the course of time the business of conjuring up a new but credible narrative on his walk home from school became the best part of his day. So that was how he had become a writer. His audience received this in silence. In their view every story must have a moral, and the moral of this one was that it need not.

If another writer had mocked their seriousness they would have denounced him to his face, but Vatsal was one of the heroes of what was then still remembered as 'the Delhi Conspiracy Trial' – an event which he turned into a comic narrative for my benefit. As told by him, the arrest, imprisonment and acquittal of a group of terrorists that he had joined when he was a student, was a three-act comedy. Weeks before he was arrested, he had already realised that, all day every day, he was being shadowed, so one morning he mounted a bicycle and rode out into the country. The fact that he was being followed by another cyclist became increasingly obvious, until at last he and his shadow were the only people on the road. He then dismounted, whereupon his shadow duly halted at a distance and dismounted too, so he wheeled his cycle round and walked back to have a word with him. It was not that he objected to the police knowing everything about his movements, he explained, but he did object to the intrusion on his privacy, so if his shadow would agree to meet him every evening, he would render him a full account of his movements over the previous twenty-four hours. In return he expected to be left to himself for the rest of the day. His shadow embraced the offer, and that was how they managed things until he was arrested.

He was arrested three times, only to be released the first two times because there was an error in the warrants. This legal nicety made a favourable impression on him and so too – as it turned out in the end – did a display of petulant violence, when he was finally arrested. It happened on the bank of a river at sunset, and involved the head of the Intelligence Bureau in the Punjab, who began to question him before he had been hand-cuffed. His hands were therefore still free when, angered by his silence, the I.B. chief switched on a torch and thrust it into his eyes. The torch did not touch him, but he automatically raised his hand and knocked it to the ground. He expected a blow in return, but the I.B. chief just picked the torch up, turned his back, and walked away to the river bank; where he stood staring at the water until Vatsal was taken away to join the other terrorists in jail.

In due course they were found not guilty and set free, but the proceedings had revealed enough about his terrorist connections for the university at which he had been studying to refuse to take him back. On leaving prison, however, he was handed a letter from All India Radio inviting him to an interview with a view to employment – on the recommendation of the Head of the Punjab Intelligence Bureau.

During the trial, the Government of India granted the accused financial aid to pay for their defence, and a leading member of the Congress Party, who was a barrister, volunteered to defend them – until they decided to keep the money in reserve to pay for a possible appeal. The patriotic lawyer then changed his mind. Instead of looking for a replacement they decided to conduct their own defence – and make it memorable.

Confined together in the same prison block they acted as a team. One of their games was to convert their journeys to and from the court house into public demonstrations. The police reacted by manacling them, but this resulted in a daily drama in the court-room, as the judge ruled that the manacles must be removed before proceedings could begin.

Vatsal appreciated this punctiliousness, rather as the one-eyed colonel in Bangalore had admired Pathan observance of the rules of hospitality, but the police resented it, and one day, to get their own back, arranged for the prison van to be unavailable at the end of the day's proceedings to take the prisoners back to jail. Their aim was to humiliate them by making them walk through the streets in manacles, but the result was to make martyrs of them. One or other of them kept falling to the ground to be hauled to his feet and shouted at, while the others lamented, lifting their fettered hands and calling on the passers-by to witness. The climax came when the judge happened by – in a modest baby car, as Vatsal noted with approval – and stopped to give the police a public reprimand.

As Vatsal told it, the prosecution case collapsed because a key witness failed to identify the accused in court. At the time which was the subject of his testimony they all had beards and they still had beards the previous evening, but were all clean-shaven on the crucial day in court. This operation was well planned. During the day they were free to pass from cell to cell unchecked, but were under observation, so they could not use the razor blade that had been smuggled in to them. They had only that one blade, however, and at night they were locked in separate cells. Before the warder came to lock them in their cells, on the night before the trial, they therefore arranged the bedding in each bunk to make it look occupied and then huddled together in the last cell in the line. I wonder now how they managed this without being seen by the warder when he locked the door of the last cell. Vatsal told me, but I have forgotten. Perhaps the cell had an attached latrine. Somehow, they did contrive to do it and then shaved one another's beards off during the night painfully, in cold water, with a hand-held safety blade.

All that remained was to wait for the warder to unlock them in the morning. He duly passed along the line of empty cells, shouting to rouse what he took to be the sleeping occupant as he unlocked each door. When he was unlocking the last cell in the line, however – the one that contained them all – no sooner did the occupants hear the key turn than they could not contain themselves and broke into giggles. Luckily, when the warder heard the giggles and realised that something was wrong, in his concern to prevent a general break-out he dashed out of the cell-block to raise the alarm without relocking the cell. By the time the governor arrived with a squad of warders the prisoners were therefore all back in their separate cells, and the warder who had reported a superfluity of prisoners was in disgrace.

For Vatsal, however, camaraderie had its limits. He began to find the company of his comrades tiring. Confinement made them quarrelsome. He was not the only political prisoner whom I heard complain of this. Mohan Kumaramangalam and Mazhar Ali Khan both commented unfavourably on the difference between the way their comrades reacted to confinement and the way in which convicted criminals did. They attributed the difference to the superior virtue of the oppressed, but it was more probably due to the difference between two kinds of imprisonment – punishment as a result of a sentence following a trial, and detention without trial or, as in Vatsal's case, awaiting it. Convicts have a penal regimen to keep them occupied. Prisoners awaiting trial, like Vatsal, or detained without trial like Mohan and Mazhar, have to occupy themselves.

Tens of thousands of Indians were subjected to this test during the last years of the Raj. A few were able to devote their enforced leisure to writing, and many more to study. As a member of the armed forces I enjoyed borrowing rights at the Royal Asiatic Society Library. So did political detainees, and more than once when I asked for a book I was told that it was out with one of them. Prison even offered opportunities that political activity had denied them when they were free. A Congress Socialist friend, who had been detained without trial in 1942, lamented that now he was free be would never be able to finish a book on the philosophy of Sankaracarya[15] which he had started to write in prison. Many detainees, however, found that idle confinement in one another's company was like group therapy. It brought out the worst in them.

In order to escape this, Vatsal asked for a period of solitary confinement when the court was not in session. The prison governor refused at first, explaining that to grant a penalty as a privilege would make a mockery of the system, but yielded when Vatsal pointed out to him that the mockery would be worse if he was compelled to commit a misdemeanour to procure a penalty.

After the Japanese surrender we went on tour together in the Punjab, without the dancers, and without addressing meetings – simply interviewing officials and notables. I saw no signs of communal tension but the communal self-consciousness was unlike anything I had witnessed in Assam. I was talking with a young Moslem official at a bazaar when a white-bearded man was dragged before him. He had been caught in the act of peeping at women, so the official broke off our conversation to deal with him, which he did by beating him. 'Do you call yourself a Moslem?' 'What enraged him was not the offence but the disgrace to his community. He was the first civil servants I had seen publicly sporting a pistol.

India's various leaders were as far apart as ever on the question of what form Independence was to take, but people were already taking it for granted. Their fear was not that the British intended to stay, but that when the British left their own particular community would be disadvantaged. Master Tara Singh, the Akali Sikh leader, visited Atma Niwas several times to persuade Kilroy that the Punjab should simply be handed back to the Sikhs when Britain left India, because the Sikhs had been ruling it when the British arrived – a view which Kilroy seemed inclined to share.

When I secured some duty or other in Lahore to visit Iftikar, I found that he too was thinking on communal lines –

although if I had said so he would have insisted that they were 'national', as the Communist Party of India had decided that Indian Moslems met the criteria for nationhood prescribed in Stalin's Marxism and the National and Colonial Question. They therefore had a right to secede from India in line with the fairy-tale right to secede which the constitution of the Soviet Union conferred on its constituent republics. He had accordingly resigned from the Congress Party, and joined the Moslem League.

Fresh evidence that times were changing was a commission, consisting of five senior Indian Army officers, to advise on the future of Viceroy's commissions. The King's commissioned officers in the army of an independent India would all be Indians, so what would be the function of *subedars* and *jemadars*? Other national armies had no place for such a rank. In due course the commission visited Jullundur, and a reception was arranged for it to meet local dignitaries. I was invited too, and what I heard the dignitaries saying made it clear that they felt threatened. They all belonged to the 'martial classes', and wanted to know how officers were going to be selected. On merit, naturally. That went without saying, but what – they anxiously inquired would count as merit? Military merit came with breeding, not with education, and its presence was not established on paper by written examinations.

Two members of the commission were Indians – both of them full colonels, who had established their military merit by winning Military Crosses in the Western Desert. 'Candidates for officer must no doubt be educated', I heard a local worthy pointing out to one of them. 'Nevertheless, the Indian Army cannot do without the martial classes'.

'I do know what you mean,' Colonel Choudhury answered. He had commanded tanks against Rommel. 'Although of course I am not martial myself. I'm a Bengali.' He was later to become Commander-in-chief.

The other Indian colonel was not 'martial' either. He was

the brother of Mohan and Parvati Kumaramangalam, so I introduced myself as a friend of theirs. He had always allowed them to assert intellectual superiority, he confided, because while all three of them had been to English schools they had gone on to Oxford and Cambridge, while he had gone to Sandhurst. Now all that was changed, however, thanks to one of his experiences as a German prisoner of war. As a regular officer of the British Army, captured in the Western Desert, he had access to Red Cross comforts which miraculously included the works of Plato. Delightedly he led me through the Socratic questioning to which he had subjected his siblings when he got home.

Q : How do you select your leaders in the Communist Party?

A: We choose the best Marxists.

Q : How do you know which Marxists are the best?

And so on.

Whatever I did that autumn was done negligently. I was one of innumerable men, who had signed up for military service for the duration of the war, lounging around India in khaki, with nothing useful left to do. Those who were British could not wait to go home and get out of uniform. If they had been conscripted, they had never wished to get into it. If they had volunteered they had only done so because their country then needed them, and it no longer did. In either case, return to the life they had lived before they found themselves in uniform was a welcome prospect.

For most of the hundreds of thousands of Indians involved, however, the case was different. None of them had been conscripted. They had all volunteered – but not because their country needed them. They had volunteered for the Indian Army because they found it difficult to make a living anywhere else. The resettlement of demobilised *sepoys* into civilian life was therefore recognised to be a major social problem, and a Resettlement Directorate was set up at G.H.Q.

There was not much it could do, however. One step it took was to circulate the official post-war development plans drawn up by the different provincial administrations. These all did make provision for servicemen returning to civilian life, although nothing like as much as would be needed. A more serious misgiving they provoked, however, was the consideration that when India achieved independence the administrations that had framed these plans would cease to exist.

Another move was to take the general public into its confidence and seek their help directly. One of its first steps, therefore, was to secure the services of the Military Public Liaison Section. The precise way in which they expected this to help them was never made clear, but just as Kilroy's circus happened to be at hand to serve as an answer when the Americans inquired what steps were being taken to prevent civilian panic in Assam, it now offered an answer to another question about civilians – how to persuade them to make room for returning soldiers. Kilroy had produced a plausible answer to the first question, but this time all he did was divide India into regions, assign one to each of us and leave the rest to us – except Vatsal, who at this point procured his release.

17: Bombay finale

I was allotted Bombay Presidency and the Central Provinces, but during my six remaining months in India my presence was of no benefit to anyone anywhere – except Delhi, where it enabled the Resettlement Directorate to point to the presence of an officer 'on the ground' when they were asked what they were doing to ease the return of demobilised *sepoys* to civilian life. The only demobilised men I heard about for whom the Indian Army provided a *man-bap* (mother-father) in this field were those commanded by Ralph Russell, a Cambridge acquaintance who later joined the staff of the School of Oriental and African Studies. He too had been commissioned in the Indian Army. Instead of going straight home when his unit was disbanded, he remained in India to canvas potential employers personally until he had found jobs for all his men. Disbanded *sepoys* did have skills with a value in the labour market, as trained mechanics, drivers, store-keepers, and security staff. Nevertheless, a similar effort on behalf of every demobilised *sepoy* would not have had the same success. Fresh employment did not exist for more than a fraction of the hundreds of thousands demobilised men. Most of them were doomed to rejoin the ranks of the periodically employed from which they had emerged. Nevertheless, Ralph Russell's personal efforts did demonstrate the perfunctory nature of other people's actions – including mine.

Even within the agencies of government the long-term prospects of employment for ex-servicemen were not bright, because when government institutions passed from British supervision to Indian their special claims would no longer be acknowledged. The only exception was the police. Policing was an area of government employment not covered in provincial post-war plans, but when I broached the subject with the Inspector-General of Police for the Central Provinces, he told me that he had already tried to recruit ex-*sepoys*. To his disgust, however, they had rejected the rate of pay. The Army, he complained, had spoiled them.

I told him that some Indian servicemen still serving in the forces felt aggrieved at being paid less than their British counterparts for performing the same duties. He was outraged that they should have thought of making the comparison! He consoled himself, however, with the reflection that experience out of uniform would teach them to think differently. He would still welcome them, in spite of everything, because he needed trained men to handle the weapons which the Army was now making available to the civil power.

Another potential employer of ex-servicemen which I contacted was the Bombay Municipality, but when I asked their Chairman about the employment of ex-servicemen, he told me that the only ex-servicemen the municipality was interested in employing were those who had joined Subhas Chanda Bose's Indian National Army. In this connection he asked for my assistance! *Sepoys* who had deserted to the Indian National Army were discharged on the same terms as those who had refused to do so, and remained prisoners of war instead. They even received their accumulated back pay! The only difference in their treatment was that their desertion was recorded on their discharge certificates. This was intended as a stigma, but it had the opposite effect. It gave its recipients an advantage in the labour market, by identifying them as patriotic heroes. Ex-servicemen who had not deserted had therefore taken to falsifying their discharge certificates to make it appear that they had. The necessary alteration was easily effected, the Chairman complained, and he wanted the Indian Army to do something about it! Surprised by his failure to imagine that the Indian Army's point of view might well be different, I assured him that I would report his difficulty and did so without comment, but with the addition of an exclamation mark.

In addition to controlling the Bombay Municipality, the Congress Party would soon be governing the entire province, so I invited Moraji Desai, then the Congress Party's provincial leader, to lunch at the Taj Hotel to discuss the role of demobilised ex-servicemen in the Presidency. The only post-war plan that he was keen to talk about, however, was his own particular favourite – total prohibition. By chance I had been picnicking with Indian friends a few days earlier, and we had drunk toddy fresh from the palm – a Garden of Eden beverage, poured into our glasses through funnels made from leaves. Its alcohol content was minimal, it was full of vitamins, and did not carry the feeblest kick. Nothing could have tasted more innocuous, although when they assured me that Gandhiji drank it regularly I did not believe my fellow topers.

Without toddy what would villagers do for vitamins? – I asked.

He might have answered that toddy laced with rubbish and left to ferment loses its innocence. Instead he replied that they would drink milk. At the time this put me in mind of Marie Antoinette's legendary suggestion that croissants might be used to remedy the scarcity of bread, but when I returned a few years later the Bombay Municipality was supplying cheap powdered milk.

Moraji Desai was probably particularly keen on total abstention that morning because he had a hang-over – probably the only one that he experienced in all his long life. The hang-over was due to no fault of his. Explaining why he had asked more than once for my assurance that his orange juice was unadulterated, he told me that he had been the guest of honour at a dinner at the Byculla Club, the previous evening, and some members had spoilt the occasion by lacing his orange juice with gin.

The fact that he had been invited showed that *box-wallahs* now saw the writing on the wall for British rule, but the louche prank that had spoilt the gesture showed that some of them – the *koi hais* – had still a long way to go. Stultified European residents were known as *koi hais* as dogs were once known as 'bow-wows'. '*Koi hai?*' was their characteristic cry when they sank exhausted into chairs in bungalows and clubs after a day's work. Its literal meaning is – 'Is anybody there?' – but it was no more a question than the cry of a thirsty infant is. Like the infant cry it was a demand, based on an assumption that a slave equipped to quench a raging thirst was waiting within earshot.

The committee of the Byculla Club that had invited Moraji Desai was clearly not entirely composed of *koi hais*. To be fair, it was Europeans who had identified the type and named it. Many indeed had long foreseen the transfer of power, but few had expected still to be in India when it did happen. 'Probably about when I reach retirement' was the date I frequently heard *sahibs* – of varying ages – set on British rule. Indians who thought in more immediate terms were regarded as impatient and ungrateful.

Nevertheless, as I had seen in Assam, 'indianization' had accelerated in the Indian Civil Service even before the war, and during it had also got under way in the Indian Army. I met an Indian officer whose regiment was now left with only two British officers – the commanding officer and his second-in-command. The second-in-command was the only British officer who ate in the mess as the C.O. was married. This situation presented no difficulties to the first second-in-command to find himself in it, but his successor had to be taught a lesson.

Fate arranged for him to travel to his new posting in the same railway compartment as an Indian captain who belonged to the same battalion, and he seized the opportunity to make his position clear. He was prepared to tolerate a mess full of Indians, but would not accept a drop in standards. The Indian captain feigned dismay. His mind had hatched a plot fully fledged in that instant, and already it was on the wing. 'I'm sorry to inform you, sir, that you have come too late. The mess has now, as you would say, *gone native*.'

On arrival he reported what had happened to their commanding officer and secured approval for his plan. When the second-in-command turned up for dinner at the mess that evening there were no chairs or tables. He had to squat on the floor, where he was served entirely with Indian food, and the choice of drinks was between whey and sherbet.

Next morning, when he complained to the Commanding Officer, he was simply told that he had asked to be made a fool of, and when he went back to the mess that evening everything was as it always had been. By 1945 the only political question was on what terms the British were going to go. Agreement on that question between the Moslem League and the Congress Party seemed impossible. In March, Sir Stafford Cripps returned to Delhi as one of the members of a Cabinet Mission despatched by the British Government to see what could be done, and Short came with him, as a personal assistant. He sent for me to see what I made of the situation. Despite his belief in sympathetic listening, he spoke approvingly of Cripps' unconcealed distaste when Jinnah had explained to him that 'Pakistan' meant 'land of the pure'. The prospect of a divided India horrified him. If the demand of Pakistan was granted there would be a civil war. With fatuous certainty I assured him that the Congress leadership could not afford to start another mass resistance movement, because it would cost them their leadership. They had all but lost it in 1942. I spoke confidently, until Woodrow Wyatt, the other assistant Cripps had brought with him, said – 'That's what I keep saying'.

My assertion was not based simply on what had happened in 1942. In Bombay I was now in touch with the lower echelons of the new leadership that was ready to replace the old one. In the course of exploring the employment prospects of discharged *sepoys*, I had been surprised to discover that a group of Congress Socialist Party activists was doing something similar on behalf of Royal Indian Navy personnel. This was surprising, as some of them had been supporters of Subhas

Chandra Bose during the war. When I met them in the India Coffee House, as I did frequently, they did not conceal what they had done in 1942, and the devotion of some of them to Subhas Chandra Bose was undimmed. They even refused to believe that he was dead. One of them, a woman, spoke of him as if he was a child. 'Then I saw my Netaji weep', she tenderly recalled, remembering the time when Gandhi had compelled him to resign the presidency of the Congress Party. 'Of course, he is not dead. He will return to us.'

Devotion to the memory of the Indian National Army did not, however, prevent these activists from seeking employment for demobilised naval personnel. Naively I assumed that they concentrated on naval personnel out of provincial patriotism. They were all either Malayalis or Bengalis, and it was from Malabar and East Bengal that the Indian Navy drew the bulk of its ratings and petty officers. I overlooked the fact that politically they were also the most volatile regions in India – the very regions where the Communist Party had claimed that it could raise anti-Japanese guerrillas in 1942, while at the same time they had also been the scene of violent pro-Japanese subversion.

Naively I did not ask myself whether their interest in Royal Indian Navy personnel might go beyond re-settling them. When one of them promised me that a day would come when the Indian Navy sailed up the Thames to shell the Houses of Parliament, I smiled indulgently.

Soon after that, however, I was driving into Bombay from a tour in Maharashtra, in time for lunch, when I was stopped by a detachment of British Military Police. Trouble had broken out in the city, and military personnel were not to enter it unnecessarily. I had to enter it, however. The Public Relations Office, where I had my desk, was situated facing Flora Fountain at the city's hub, and I was quartered close by in a hotel on the sea front. The M.P.s therefore directed me to follow a circuitous route through back streets, guided by other military personnel posted at intervals.

There was hardly any traffic, but more pedestrians than usual in the streets, and when I sat down for lunch at my hotel I learned the reason. The Indian Navy contingent stationed at Bombay had mutinied, the citizens had gone on strike in their support, and sporadic rioting had broken out.

Walking from the hotel towards Flora Fountain after lunch was like drifting with a crowd of holiday-makers towards some festival, except that everyone was silent and they were walking all over the road, because there was no motor traffic. There were as many people on the road as on the footpaths, and an unaccustomed sound of feet. I suddenly realised that I was the only European. Over the past three years I had grown accustomed to being the only European in a crowd of Indian civilians, but had never felt this position, as I did now, as one of isolation. Inevitably when I had mustered the crowd myself I was the centre of attention, but at other times when I was in an Indian crowd I had seemed to be part of it. Even visiting a temple I had not been made to feel that I had no business to be there – although no doubt that is what I would have been made to feel during the 1942 disturbances, if Short had not sent me away to a hill station.

When I reached the open space where roads converge at Flora Fountain I found people standing around in silent groups. Those I had been walking with slowed down and spread around among them. I had to thread my way through them to reach the office. People did not move aside to let me through, as they had always done before, but there was no harm in that.

Why should they? The two British captains with whom I shared the office – ex-journalists, now Public Relation Officers – behaved as if they were re-enacting the siege of Lucknow. They told me that for the past two days they had been eating and sleeping on the premises, standing by the telephone and teleprinter, and so had run out of cigarettes. In those days we all walked around with tins of fifty. I offered mine, and asked them why they had not gone out to buy themselves some more. It would be dangerous, they answered, to go out.

Before my break with Communism I would have welcomed a suggestion that the streets were no longer safe for Europeans. Now I rejected it as absurd, and to show them how silly they were being, I offered to slip round to the tobacconist down the road. They warned me not to try. Airily I told them to leave it to me. Macropolo's was barely a hundred yards away. I knew what I was doing.

No sooner was 1 out on the pavement than I felt less sure of that. Hornby Road was transformed. There was no wheeled traffic, only men on foot, and even they were not going anywhere. They were not even talking. They were just hanging around silently, hoping that if they waited long enough there would be something interesting for them to see. At last – although the thought did not then occur to me – I was face to face with the *tamasha-wallahs* I had read about in the manual on aid to the civil power. The shops were all shuttered. Macropolo's would not be open. But then again it just might be, in which case I would look silly later if I gave up now, so it was up to me at least to walk the distance. I set off down the road.

As there was no traffic, and nobody in my vicinity was talking, all I could hear was the sound of feet behind me. I did not look back, but knew that I was being followed by a crowd. It was only when I turned to retrace my steps, having arrived to find Macropolo's shut and protected by an iron grille, that I faced them.

As I had stopped, they had stopped too. It was a critical moment. Luckily for me, as it happened they really were all mere *tamasha-wallahs*. They had no designs on me themselves, but they did not want to miss the spectacle if someone else had. None of the faces in front of me was threatening, but they all wore the look of members of a patient audience, waiting to see fireworks. If I suggested, by hesitating, that I too expected fireworks I might start them off.

They were all men, and the footpath was packed with them. They were even thick on the road alongside it, so that to find an unobstructed passage back to Flora Fountain I would have to cross to the other side. But that would be asking for trouble as it would, quite literally, mean giving way, so I walked straight back along the footpath as if the men who were crowding it, with the nearest only a few feet away, did not exist. Just before I would have had to stop walking to avoid colliding with them they did open a pathway, but they only gave way at the very last moment, and went on doing so at each step I took, without clearing a way well in advance for me. Every step I took forwards therefore had to be a challenge. It was only at the point of collision that the men I was stepping into moved to let me through – and yet I do not think I brushed a single body.

Macropolo's was not far from the office, but covering the distance seemed to take an hour. In this instance the trope does not exaggerate. I had no anticipation that this walk would ever end. Experiences are often said to be dream-like, but this one really was. The path that had opened for me closed in behind me as those I passed turned round and followed at my heels. No matter how far I went into the crowd the number of men I had to pass through was not reduced, as people pressed round from the street ahead to see what was going on.

That evening a European was murdered coming out of a cinema on the road along which I had walked from the hotel after lunch, and I believe that two other Europeans were killed. In comparison with the Indian death roll, this was nothing. With Indian armed forces now in revolt, it had seemed to many Bombay citizens that this might be the dawn of Indian freedom, so they rioted in the mutineers' support and in some places attacked the troops that patrolled the streets. When it was all over, my Congress Socialist friends told me proudly how small boys had joined in. When a military vehicle was held up in a street, a child could open the cap of its petrol tank, dip a rag into it, and set it ablaze as effectively as an adult.

That does not merit death, however, and from eye-witness accounts I fear that many of some two hundred people who were killed were guilty of no more than congregating unlawfully – or not even that. Not every opening of fire was a text-book operation. I heard of an authenticated case of an old man alone in an upstairs room being killed by a stray shot from a military truck driving past in the street below. British troops, brought onto the streets 'in aid of the civil power', were directly responsible for much of this. A British Army officer whose unit had been involved sadly told me that his men had been trigger-happy, fearing that if this trouble turned into a revolution, their demobilisation would be postponed. It was the fact that they were not regulars that made them so ready to shoot. They wanted to get out of uniform.

Weeks later, when General Rees presided over a full inquiry into the mutiny, it transpired that before it started my Congress Socialist acquaintances had been in close contact with the mutineers and they were summoned to be questioned. None of them mentioned this to me. Indeed I rarely saw them once General Rees had opened his inquiry. I only learned what had been happening when I was starting on the first leg of my journey back to England for demobilisation.

I had hardly set foot in a compartment on the train to legendary Deolali and the Homeward Bound Trooping Depot, when a staff officer already seated there cried: ' At last! The mystery man!' He had read my name on my luggage. It was a name, he informed me, that had appeared repeatedly in the evidence given by subversives to the Mutiny Inquiry and he had been trying to trace its owner for weeks. General Rees had been keen to question him. When a subversive was asked to explain his business with naval personnel, he had always protested that Major Bolt knew all about it. Nobody in Bombay Area H.Q., however, knew anything about Major Bolt. In vain they had done everything to trace me. Unfortunately it was too late now. The inquiry was closed.

As it happened I had met members of a preliminary inquiry team that came from Delhi to question the mutineers immediately after they had surrendered. One member of this earlier team was Unni Nair, a young Indian lieutenant-colonel soon to be killed serving in Korea as a U.N. observer. He was a Malayali. 'Half these chaps hail from your neck of the woods, Unni. What do you make of that, eh?' asked the general in charge. Unni confirmed the finding but stopped short of adding that it pleased him.

It pleased me too. I had developed a lasting link with Malabar. If the British Communist Party had provided me with a contact in Bangalore, I would have met Jaya, my wife, as soon as I arrived in India. She was a staunch communist supporter in regular touch with party members there. As things were, our meeting had to wait until the eve of my departure. We met in New Delhi where I was attending a course on resettlement, prior to taking up my new appointment. She was a senior commander in the Women's Auxiliary Corps, attending another course there, and once I had seen her I resolved to go on doing so. My new appointment made this easy. She was on the staff of Central Command H.Q. and, although I was based in Bombay, the Central Provinces fell within my area too, and Nagpur, where Central Command was situated, was also the seat of the provincial administration, so it would always be easy to find a reason to go there on duty.

As I could not stretch my duties to include a trip to Malabar, the land of her birth, I did the next best thing and went out of my way to meet Malayalis. That was another reason why I spent so much time with the young Congress Socialists: so many of them were from Malabar. One was the political detainee who regretted having been released before completing a book that he had started writing in detention. He often lectured me on the philosophy of Sankaracarya, which had been its subject, but was just as ready to explain how different Malayalis were from everybody else. I remember my surprise when he told me how he used to run home from school to be suckled.

He had a fund of Malayali folk tales, about an eccentric holy man named Narayan, who spent his day rolling a boulder up a hill and then, roaring with laughter, let it roll back down again. Camus's dictum – 'We have to picture Sisyphus as a happy man' – was then a thought-provoking paradox. I was almost as impressed as my French brother-in-law was, a few years later, when he discovered that his Malayali cook, was reading Sartre in a Malayalam translation.

The best story about Narayan told how he used to sleep in cremation grounds. It is also the *dharma* of the terrible mother goddess, Kali, to dance in a cremation ground every night, and one night she arrived in one where Narayan had just fallen asleep. As usual she was accompanied by demons, and as her *dharma* does not permit her to dance in the presence of a mortal, she ordered them to scare him away, and they duly gibbered, gesticulated, howled and bared their fangs. Anyone else would have been terrified, but the only effect of this performance on Narayan was to irritate him, because it had spoiled his sleep, so they had to return to the goddess and report failure. Contemptuously she commanded them to try harder, but when they did, as Narayan had meanwhile gone back to sleep, this only made him more annoyed, so there was only one thing for it. The goddess must go to him herself.

It was clearly no use trying to scare him, so after apologising for disturbing him again she appealed to his good nature, explaining that she simply had to dance there. 'Don't mind me', replied Narayan. 'Just let me sleep.' But he did begin to grumble when she then told him that her *dharma* prevented her from dancing in the presence of a mortal. Eventually, however, he did get up and made to go.

'Wait!' she commanded. 'Now you make a wish.'

First she disturbed his sleep, then she drove him away, and now this!

'It isn't my fault', the goddess pleaded. 'It's my *dharma* again. When I manifest myself to a mortal, I have to grant him a wish.'

The holy man suffered from elephantiasis in one leg. 'Oh, very well!', he told her. 'Shift it across to the other one.'

Holy men were not only found in stories. Under Abe's tutelage in Assam I had become interested in the teaching of Ramana Maharshi. He was still alive in Southern India, surrounded by disciples and granting audience to visitors, and before I left Bombay I heard of a convincing demonstration of his powers. A Swedish woman journalist, whose Indian friends told her about the Maharshi, lamented – or boasted – that he might be able to straighten out the tangles simple peasants got their lives into, but the tangle of her love life was beyond the comprehension of anybody, least of all a holy man. Eventually, however, she made quite a long journey to visit him, and was shown into a room where he was sitting.

She sat down too, expecting him to ask her what she wanted, but he said nothing, so neither did she. She sat there, waiting for him to speak and looking at him, while she waited, and the longer she looked at his face, the more she realised that she would be ashamed to put the question she had come to ask. The answer was obvious, and she had always known what it was. There had really been no point in going there, and there was even less point now in staying. Nevertheless, she stayed for two hours, during which neither of them spoke.

I heard of this incident from a circle of young Hindu journalists and business men who met informally but almost continually, and yet irregularly, in a bachelor flat where visitors dropped in even when its owners had gone out, and sat around drinking tea and eating sweets and savouries provided by the servant. They discussed most things, but their attitude to spiritual life was what intrigued me. They regarded it as a retirement pursuit. This was not to trivialise it, they insisted. According to an ancient Hindu tradition that divided life into four stages, the final, contemplative stage should be engaged in only when the first three had been passed through satisfactorily. When that time came they could put their workaday concerns behind them and dissolve their egos by following instructions now available in paper back at all good newsagents.

Nobody offered to introduce me to someone who had done this, but one member of the circle – an accountant who suffered from migraines – did claim to be benefiting from *yoga*. When he suffered an attack he practised *inana-yoga* – which offers union with eternity through meditation on metaphysical truth. He meditated on the doctrine that all was one, consciousness of this truth was endless bliss and anything else was an illusion. This meant that anything that fell short of bliss – which was certainly the case with his migraine attacks – was an illusion. This realization, he admitted, did nothing to reduce his agony when he suffered an attack, but the greater the agony the greater the satisfaction in knowing that it was not real.

I expressed an interest in Tantra – esoteric Hinduism – and was introduced to an alcoholic lawyer who claimed to have received instruction in its secrets. He drew a mystic diagram for me and taught me a *mantra* to go with it. I still remember them both, but what has stayed with me most vividly is his story of how once, when he was living in Calcutta, he joined other devotees – including an eccentric British army officer – to sit at the feet of a visiting Tantric adept. Naked, with his hair falling in snake-like coils and his body smeared with ash, the adept had converted himself into a living image of Shiva, the divine annihilator, complete with trident. They all sat literally at his feet, squatting on the floor.

Questions were put to him but he ignored them – until one stung him and, swinging back his arm he flung his trident straight at the questioner. Those squatting in front of its target ducked as it whizzed overhead – all except the British officer, who caught it in mid-flight. This exemplary piece of fielding seemed to be the most impressive memory the lawyer had brought away. India was already a cricketing nation.

I was absurdly pleased by this story of British fielding skill. Patriotic feelings came more easily, now that the new British government was demonstrably trying to arrange a hand-over of power, and I found myself defending my compatriots, in a way that I had never done before. A case in point was the behaviour of British passengers on railway journeys. In their efforts to find employment for ex-naval personnel, my Congress Socialists had won the confidence of a millionaire manufacturer who was eager to meet me, or so they said. As there this might mean an opening for *sepoys* as well as sailors, I declared a corresponding eagerness, but nothing came of it for weeks. Then one evening they arrived at my hotel, without warning, and took me to his house. There was nothing in the visit for me. The magnate only wanted to meet me to complain about the rudeness of the British to Indian fellow-passengers on trains.

Needless to say, there was no official *apartheid* on the railways, but it so rarely happened that passengers of different races found themselves in the same compartment that some sort of discreet convention must have governed the allocation of compartments. I heard of more than one case of a *sahib* complaining before the train started, when he found that he had an Indian for his fellow-passenger. In such cases the guard requested the Indian passenger to remove himself to another compartment. He could not order him to do so, however and when this happened to Iftikar he announced that he had no objection to the company he had been allotted and was staying where he was. If his fellow passenger objected to his presence, it was up to his fellow passenger to go somewhere else. (His fellow-passenger did not agree, and remained in the two-berth compartment to fume in silence throughout the journey.)

Although uncommon, it was therefore not unheard of for Indians and British to find themselves in the same compartment, and when this happened the Indians were usually conscious of an unmistakable coldness in the behaviour of their fellow-travellers. Instead of disassociating myself from this behaviour, however, let alone condemning it, I found myself explaining it away. If they were bound to travel together for fifty hours in close proximity, the British avoided eye contact with one another and exchanged the minimum number of words. Indians who received the same treatment were therefore mistaken to interpret it as a sign of racial prejudice. My interrogator refused to accept this half-truth.

I even had a brush with Mohan Kumaramangalam, when he expressed distrust of Lord Wavell, the viceroy. If Wavell had not offered terms for a hand-over of power that both Congress Party and Moslem League could agree to, I insisted, it was not because he was withholding them but because as yet no such terms existed. After a pause he conceded that this was probably true. Nevertheless, the task of throwing out the British remained. My reply to that was that there was no need to throw them. They were keen to go because the imperial game was longer worth the candle. He forgave me my defection, and years later I named my first son Mohan after him.

He was now living in a commune at Communist Party headquarters in Bombay. I went there once to visit him when he was ill, but I had nothing more to do with the Communist Party – personally because I had lost my enthusiasm for the Soviet Union and professionally because, unlike the Congress Socialists, they had no interest in the resettlement of ex-servicemen.

This break was just as well. A few days after the naval mutiny was over – in a repetition of my meeting with the Intelligence Bureau chief in Madras – I was invited by a colonel I had never heard of to visit him in his flat. It was in a residential area, and the door was opened by his wife, but after leading me through an everyday living room she directed me through a room where a uniformed British warrant officer was operating radio equipment, into a bedroom which was now an office where her husband was sitting at a desk. Unlike the staff of Bombay Sub-area Headquarters, he clearly knew a lot about me. He had just one question to put to me. Had

P.C. Joshi been present in Bombay during the naval mutiny? I wonder whether I would have told him if I had known.

I had no notion of the catastrophe that would accompany the partition of India. Morris told me about a dinner he had attended where E.M. Forster, who was then visiting India, had been the guest of honour. The conversation – when the ladies had retired – was about the coming transfer of power. The other guests were British residents of long standing, and as they predicted murder, loot and arson Forster's head sank into his hands. 'Nevertheless,' Morris said to cheer him up, 'we have to leave.'

'Leaving cities in flames?' somebody protested.

'Yes', Morris said promptly, and Forster asked him to say it again.

At the time, although I considered this the proper thing to say, I doubted whether assent to flaming cities could be so easily given, but now, in spite of the havoc that did accompany the partition of India, I am sure there was no other answer.

My last tour took me to Poona, and Y.K. Menon gave me the name of a young Gandhian to contact there – an invalid who had been detained with him in 1942. He was already consumptive when he was arrested, and while he was in detention his condition had grown worse. Nevertheless, he still believed in loving his enemies, and would welcome a visit from one.

This proved true. The Gandhian was overjoyed to see me. He had always believed in the existence of European sympathisers, but had never met one. My appearance at his lodging caused an overflow of feeling which demanded reciprocation. I took him out for an evening meal, and then on to a cinema. During the long interval, half way through the film, we joined other members of the audience for refreshment on a verandah. Although the drinks were all non-alcoholic, nearly all the patrons were British. My new friend was not just the only man there wearing a *dhoti*, but also the only one capable of taking my hand, in an unaffected manner. Despite the interest this caused, I let him keep it, remembering the wise words of Colonel Kelly on the troopship – although I doubt whether Colonel Kelly would have done the same.

By the end of 1946, Jaya and I were in Britain – a country where rice was not even available on the ration – but East and West were already changing places. When a passenger, seated opposite Jaya in a railway carriage, held out his palm to her, and asked her to read it, she burst out laughing. But a *sari* was a rare sight in England then.

My parents and Jaya, my bride

Notes

1 Étaples mutiny – 9.9.1917. One of the many mutinies among the British troops as World War I drew to a close. Étaples was a notorious base where conditions and treatment were so appalling that wounded men preferred to return to the Front rather than remain and on one occasion mutinied.

2 *Hobson-Jobson* by Henry Yule and A.C. Burnell, first published in 1886. It is a "Glossary of Anglo-Indian Colloquial Words and Phrases", many derived from Indian languages and probably the most amusing dictionary ever written.

3 In bathrooms in the countryside the bath was not plumbed in but was emptied by being tipped over, the water flowing out into the garden through a hole in the wall. Snakes in search of coolness sometimes entered the bathroom through the hole in the hot weather, to lie on the cold cement, and according to legend this once happened when the bath was occupied. Accordingly, the snake made to depart as it had come, but when only its tail remained sticking out of the hole the bather seized it and flung the snake back into the room. After this had happened twice the snake went out backwards.

4 Mirza Ali Khan, a Pashtun from N.W. Pakistan, known as the Fakir of Ipi, waged guerrilla warfare against the British throughout the 1930s and until 1947, often tying up substantial numbers of soldiers, particularly in Waziristan. He was never found. After Independence, interest in him vanished; it was rumoured that he died in the 1970s. His *jihad* demanding *shari'a* rule was apparently triggered by the rescue by the British, within the war-lord's territory, of a Hindu girl forcibly converted and married to a Muslim.

5 A group of social reformers, active c.1790-1835, largely Evangelical Anglicans, who met in Clapham, where one of their number, William Wilberforce, lived and worked for social change, especially the abolition of slavery and the reform of the penal system. Among them were Hannah More, the author, and William Smith, the grandfather of Florence Nightingale.

6 Marie Corelli – 1855-1924. Best selling author of melodramatic and emotional novels with a strong occult component, appreciated by 20th century New Age cults.

7 Subhas Chandra Bose (Netaji) – 1897- ?1945. A revolutionary young Congress Party leader, who challenged Gandhi's leadership before the war, which he welcomed when it broke out as an opportunity for revolution, ending up as the leader of the pro-Japanese Indian National

Army, largely composed of Indian Army soldiers who had been taken prisoner by the Japanese. At the end of the war he disappeared.

[8] The editors have been unable to trace a photograph of Bill Short. Should anyone reading this have a picture of him, please do contact the Centre of South Asian Studies.

[9] This was a social experiment designed to improve physical and mental health by providing preventive care, including medical check-ups, sports facilities, etc. in a deprived area of London. The project closed in 1950 through lack of funding.

[10] Bharat Natyam. Probably the oldest dance form in India, this classical school originated with the temple dances of Tamil Nadu (Southern India) and many of the postures can be seen in Indian temple sculpture. It enjoyed a major revival in the twentieth century.

[11] The Hump or Camel's Hump was the name given by pilots to the 530 mile passage over the Himalayas. The route was used to create an air bridge linking India, Burma and China from 1942 until 1945 when the Burma Road was reopened. Some 1000 men and 600 planes were lost over this period.

[12] Ursula Bower's (1914-1988) books *Naga Path* and *The Hidden Land* also offer a vivid description of this effort to rally the tribes against the Japanese in the Naga country, across the mountains from Assam and a heartbreaking picture of the effects of the disappearance of the Raj from their perspective.

[13] The Centre of South Asian Studies, University of Cambridge, holds a typescript of Michael Stratton's *War diary* (April 6th-July 8th 1942).

[14] The rulers of Oudh. For further details on his ancestor, chess and dance, see Satyajit Ray's film, *The Chess Players* (1977).

[15] Named after the 8th century Hindu philosopher who stressed the greatness of the Hindu scriptures and was a major influence on the revival of Hinduism at a period when Buddhism was gaining in popularity.

Glossary

Ayah – lady's maid or nanny (Portuguese)

Ayurvedic – traditional system of medicine practised in India (Sanskrit)

Babu – office worker, clerk, often used somewhat disparagingly under the Raj *see p. 74* (Hindi from Sanskrit)

Banya – Hindu trader (Gujerati from Sanskrit)

Burra mem-sahib – literally 'great or senior mem-sahib', European wife of the head of any European organization (Anglo-Indian)

Bearer – personal domestic servant in charge of clothes and arrangements, comparable to a valet or batman

Biwi – Indian mistress, from Persian *bibi* – lady, versions of this word have meanings ranging from highly honorific to prostitute *see p.63*

Biwi-khana – residence of a *biwi* from Persian *han* – a building, generally public.

Bolshy – from 'Bolshevik' – majority faction. Although this originally meant a follower of Lenin, in army slang it applied to anyone who rejected discipline. (Russian)

Box-wallah – itinerant pedlar, used somewhat disparagingly for business men under the Raj (Anglo-Indian)

Brahmin – member of the Hindu priestly caste (Sanskrit)

Bullshido – a modification of army slang 'bull-shit', meaning the exaggeration of the importance of trivial features of life such as the brightness of buttons. The modification implies this is ritualistic and Japanese.

Bushido – "way of the warrior", martial code (Japanese)

Carrom – a blend of billiards and shove-halfpenny (?uncertain)

Casbah – citadel (Arabic)

Chhaoni – cantonment or military station

Chha-wallah – man who supplies tea

Chhota mem-sahib – literally 'small mem-sahib', wife of a junior European manager or officer (Anglo- Indian)

Chillum – bowl of a hookah

Cooly – hired labourer, unskilled workman (perhaps from Tamil – wage or from the word for slave in various Turkic languages.)

Dak bungalow – one of a network of government bungalows in every province of India, for the accommodation of officials on tour (from Hindi- post)

Dhoti – loin-cloth (Hindi)

dilally, to go – to procure discharge from military service by feigning madness, derived from Deolali, the location of the Homeward Bound Trooping Depot. *see p. 36*

Fawji Sewardani – Military Female Helper *see p. 128*

Goonda – ruffian

Havildar – non-commissioned officer corresponding to sergeant (Hindi from Persian)

Jehad – Muslim Holy War (jihad – Arabic)

Jemadar – Second rank native officer in the Indian army under the *subedar* (Hindi from Persian)

Kismet – destiny, fate (Arabic and Persian)

Lathi – quarter staff, used by the Indian police for keeping order (Hindi)

Maidan – parade ground, open space (Persian)

Man-bap – "My father and mother" term of respect and appeal to a person in authority. (Hindi and other languages)

Mantra – sacred formula repeated as an invocation (Sanskrit)

Mazri – coarse grey cotton cloth

Milagu-tannir – (Tamil) pepper soup, became a Raj favourite as Mulligatawny, a thick hot vegetable soup

Munshi – clerk, teacher under the Raj particularly of Indian languages to Europeans, (from Arabic, Persian, Urdu – secretary, writer etc.)

Naik – corporal (from Hindi – leader)

Nimat-halal – true to his salt

Pan – chopped areca nut, tobacco, spices, etc wrapped in a betel leaf and chewed

Pan-wallah – pan seller

Punkah – sheet of cloth or matting used as a hanging fan, swung back and forth by a *punkah-wallah* (Anglo-Indian from Hindi)

Pukka sahib – a ripe or full-blown, in other words a genuine *sahib see p. 6-7*

Purana sahib – a mature *sahib. see p. 87*

Sam Browne – a belt to take pistol or, earlier, a sword, with a shoulder strap to help support the weight. The Sam Browne belt was named after General Sir Samuel J. Browne, 1824-1901, of the Indian Army.

Sarode – a many-stringed lute played with a plectrum from North India (Urdu from Persian)

Sepoy – native soldier trained in the European manner (Hindi from Persian)

Seth – important merchant, banker (Hindi)

Shahr – city

Sitar – a very complicated Indian instrument made of gourds and teak with numerous strings and moveable frets (Hindi from Persian)

Subedar – chief native officer of a company of *sepoy*s (Hindi from Persian)

Syce – groom (Hindi from Arabic)

Tabla – small hand drum from North India (Hindi from Arabic)

Tamasha – public show

Tamasha-wallah – street entertainer, vagabond or innocent bystander *see* *p. 39-40*

Tatty – window screens made of matting (Hindi) *see p. 57*

Tonga – light two-wheeled vehicle drawn by a pony (Hindi from Sanskrit)

Victoria – four-wheeled vehicle with a double seat for passengers

Yggdrasil – the world tree, central to the myths of Ragnarok or the end of time (Norse)

Picture Credits

Front cover: Author's own photograph

Picture 1: Author's own photograph

Picture 2: University of Cambridge, Centre of South Asian Studies; Sir Charles Pawsey Collection, 102/16/125

Picture 3: University of Cambridge, Centre of South Asian Studies; Sir Charles Pawsey Collection, 102/1/22c

Picture 4: University of Cambridge, Centre of South Asian Studies; Sir Charles Pawsey Collection, 28/10/1

Picture 5: University of Cambridge, Centre of South Asian Studies; Sir Frank Engeldow Collection, 9/4/2

Picture 6: University of Cambridge, Centre of South Asian Studies; Sir Charles Pawsey Collection, 102/1/4d

Picture 7: Author's own photograph

Picture 8: University of Cambridge, Centre of South Asian Studies; Sir Frank Engeldow Collection, 9/2/2

Picture 9: University of Cambridge, Centre of South Asian Studies; Sir Frank Engeldow Collection, 9/3/2

Picture 10: University of Cambridge, Centre of South Asian Studies; Sir Frank Engeldow Collection, 9/8/2

Picture 11: University of Cambridge, Centre of South Asian Studies; Sir Charles Pawsey Collection, 28/1

Picture 12: Author's own photograph

Back Cover: Author's own photograph

Index

Printed in the United Kingdom
by Lightning Source UK Ltd.
120446UK00001B/104